His Road Trip 3

a continuing…

Aspiring Adventure

Across America

By Lugene Hessler Hammond

Published by WebPowerPros, Inc.,
POBox 51654, Myrtle Beach, SC 29579
Copyright 2018 by Lugene Hessler Hammond

www.HisRoadTrip.com

Thanks for purchasing our little book. Funds from this sale will enable us to continue our ministry and keep us on the road for Him.

www.MotorHomeMinistry.com, a ministry for connecting the Bible to kids and parents.

Printed in the United States of America

ISBN 978-0-692-05653-0

Unless otherwise indicated. Bible quotations are taken from:

Most Bible quotations are taken from the New International Version (NIV) Holy Bible, New International Version®, NIV® Copyright ©1973, 1978, 1984, 2011 by Biblica, Inc.® Used by permission. All rights reserved worldwide.

Introduction Bible quotations are taken from the Holman Christian Standard Bible (HCSB) Copyright © 1999, 2000, 2002, 2003, 2009 by Holman Bible Publishers, Nashville Tennessee. All rights reserved.

This book is dedicated in sweet memory of:

Dixie Lee Whitehouse Hessler

Harlan Alan Hessler

Wanda Dutton Bryant Hessler

Lois Ann Berne Hammond

Charles Davis Hammond

All of them were loving parents to me, and each one

left this earth

long before I was ready to let them go.

I am grateful for everything they did or tried to do

that turned me into the woman I am today.

I MISS ALL OF YOU

Isaiah 58:11
The LORD will guide you always;
he will satisfy your needs in a sun-scorched land
and will strengthen your frame.
You will be like a well-watered garden,
like a spring whose waters never fail.

1 Peter 1:3
Praise be to the God and Father of our Lord Jesus Christ!
In his great mercy he has given us new birth
into a living hope through the
resurrection of Jesus Christ from the dead

Jeremiah 29:11
For I know the plans I have for you," declares the LORD,
"plans to prosper you and not to harm you,
plans to give you hope and a future."

PREFACE

When I wrote my first book, I felt it necessary to present a detailed history of our lives leading up to our embarking on a personal mission for the Lord named Motorhome Ministry. No one could truly appreciate the personal importance of doing such a thing, unless they could understand what life experiences had brought us to that point.

And especially, our faith experiences.

I boiled all that history down to a few pages for His Road Trip 2. I've included that same boiled-down version of Background in His Road Trip 3, for the sake of latecomers, or simply a refresher.

There are a few other things worth repeating.

As I did in my first book, I will apologize in advance for the number of times I will use the words *wow, amazing, beautiful, breathtaking, awesome, terrific, spectacular, remarkable, stupendous,* and other such superlatives. Even these words do not do justice to God's beautiful creations.

There are Bible verses throughout this book. As Christians, the Bible is our instruction manual and I feel these scriptures bring our story to life.

One important note as you read this book, when I refer to Him with a capital "H", I'm referring to my Holy Father God above, our Lord and Savior, Jesus Christ. Anybody else, is just a plain him.

To bring this book to life, we've uploaded thousands of beautiful photos, in date order, on our web site www.HisRoadTrip.com. You will find some of the most amazing scenery, architecture, historic landmarks, flowers and plants, and wildlife across North America. There are some blurry ones, many of which were taken through a bug-specked windshield at highway speeds. We chose not to delete these, because they still help to tell our story.

We probably need to remind everyone of the complex collection of navigation electronics with which we travel, as we've named each one. Frick was our first, our Garmin. He was okay in the days that he was the best technology available, and we always keep him on standby, in the motorhome cockpit.

Then there's Frack, my iPhone Google Maps app. I really like Frack, but he does have his limitations. And Frick and Frack used to argue relentlessly. That's why my husband insisted we needed yet another app.

Frank is our Sygic program designed for truckers. He's really got some terrific options, when they work. Larry, my husband of nearly 45 years, set it up to know that we are indeed a big rig, and supplied it with our length, our height, our width, and our weight. Frank contemplates our destination from our origin and finds the perfect route, taking into consideration all the parameters described above. Or sometimes, he just screws up. And when he does, he screws up BIG time.

At some point however, Larry changed Frank's voice to that of a lilting Aussie female. We deemed it proper to rename it Frankie.

Then, of course, there Suri. You know her. Apple Computer's AI (Artificial Intelligent) alter ego.

The newest addition is the nav app in my new Ford Escape; she's Apple-based, as well. I chose to name her Alice, as in Alice in Wonderland. As in, where in the world are we?

I talk a lot about getting a "stamp in my Passport", when we visit National Parks. Well, it's not the same Passport I'd present to

Homeland Security when I travel. It's a Centennial Passport issued by the National Park Service in 2016, in celebration of their 100th Anniversary. Each Park has their own set of rubber stamps with old-fashioned ink pads, so that you can stamp where you've visited. Mine is so full in certain regions, that I had to add pages in the back!

There are also references to doing a "shop." We have done work based on an app named "Easy Shift." They offer a set sum of money for going into a place of business, answering a few or many questions regarding certain products, and taking pictures. We have searched for shops available in an area where we were visiting, reviewed the basics of the shop versus the amount of cash it pays, then decided whether or not to reserve it. Some were shops about cookie and cracker brands. Some were about beer brands and how the store has them on display. The toughest ones (but pay well) were about wine—label names and types—but they were so time consuming! Stores usually have wine displays all over! The cash we earned appeared in our checking account, usually the next day. We found it a great way to make some extra cash, when we had the time to spare.

I pray this book will encourage you to not only go out and see this beautiful land that we have the freedom to roam without restraint, but to also encourage you to seek His amazing grace and enjoy a greater personal relationship with our living Lord and Savior, Jesus Christ.

Psalm 19:14
May the words of my mouth and the meditation of my heart
be pleasing in your sight, O Lord,
my Rock and my Redeemer.

BACKGROUND

Larry and I grew up in a then-small suburb of Cincinnati, met in high school band class, graduated, and were married in 1973. I worked 2 jobs while Larry attended college and worked full time. A new job for Larry moved us to Winston-Salem, North Carolina, where we bought our first new car, our first house, and had our first baby. When Diana was born in 1976, I was terribly homesick, and we moved back to Ohio late that year. We purchased my childhood home and Diana's brother Bobby arrived in 1979. We were close to friends and family. We were active in a wonderful church. Life was good.

I've enjoyed a personal relationship with my Heavenly Father since I was a small child. Larry did not. Some would have said that we were unequally yoked from the start. But we did okay.

Several years later, another job opportunity took us to Louisville, Kentucky, then quickly on to Indianapolis, Indiana. By Christmas, 1985, the kids were doing great in school, Larry and I both had great jobs, we loved our house, the neighborhood, and our church was only a mile away. Everything was perfect. Until disaster struck.

On New Year's Eve, our new best neighbors, Jim and Jill would arrive at any minute. We had agreed earlier to spend the celebration here at our house, with all four of our kids. They would cut through a couple of back yards to get here, and we would play games, watch movies, and stuff our faces until midnight. It would keep us all off the roads. We would be safe against the world.

Our friends would be arriving soon, so I sent the kids off to tidy their rooms, telling them, "I don't want our new friends to think we live like heathens!" Excited about the upcoming evening, they scooted off quickly. Diana skipped her way back to the kitchen after about 5 minutes, proud that her room didn't need much work. I sent her back to check on her brother. Larry and I will never forget her words, as she ran back: "Bobby had an accident and I think he's dead."

Why on earth would she say such a thing?

Larry and I rushed back to Bobby's bedroom. He had received a bicycle lock chain for Christmas and had been "locking up" all sorts of things earlier that week. We found him hanging from the chain on his bunkbed, not breathing. I ran to call 911.

Larry, alone then with Bobby: *I ran into the room, carefully removed him from the chain, then started to give him CPR and mouth to mouth. As I was desperately trying to bring him back to life, God spoke to me directly for the very first time in my life. I heard Him say clearly, "He's okay. He's with Me. Let him go." I didn't hear this through my ears or thought it through my mind it was just there. Loud and clear. A strong presence was with me. But I just kept on going. I couldn't stop! I had to be in control! I stopped only when the first responders poured into the room and took over. I felt emotionally broken, almost to the point of collapsing.*

I phoned for our new friends to come quickly, as something terrible had happened. Without question, they arrived in minutes. The ambulance and police had already arrived. Other neighbors were out on the street, wondering what could be happening to the new folks in their quiet little neighborhood.

The paramedics quickly loaded Bobby into the ambulance, and leaving Diana with our friends, we were quickly whisked away in a police car. The officer driving was male; his partner a woman. I was sitting right behind her in the patrol car, with Larry to my left. As uncomfortable as it must have been, she reached over the high bench seat to firmly hold my hand the entire ride downtown. My other hand was holding onto Larry's. No one spoke.

Traffic was horrible, as expected. There was no easy way to get to the hospital district in downtown Indianapolis. The ambulance eventually radioed the cruiser and asked that we run ahead of them with lights and sirens, to cut a path in the traffic. Both sets of blue and red lights pulsated against the close buildings. There were sirens, white lights, and traffic lights. We would race up the block, screech to a stop in the middle of the intersection, wait for the ambulance to catch up, then speed ahead to the next light, over and over again. It was total and complete mayhem.

While we had followed the ambulance, I could see everything through the glass windows in the back. I was glad when we pulled ahead of them. I no longer had to witness their futile efforts.

So, while sitting and holding hands, my mind is racing, shooting questions one after another: "Where's my Mom and Dad? I've got to call them. Oh, they're in Florida, at a campground. What campground? It's late and the campground office might be closed. Maybe I can call the local police. Where are they in Florida? I need to call Larry's Mom and Dad to tell them. No. I'll call my sister-in-law and let her and her husband drive over to tell my in-laws. What if he dies? What if he lives and needs special care? OH, MY GOD, WHAT IF?"

And my world stopped. All the flashing lights, all the sirens, all the traffic and holiday lights, all the mayhem. My mind was completely still. Then God explained that this was no one's fault, no accident. Everything was going according to His plan. I had indeed called upon the Lord with a plea and He had immediately answered. That was different, and He had my complete attention.

Jeremiah 29:11
"For I know the plans I have for you," declares the Lord,
"Plans to prosper you and not to harm you,
plans to give you hope and a future."

Larry didn't share with me his experience with God's words until years later, but I knew at that very moment God had already called Bobby home to be with Him. I knew the doctors would not be able to revive him. At the hospital, they worked on him for another hour or so, to no avail.

Sweet Bobby, full of smiles and giggles, who had been stealing Baby Jesus out of the manger scene just a few days ago, was gone. He was only six years old.

The next few months were agonizing. After such a loss, I immediately began taking Diana to counseling, and I participated, as well. Larry claimed that "men don't talk about touchy-feely emotions with other men." Nope. Forget it.

With that said, Diana and I did pretty well in working through our grief together, but Larry did not. And the greatest problem was that Larry was angry with God.

But God had others plans to convince him. Christmas, 1986 quickly arrived.

Larry: *"Christmas is almost here again Dad, get out the decorations," my 10-year old daughter, Diana insisted. When I'd put away the Christmas things last year, we'd just buried Bobby. My wife had carefully packed each item in its labeled box and I'd lugged everything out to the storage shed. I didn't want to face those sad memories again. But Diana wanted Christmas as usual, with the tree and all the trimmings. She was absolutely right. Life goes on. I steeled myself and headed out to the shed. It was a crisp, clear, windless day, with the sun high in the sky, but the beauty was lost on me. I thought I would never again enjoy Christmas.*

How can I, without all of us here together?

I yanked open the shed door and a cold wind swooshed out. A sheet of paper floated toward me, slowly coming to rest at my feet. Then the air was still once more. I bent down to pick up the paper— a handmade Christmas card. How did this get here? I wondered. We had a special box for cards we'd saved, cards whose messages were worth reading year after year. We cherished those. Especially this one from last year, the one I held in my hands. As I reread his penciled message, I could hear Bobby's voice see his face on Christmas morning.

His card read...from first grade 1986:

"Have a Merry Christmas Mommy and Daddy. Happy New Year." Love, Bobby

Bobby would always be with us, and one day we'd be with him."[1]

HE would always be with us, too.

I was pale as I went inside and recounted this incident to Lugene. I started to question in my mind. What? Why did this happen? This would be the second encounter with God, and a turning point in my faith.

Psalm 91:11
For He will command his angels
concerning you to guard you in all ways.

Within months, we could see the people closest to us undergoing changes in their lies—amazing changes. We had been the only members of our extended families that regularly attended church. Over the months and years, one by one, family members began to attend church, accept Christ, and were baptized. A marriage was saved. New children were born. One began singing praise in churches. A few played in praise bands. One became a minister. One is a church secretary, another works for the church. One is studying

---

[1] This story was submitted by Larry Hammond to Angels on Earth, A Guidepost Publication, printed and published in Nov/Dec 2000 Christmas issue.

to become a missionary. A couple created and ran ministries for the poor, the elderly, and those with special needs.

God had assured me that He had a plan, and that Bobby's death was part of the plan. I had accepted His assurance and although I grieved, I sat back and patiently waited for His plan to be revealed.

I am happy to say that, as this story continues, you will learn of many other lives that are changed daily, even to this very day. And, God willing, every tomorrow ahead. Every day of every one of our lives is spent in service of Jesus and bringing new souls to Christ.

John 16:20
Very truly I tell you, you will weep and mourn
while the world rejoices. You will grieve,
but your grief will turn to joy.

God is good. All the time.

By 1988, still struggling with his relationship with God, Larry decided that his corporate life had no meaning for him anymore. We sold our home in Indianapolis and moved to Gatlinburg, Tennessee to open a little gourmet popcorn and candy store. There were some lean years, but Diana especially flourished, away from the constant reminders of the tragedy that occurred there in our home.

By 1995, we moved to Myrtle Beach, South Carolina to open a larger store at a new entertainment complex called Broadway at the Beach. Diana started college at Coastal Carolina University and we all nearly worked ourselves to death. Diana graduated in 2000.

We learned in 2004 that our landlords had no intention of renewing the lease for our store. By the time it expired in 2005, we had gone tens of thousands of dollars in debt to build another store close by, but there just wasn't enough foot traffic to make it successful. In the meantime, Larry had been afflicted with an autoimmune disorder that no doctor or specialist could figure out. He was much too sick to work, and that left everything up to me and Diana. The store died a slow and painful death, until we closed it in September 2006.

Along with Larry's mother and sister, Lisa, we fell in love with Langston Baptist Church in nearby Conway. It was the largest church we had ever attended. We were encouraged to join a Sunday School class, and it was the best decision we ever made. I had quit going to Sunday School when I graduated high school, and I taught for a while after that. I always considered Sunday School was for school kids. I was so wrong.

The study of God's word is a very important thing, and should be done daily. There was an average of 30-40 members in that class and they welcomed us with open arms. We got to know them well. We prayed for one another, rejoiced with them in good times, and interceded in their troubled times. We had pot lucks once a month and a grand but silly Christmas party every year. Once we were comfortable in there, other relationships began to form.

Ever since junior high, I've been a back-row Alto. I love to sing in large groups, but you will never hear me sing solo. Langston had 60+ in their adult choir and I loved being a part of their back row.

Going on a mission trip is what first caught Larry's eye. Another member of our Sunday School class had taken a group the year before and she planned to take another. Larry jumped right in. It was something he'd never done before, and he loved it so much, that he went each year for 6 more years. It pushed him to the limit of his poor health, but he loved it.

As time went on, we both participated in seasonal dramas, I assisted with the children's choir, and Larry was voted in as a Deacon. There were programs to help the poor, benevolence meals to prepare, special evangelism events, special choirs, and the need for golf cart drivers for the crowds that attended. We enjoyed every minute of service.

During that same time, Langston decided to sponsor nearby Waccamaw Elementary School for a Good News Club. A national program of Child Evangelism Fellowship, it was difficult to find volunteers. It took place after school, but still during the typical workday. Being disabled, and not on a schedule, Larry showed up to see if he could help.

The Club invited kindergarteners through fifth graders. I will never forget when he came to my office after his first Club. I was sitting in my desk chair. He stood close to me, looked down and said, "I don't think the kids like me." I looked up at him and checked him up and down. Larry's a big man, 6' 3" and at that time, weighed over 300 pounds. That day he had chosen to dress all in black. I replied, "Well, looking up at you from this angle, dressed all in black, you look pretty scary to me, too." It was agreed that he would wear something less imposing the next week, and he wore a comically-illustrated jungle animal shirt. It made all the difference. They loved him, and he loved them! He volunteered with the same club for 6 years, until we went on the road for Him.

Also during that time, I began to keep the books for our county Baptist Association. The woman I worked with, Diane, had led Larry's mission team to Guatemala. They went there to accompany a team of doctors and dentists through Medical Missions Ministries, based in Guatemala City, Guatemala. She had since then become a local leader for Operation Christmas Child and enjoyed it so much. During her annual recruitment, she invited me to become a member of her team. Those couple of years as a full-time volunteer introduced me to an amazing group of people who accomplish amazing things. The millions they reach worldwide are kids who would not otherwise hear the Gospel. You should participate, too. Check out samaritanspurse.org, Operation Christmas Child.

I'd known for years that my primary gift was the gift of service. I was always happiest when I was serving others. Larry had come to realize, over these past 10 years, that Evangelism was his primary gift. He also realized that offering up his life in such service gave him amazing fulfillment, too. God was finally getting through to his heart.

And if that hadn't been enough, one night he paid a visit to Heaven. All the precious details are in the original *His Road Trip.* He choked to death in his sleep, and awoke pain-free in Heaven. But God motioned for him to go back; it wasn't yet his time. When he awoke, struggling for breath, he considered what he had seen. Not an earthly word had been spoken to him, but he knew without a doubt that God had bigger plans for him. It would still be another couple of years before that life mission would be revealed, but that encounter brought him so much closer to God. His anger was finally gone. That burden lifted, it was time to get to work on his personal relationship with God.

We continued to struggle in the years that followed. The real estate market collapsed and the home we loved so much was breaking us financially. Larry couldn't work, that was a fact. Finding a permanent, decent job in the fluctuating tourist job market of Myrtle Beach was next to impossible, much less for this 60'ish grey-haired woman, who'd been self-employed the last 2 decades. I was a little short on job references. Something had to give.

By now, Larry had a much clearer idea of what God wanted him to do. He wanted us to sell everything and commit our lives in service to Him. Larry's impression was to do this on the road. We found a motorhome to lease, and gave our house back to the mortgage company. Anything that couldn't fit in the motorhome was either sold or given to charity.

He tediously laid out plans for our Motorhome Ministry. We would travel the United States and parts of Canada to spread the Gospel. His original plans were to offer a Campfire, at an established day and time. We would offer a video, songs, activities, and marshmallows by our portable gas campfire.

Many of our first campgrounds had a problem with our plans, and I guess, in hindsight, I can't blame them. In this day and age, any activities involving children and strangers are no-go. We changed our tactics to hanging out a banner and ministry packets on the front of the motorhome with a FREE sign. To date, we've given out over 700 of those precious packets.

But, back to the story. I had told Larry that hitting the road without some money in the bank was just plain foolish. I have always trusted the Lord to take care of me, but what if this mission of his was not a mission of His? I was adamant: we would not leave with an empty bank account.

By November 2014, I was finally working full-time. We were living in Myrtle Beach, in that rig when disaster eventually struck.

It was October 20, 2015. We were beginning our long drive to the 2015 Spyder Rally in Fontana Village, North Carolina. We were the sponsors, and our Rally the previous year had been a great success. There were over 1,000 people pre-registered this year, and others were free to drop in as they wished. We were so excited.

We were still in our home county, when we realized I had failed to secure the bathroom door and with every bump and turn, it banged open, then banged closed. I am a firm seatbelt advocate. My car doesn't move without my seat belt buckled. I reasoned that we were on an open stretch of highway we were quite familiar with. There wouldn't be another stop light—or car—for miles. I unlatched my seatbelt and ran to the back to secure the door.

I was back in less than 8 seconds, but a moped had appeared out of nowhere and yanked right in front of Larry, who slammed on the brakes to spare the life of the kamikaze driver. In a heartbeat, I had been thrown head-first into the windshield and fallen to the floor.

Long story short, after 2 ambulance rides, 2 hospital emergency rooms, and lots of tests, it was confirmed I had fractured my C-2. I just know it hurt like hell.

I called Diana at work, to explain what had happened. She needed to go with her dad to Fontana—there was absolutely no way Larry could handle such a crowd on his own. Her new boss was admirably cooperative and in a few hours, they were repacked and on their way, the windshield reinforced with clear tape.

I spent 5 days in the hospital, with the neurosurgeon's promise that if I keep the cervical collar on, it will heal itself in 3 months.

Well, 3 months later, tests revealed that not only had the fracture not healed together, it had actually separated, and completely unstable. I would need immediate surgery.

After that surgery was performed, the pain was unbearable. But even more unbearable was the news the neurosurgeon brought later that evening: we will have to operate again. So, 3 days later, on Valentine's Day, 2016, he did.

Even birthing 2 babies, I had never known that level of pain. It's amazing how much physical strength is required to hold up your own head. I couldn't return to work for weeks, as the pain was so bad. Financial woes continued to worsen.

A couple of weeks after the accident, I received a telephone call from an attorney in Charleston. He made the 3-hour trip to explain that I might have settlement options available that we may not be aware of. At the end of the meeting, I asked him how he had learned about me. He had seen the Go Fund Me page on Facebook that my dear supervisor had set up for me. What an angel she was.

In short, God had turned that 8-second trip into something life-changing in more than one way. He used that painful event to provide for all our needs—we now had cash in the bank to hit the road for

Motorhome Ministry. My one and only concern had been addressed in a mighty way.

We said goodbyes to our church family and left Myrtle Beach on March 30, 2016. The rest, as they say, is history.

Proverbs 16:3
Commit your activities to the Lord,
and your plans will be achieved.

"The greatest legacy one can pass on to
one's children and grandchildren
is not money
or other material things accumulated in one's life,
but rather a legacy of character and faith."

--Billy Graham--

AND THE JOURNEY CONTINUES...

FEBRUARY 24

Larry was still working hard to secure alternative Florida State Park reservations for next winter. Early this morning, he had 4 different campgrounds and a dozen campsites open on his browser, ready for the split-second when the time struck 8am. He managed to win another one!

We now have reservations to camp in Florida from January 2, to February 6, 2018. The Florida State Parks and National Parks within Florida fill up very fast, because the private campgrounds are all so expensive—again, factor in supply and demand. In Key West, for example, a private campground can cost upwards of $110 per night, whereas a public site will cost you around $38. Perhaps Larry will fret a bit less now.

But, as my fingers sit here, poised to write about Friday, February 24, 2017, I simply don't know where to begin. It was an absolutely amazing day of sights and smells and tastes that I will never forget.

It started later than usual. The pain in my lower back was already there when I awoke, so I took some over-the-counter meds and went back to bed, hoping it would feel better. When I finally gave up and got up, it was bad.

Larry had been up for a while and wondered when we would get going. It was our first day in New Orleans and we wanted to explore, to get the feel for the French Quarter long before Mardi Gras arrives in four days.

I ate breakfast and was finally ready to go. I slathered my lower back in Capzasin cream, then wrapped myself tightly in my trusty back brace. I packed a couple of pain pills left over from my neck surgery and was ready to face the day.

We sprinted across the four-lane divided highway to the bus stop, only to wait another fifteen minutes for it to arrive. We bought two Jazzy Passes, which would give us unlimited public transportation service for the next twenty-four hours. As seniors, we could have paid eighty cents for each trip, but we figured this was best. Hindsight being 20/20, we should have paid the eighty cents. The bus was clean, and we sat in the "reserved for handicapped and elderly" seats in the front. People got off and on along the route at the various stops.

We got off the bus as they switched drivers and walked to the trolley rails nearby. Larry had already done his research and knew the Red Line trolley would deliver us right down into the French Quarter. It was a short walk to the rails, but I quickly realized that the rails were blocked in both directions with yellow tape—there would be no trolleys on these rails any time soon.

We crossed the street with hordes of pedestrian traffic and found an RTA employee standing there. We asked him how to get to our destination. He explained that the rails were shut down all day today, in preparation of the parades tonight. But they had put bus service in place of the Red trolley route. He pointed back across the street and told us to wait for the next bus.

There were lots of people waiting and the bus was already crowded when it arrived. There I entered, all silver-haired and wearing a back brace, one thirty-something gentleman quickly rose to offer me his seat. I thanked him and blessed him profusely. The woman who was seated next to me spotted Larry's cane and offered him her seat, as well. Yes, there are still good people in this world.

Everyone was from someplace else and everyone was in a great, festive mood. Goodness and graciousness were wonderful things to behold. Each time we stopped, we picked up more folks than we left off, and by the time we arrived in the French Quarter, it was shoulder to shoulder, packed in like sardines.

We had no specific plans for the day. We finally arrived on Bourbon Street, four days from Mardi Gras and the party had obviously started without us.

There was so much going on at every moment, that it's difficult to describe in words. The streets were already crowded with people, young and old, some dressed plainly (like us), some a bit immodest, and others downright lewd and improper. Many of the Krewes (pronounced "crews"), the organizations who would be sponsoring parades this weekend, were already partying up on the balconies overlooking the street. They were throwing all sorts of prizes to the crowds below. Most were strings of beads, but also included feather boas, bead-covered bikini tops, plastic cups, rubber balls, and foam footballs.

I remember one Krewe specifically, in addition to the regular strings of beads, offered strings of much larger beads, each the size of softballs. As my back was really hurting, we would have to stop occasionally and let me lean my back against a building to rest. I could see that the men would hold these huge beads out over the railings on the second floor, taunting the crowds below. I couldn't hear their words, but their gestures implicated that those down below would have to reveal their boobies to earn these special beads. I could only see the backs of the crowd, but it was clear to me that young and old ladies alike were showing them what they requested, as each walked away with a ginormous set of beads.

Proverbs 5:17
Let them be yours alone, never to be shared with strangers.

I, on the other hand, didn't even rate a throw of little beads. But, I would never reduce myself to be so immodest for a 5-cent string of beads—even in front of strangers. We picked plenty of beads up off the ground, and I was content with that. After a quick lunch at Krystal, we again ventured outside. We heard a marching band playing and walked toward the music, passing a horse-drawn carriage on the way. There was no parade scheduled for this time of day, but someone was having a small, impromptu event anyway. There were lots of men in handsome suits, walking alongside the band. Most had a couple of strings of beads around their necks, but carried dozens of beads on their arm, much as a waiter holds a napkin. Occasionally, they would throw some beads into the crowd.

Larry and I were leaning back against the corner building, trying to stay out of the way, when a forty-something man walked straight through the crowd and put a special necklace into my hand. I wasn't even asking for one, yet he knew. I blessed him profusely. The handsome string of white, navy, and gold beads held a flashing medallion of *The Tempest, Hermes MMXVI*. I realized later that it was last year's medallion, but I didn't care. That man sought me out of the crowd and gave it to ME. That made the whole day so special; perhaps I reminded him of his dear old mom.

The alcohol was flowing as the afternoon progressed and the constant roar of the streets was getting louder. The alcohol was clearly having its effect, and it was still so early in the day.

---

1 Peter 5:8
Be alert and of sober mind.
Your enemy the devil prowls around
like a roaring lion looking for someone to devour.

There was a group from a local church holding a large cross and preaching the gospel in the middle of the chaos. I gave them a lot of credit for doing that where they did, because they were taking a lot of verbal abuse and finger-gestures from the crowd. But they stood firm and continued their warnings to repent and be saved.

As in most places since 9/11, it is illegal to wear a mask in public here in New Orleans…except during Mardi Gras. There were only a few with masks today, but I'm sure Tuesday will be very different. Marijuana was also present today, here and there. It smells like day-old skunk to me. As we continued to walk Bourbon Street, a four-piece brass band was playing the slow jazz songs that are traditional for New Orleans. They were strolling the streets playing for the crowds.

> 2 Chronicles 5:13
> The trumpeters and musicians joined in unison
> to give praise and thanks to the LORD.
> Accompanied by trumpets, cymbals and other instruments,
> the singers raised their voices in praise to the LORD and sang:
> "He is good; his love endures forever."
> Then the temple of the LORD was filled with the cloud.

We were shocked at the number of face painters on the streets. Not shocked because they offered to paint faces, but shocked because every one of the female artists were topless and had their important parts covered only in paint and glitter. Public nudity is illegal always, including Mardi Gras, and there were plenty of police around, so why was this an exception? And we saw dozens of them throughout the day. My, oh my. Some people were really having way too much fun.

Bourbon Street was filled with foot traffic and only occasionally would a car attempt to come through. As we continued to walk, I glanced into a corner bar and was surprised to see a pair of hairy legs dancing up on the counter. As I dragged Larry with me to see what was going on, there were actually two men up there dancing, wearing only Speedos and dollar bills. Whether they were appealing to the women or the men of the crowd, I didn't care to know. Yikes.

When it became obvious we were still going to be here for the 6pm parade, I begged for an early supper. As we walked up Bourbon Street, I glanced into one open-air restaurant and saw a single table empty. I stopped at the door of Bayou Burger & Sports Company and asked the Host if we could have that table right there? And like that, it was ours. We had a delightful young waitress who encouraged us to stay as long as we wanted. We ordered their Trifecta, which included red beans and rice, crawfish etouffee, as well as chicken and andouille gumbo with fresh bread. It was delicious! We almost ate it all, and left a Motorhome Ministry brochure with a seed packet next to her tip.

Back out on the streets, after asking a policeman where we should be to watch the 6pm Hermes parade, we arrived at a police barricade fence at St. Charles and Canal Streets at 5:15. There was a Starbucks on that corner, and I went in to get us a couple of cold, bottled soft drinks. We were getting concerned that not only were the trolleys not running down here, the bus routes would be closed because of the three parades scheduled for this evening.

We voiced aloud our concerns to a nice couple from Boston to our left, who had arrived just after us. We had all claimed "front row seats" to the parade, which were actually "front row stands". They began telling us about Uber and the woman showed Larry her app. Larry's upset now, because his iPhone is low on battery power, and mine's down to like 3%. It had been a forty-five-minute bus ride down here—how were we going to get back, at least before the wee hours of the morning?

It's amazing how we all depend on these little phone computers for all important information and being able to get information instantly. What has happened to maps, pay phones, telephone books, guides? Remember tearing pages out of phone books? Now all we need is our phones and a power source. A dead phone in a strange city is asking for trouble.

I had told him many times to spend the money for a supplemental power source for his phone, but he never has. I had seen a small electronics place just a couple of stores back, so I grabbed my wallet and cell phone and walked there. I was hoping they would allow me to charge my own phone, but it was no surprise that he said no. I told him my problem and he quickly showed me a power supply that was already fully-charged and ready to work. He plugged my phone into it and it was charging quickly. Sold. Now Larry would hush and enjoy the parade.

There was a high presence of law enforcement visible. And the folks from Boston said their local friends had told them that there would be great numbers of undercover law enforcement, as well. We saw local police, county Sheriff, State Troopers, and FBI all in uniform. We saw vehicles marked Department of Homeland Security. The thought had never crossed my naïve little mind that we could be a target for terrorism, just by attending a parade. What a frightening world we live in now.

We stood in that same spot for hours, the young children to our right never standing still, and the folks behind us never crowding forward. And as long as I was leaning against the police fence, my back didn't even hurt. As Larry's bedtime came and went, he complained of the delay, and grumbled that it had better be worth the wait. Much to our surprise, that parade didn't get to our part of the route until 8:45, but it did not disappoint! The Hermes parade floats were bigger than life, each manned with a couple dozen masked and costumed riders throwing stuff everywhere they could. Larry and I both caught a few things in the air—but one struck him right in the head. He said, "That hurt!" and wondered if the thrower had singled him out, like a pitcher throwing a baseball. I have a new collection of four Hermes Parade cups, another different flashing necklace and a cool flashing LED bracelet.

I must note that one attractive young "lady"—and I use that term loosely—sure stood out from the rest of the crowd. She was costumed in a bright green bustier and had taken her place right across the street from us. Her breasts were completely out of the bustier, and were decorated with pasties and glitter; she offered herself up to take photographs with anyone who asked. She stayed busy the entire five hours we stood there. She had a small basket of Dum Dum suckers and was offering them personally to everyone in the area, especially the policemen nearby. We politely said, "No, thank you," when she offered us suckers, but we heard her tell the small children nearby, "They're wrapped, so they're safe. I'm a teacher." Larry's eyebrows shot up he commented quietly to me, "I sure didn't have any teachers that dressed like that!"

As the crowd dispersed, everyone was happy and had enjoyed the event. I didn't see one drunkard in the bunch, but I'm sure there were plenty of them down on Bourbon Street.

Galatians 5:19-21
The acts of the flesh are obvious: sexual immorality,
impurity and debauchery;
[20] idolatry and witchcraft; hatred, discord, jealousy,
fits of rage, selfish ambition, dissensions, factions
[21] and envy; drunkenness, orgies, and the like.
I warn you, as I did before, that those who live like this
will not inherit the kingdom of God.

No busses were to be seen anywhere along the parade route. Larry used the Uber app for the very first time, and within five minutes, Erold had arrived. At first, he was a bit dismayed that we were taking him so far out of the city, but it was only about six miles. We quickly learned that he was a pastor from Haiti, and driving for Uber was one of the ways his mission team of twenty-three earned monies for their mission projects here. We had such an uplifting conversation all the way back to the campground. What a God-sanctioned meeting it was for all of us, to encourage each other in our ministries. We tipped him well and gave him a brochure about our ministry.

Larry had passed brochures and seeds today to our supper waitress, the couple from Boston, and Erold. Hopefully, those seeds will sprout new fruit for the Lord. There was certainly a reason that He guided us to New Orleans during Mardi Gras, if not only to open our eyes to the evils that still exist out in the world—a world that we normally do not see. As you might have guessed, we are most definitely not the party-hardy type.

Romans 13:13
Let us behave decently, as in the daytime,
not in carousing and drunkenness, not in sexual immorality
and debauchery, not in dissension and jealousy.

FEBRUARY 25

After about ten hours on my feet yesterday (save 2 sit-down meals), I was completely and thoroughly exhausted. Every part of my body hurt. And I wasn't even out of bed yet! I got up long enough to announce to my husband that I was taking some over-the-counter meds and going right back to sleep, which I did. We stayed in the motorhome almost the entire day. I didn't even write, because it hurt too bad to sit. I laugh as I write this, but it's h*** to get old. You have great fun one day, then it takes you an entire day to recover from it! I put a nice little pot roast in my mini Crock Pot and went back to sleep some more.

When I arose the next time, I was beginning to feel a bit better. I added some carrots and sliced potatoes to the pot roast and asked Larry to go over to the hot tub with me. The water temperature was perfect and helped to further ease my pain. The pot roast was excellent, and we watched *Travelers* on Netflix—then it was bedtime once again.

FEBRUARY 26

After a day of rest, Larry decided that we would drive our car around the city today, perhaps set out to see the beautiful historic cemeteries of the Garden District. Unbeknownst to either of us, we had chosen to set off on a horribly frustrating and impossible mission.

It was a short trip on the city map. It would be simple. Although there were a couple of orange and red delays on the Google Map, it should still be okay. But what Frack failed to know and illustrate was there were many, many roads completely closed because of the four parades today. We quickly made it down within just a couple of blocks of the noon parade. In hindsight, what we *should* have done was parked the car and enjoyed the day. BUT, Larry wanted to see the Garden District.

So, picture that West to East St. Charles Avenue is the basic parade route. But, the parade staging areas are north and south of the western beginning. And the streets that people use for parking are yet another few blocks north and south of that entire west to east area. But if you keep driving south to go around the parades, you hit Tchourtoulas, which is where many of the parades end. Have you ever been at the end of a parade route? I have, many times. And it's chaos.

So, you just can't get to the southwestern Garden District by going south, so still stuck on the western side, we begin heading north. We drove on a hundred short, tiny streets, past dozens of block parties, and cars parked everywhere. Every road was lined, both sides up and down, with parked cars. If you tried to go down one road someone is coming up the other direction towards you. Someone has to back up if you can and don't have any traffic behind you. We got stuck in a turn, with traffic coming towards us in three directions and nowhere to go unless someone backed up. We were gridlocked.

People were everywhere, walking on the streets, sidewalks, in between the cars and traffic. No one was directing the masses of traffic. The city shuts down some of their main arteries of roads for the parades. If you lived here you would know the back roads and the way to go around the parade routes, but since we didn't, we were tightly entangled in the maze of traffic on the roads.

We passed the Mercedes-Benz Superdome for the third time. Larry's ADHD is kicking in big time and we're both upset by now. Next time—if there is a next time—public transportation and Uber will be the mode of transportation of choice. You can't sightsee in New Orleans during Mardi Gras, it's IMPOSSIBLE!

I suggested we forget the Garden District today and go see a movie. Larry likes movies, so the bone worked. I set the GPS for a cinema in the nearby town of Metairie, then struggled to find a way out of the city of New Orleans. We arrive at the cinema just in time for the 2:30 IMAX 3-D showing of *The Great Wall*, with Matt Damon. It wasn't anything like what we expected, but it did keep us entertained for a while. But, as we walked back out into the parking lot, we could hear drums. We looked across the street to our left and lo and behold, the Metairie parade was about to begin!

There was no way to escape parades today. We slowly crawled through the traffic and set Google Maps for a straight route to the campground. Oh my, we ran into another parade on the way back. We breathed a sigh of relief when we parked and went inside. Thank you, God for that hedge of protection.

I nuked some Stouffers Lasagna and we finished off the Oriental Salad we'd started a couple of days before. We watched *Travelers*, until we saw the end of Season 1.

Larry mentioned during watching the episode if I remembered where that Chinese Garden is at that we just saw in a scene. Larry said we walked that same path; it was in Vancouver back in June. Then there was another scene that was in a park that we'd visited in Vancouver along the bay. We had been on that very same walking bridge as the characters were at that very moment. As we travel more and more, our trip is coming to life even in the movies and TV series we watch. We both chime in, "We've been there," as we recognize the landscape or landmark.

At that very moment, the wifi died, so we took it as a sign that it was time to call it a day. And what a day it had been.

FEBRUARY 27

After I was up and ready, I told Larry that I needed to get to CVS, because I had prescriptions that needed filled today. He reminded me that this wasn't a very good part of town and told me that he wouldn't allow me to go alone. The CVS was only a couple of miles away, but in an area, we had not yet traveled. We had driven only a few blocks from the campground, when Larry loudly complained of piles of junk and trash by the sides of the highway; he just didn't know how people could live this way.

Halfway to CVS, Frack took us into another residential neighborhood, where I began to see blue tarps atop many of the houses. I pointed them out to Larry. I wondered aloud if this could be the area that was hit just a few weeks ago by tornadoes, while we were staying further north in Louisiana.

When I saw the black semis from Samaritan's Purse, it confirmed what I'd feared. It was so sad to see the area looking like this, nearly three weeks after the storm.

At first, we were very upset that there seemed to be no one working today. And why was the only disaster relief that we saw in the area was Samaritan's Purse? Where was the Red Cross? Where was FEMA?

When we returned to the motorhome, I did some research. Immediately following the storm, NOAA reported: "25 injured. Emergency management preliminarily report approximately 60 houses and structures with varying degrees of damage.

31

Approximately 25 injuries reported."[2] Those were the houses we'd seen firsthand.

The Weather Channel reported the following day that: "a separate supercell spawned a large EF3 tornado on the East side of New Orleans, causing moderate to severe damage to 638 homes and at least 40 businesses, including NASA's Michoud facility. The NWS estimated peak winds reached 150 mph in this tornado along its ten-mile path."[3] It was the strongest tornado on record to hit New Orleans.

As we pondered all of that, it then dawned on me that it was a Sunday. We looked up the disaster response to find out that everyone had been there since the storm. Samaritan's Purse was leaving that very day, having arrived the day after the tornadoes. God bless Disaster Relief.

After all the frivolity, we've witnessed these past few days, it's sobering to imagine how terrible that day was in this neighborhood, just a few weeks ago. Once we returned to the motorhome, I wrote most of the afternoon. I don't know if there's a hospital east of here, but emergency vehicles with lights and sirens have been screaming past the campground entrance every few minutes all afternoon. I have been praying for all law enforcement and public servants who worked so hard this week, so others can have so much fun. Friday evening, I stopped several times to tell officers to "Be safe." Each smiled and thanked me. God bless them all, indeed.

Stouffers makes amazing frozen stuffed peppers and that's what we enjoyed for supper tonight, along with some leftover Popeye's Shrimp. Yum. Larry surprised me by finding *Contact* with Jodi Foster, Matthew McConaughey and many other stars. I'd been

---

[2]spc.noaa.gov/climo/reports/170207_rpts.html

[3]weather.com/storms/tornado/news/severe-weather-forecast-south-early-february-2017

looking for that movie since we visited the Very Large Array (VLA) in New Mexico months ago, I had forgotten much of it and we thoroughly enjoyed seeing it again. It is so awesome when you're watching a movie and know that you have stood in exactly the same spot that the characters are standing.

I wrote some more after Larry went to bed and then retired myself. I keep thinking about the tornado victims. Their situation really touched my heart. I prayed for them.

FEBRUARY 28

Today is Tuesday, we're in New Orleans, and it was MARDI GRAS! I was ready early, wanting to jump start the day. Parades had begun at 8am. I knew we wouldn't last the entire day, and I wanted to see the day progress. There were four parades this morning, one right after the other; they had different staging areas, but the main parade route was the same for each, right down St. Charles Avenue.

We would catch the bus and let them do the driving today, but several things delayed our liftoff: Larry's cell phone was down to 40% and wouldn't charge, and his RTA app said the bus wouldn't arrive for another forty minutes, anyway.

We caught the #94 bus into downtown and were finally on our way. Larry had the route all figured out: we would take this bus all the way to catch the Red Trolley Line, which would take us right down to the riverfront. Perfect. We eventually hopped the Red Trolley, which lurched to a stop only two blocks later. We assumed it was making a scheduled stop, but the driver announced loudly, "This is as far as I go today." What? Sure enough, the rails ahead were blocked with other trolleys, who had already parked on the line.

We asked the driver if a bus was running the rest of the route and she said that this was as close as any of the public transit went today. We could see the parade route in the far distance—and I do mean far—and dismayed that we would have to walk the rest of the way. I'd bet it was more than ten city blocks to get to the parade, and despite my brace, my back was screaming loudly by the time we arrived. We walked and walked, stopped to rest and then walked some more. We finally arrived at the parade!

The final parade today, the Zulu Parade, was already in progress and the route was packed, at least ten people deep. Many of the folks had been there for hours, many with folding chairs, coolers, and big bags of stuff they'd caught off the floats. It was going to be difficult to catch anything back against the buildings.

But eventually there was a lull in the parade—one of the policemen explained there had been a breakdown—and many decided they had been here long enough. They began to gather their prizes and headed in any direction they could. Suddenly, there were openings close to the street, so I grabbed Larry and dragged him down with me to the police barricades.

Catching stuff was easy now that I was in the front row. We caught dozens of strings of beads, some beads with special pendants, Larry caught a plush Smiley, a giant toothbrush, and a collapsible sword, which he promptly handed over to the little boy standing next to us.

As another float approached, I stretched out both of my arms and one man in costume locked eyes with me. He threw carefully and straight to me, and I caught the prize squarely. He was happy that I'd caught it and gave me a big smile and thumbs up.

The young lady next to me was in awe at my catch and said, "Oh, my. You are really lucky!" I asked her to explain. She said to catch a Zulu coconut was a rare treat, indeed. NewOrleansOnline.com describes, "Of all the throws to rain down from the many flats in the parades during Carnival, the Zulu coconut or "golden nugget" is the most sought after."[4]

Since we returned to the motorhome, I've looked at photographs of many of the coconuts online, and I think mine is the best one of all. It's painted with a background base of shiny black, and glittered in silver, gold, red, blue, and green. Painted atop the glitter, the word "Zulu" is on it twice, once in silver and once in gold. Its face includes two eyes: one outlined in white with a gold center, and the other outlined in gold with a silver center. It has a gold triangle for a nose and a large white, smiling mouth. Its hair is composed of straight spikes painted in silver, white, and hot pink. Whoever painted it really put some thought into the personality it would convey.

Thank you, whoever you are, for making it so special. I will always remember how this coconut came to me from the gentleman of Zulu. President Obama was given one in 2009 and displayed it in his private office. I'd bet mine is way cooler than his!

When the parade finally ended, we began to work our way toward the French Quarter, along with thousands of others. You cannot get anywhere easily as the crowds of people are everywhere. We were hungry and ready to sit down and cool off. At the first tiny restaurant we came to, we stepped inside and requested a table for two. The hostess asked if we had reservations. Uh, no. The first opening she had was like five hours away. We walked on, but every place was packed, and their story was the same.

We walked a block off the main streets onto Charles Street, which was a bit less crowded. I peeked inside The Grill and saw three u-shaped counters with revolving stools, like those popular back in the 1950's. I quickly decided this was where I wanted to eat lunch. Their

---

[4] neworleansonline.com/neworleans/mardigras/krewes/zulu.html

wonderful air conditioning hit us as we walked in and stood in line. Their seating probably accommodated fifty, and there were only four people ahead of us in line.

The short wait was worth it. We ordered a turkey club sandwich, with an egg added, with fries and a Diet Coke. There was so much food that the two of us together couldn't eat it all. Our waiter, Louis was older and a bit on the shuffling, disorganized side, but I heard him muttering aloud that it was his birthday and here he was, working on Mardi Gras. No wonder he was in no mood to turn his orders quickly. We paid the bill and left our MHM brochure and seeds.

Finally rested and fed, we walked down to the waterfront. It was also packed with people who were definitely enjoying the day of costume. I cannot begin to describe how everyone in the crowds was dressed. Unique, crazy, historic, amazing, elegant, sassy, vulgar, revealing…are just a few words that begin to describe their costumes.

Fishnet hosiery, sequined masks, neon wigs, flowers, umbrellas…were just a few of their accessories. Yelling, singing, and dancing in the streets…just a few of their behaviors. Most were drinking beer or margaritas, some drank hard liquor straight from the bottle, some were smoking marijuana, (the skunky smell was everywhere), and there were a few like us—dressed plainly, covered in beads, and stood gawking at everyone else.

We caught the River Street trolley south, back down to Canal Street, which should have taken us to the #55 bus. When we discovered that the signs at the bus stop had been removed, I called RTA and spoke to a woman to ask her where to catch the bus. She explained that the Red Line and Canal Street trolleys would not run until tomorrow. Then she told us to take the River Street Trolley back the other way until the end and walk twelve blocks to catch the #55 bus. Whaaaat? Forget that! We did walk to take the trolley back the other way, but I insisted that we had to make one more stop before we left the city.

We were only two blocks from the Café Du Monde Coffee Stand, in the French Market area. We just had to purchase some Beignets. The place was packed, but a young waiter took my to-go order, and was back with my two small bags of Beignets in minutes. I paid and we continued our way to the train. Café De Monde has been selling these square French-style doughnuts, covered in powdered in sugar since 1862. The only other time I'd been in New Orleans I tried them and loved them. A trip to this city would not be complete without Beignets. Yum.

Larry was more prepared with his RTA app than the RTA employee had been, because when we hopped off the trolley, it was only two blocks to catch the #55 bus. We had to walk through a very seedy part of the French Market and the effects of alcohol were beginning to show in the crowd. It was getting "scary" to say the least and it was only the late afternoon. I had absolutely no desire to stay and watch the party progress.

A few miles later, we had to wait at a stop to transfer to the #94 bus, so I ran inside the CVS on the corner to buy a liter of cold water and something sweet. When I returned, Larry was in a conversation with other travelers about God, and being in a relationship with Him. Go figure, there on a corner bus stop!

Some of the people were not in church because one woman said, "it is full of hypocrites." Larry said, "Yes, it's full of sinners." One African immigrant said that he couldn't find a church that preached the Bible, and was frustrated by the sugar-coated versions many popular preachers deliver. Larry explained "good preachers are out there, but you have to seek out one who preaches the word, not just what his congregation wants to hear. He must be willing to follow God and His commandments, not bending the word to fit what society wants to hear. But again, it's not about the church, it's more about your personal relationship with Him. First seek Him then seek a church to be a part of the "body", which is the church". God brings people into your midst that need something special to hear. He uses both of us for his purpose. We have to be ready for those moments. We have to be obedient to those moments as well.

> John 1:18
> No one has ever seen God, but the one and only Son,
> who is himself God and is in closest relationship
> with the Father, has made him known.

The bus arrived as scheduled, and quickly delivered us right to the entrance of the campground.

We were pooped; nearly dead on our feet. I was hot and dehydrated, despite drinking water all day. I took a nice, cool shower and fixed us something small for supper, and finished that liter of water. Larry collapsed into bed around 8pm, and I was asleep by 8:30. What an absolutely amazing day.

Larry posted the following on Facebook that day: "The 'Real' Mardi Gras, lots and lots of people and lots and lots of walking, public transportation was down and you had to walk into and out of the French Quarter to catch a running bus or trolley. Traffic was at a standstill, and parking was not to be found. But it was an experience; God wanted us to see the real world away from the church, for us to see how much work remains to be done (there is lots and lots of work to be done in His creation.

"In reflection, Mardi Gras is about having fun, dancing in the streets, the music, the food, the parades, and the culture. There is drinking, lewdness, and partying to the EXTREME. There are people of all ages, rich and poor, all types of backgrounds, sexual preferences, skin colors, and cultures. Some may be in the church, but most are lost.

"Sometimes, I think you must step away from the church to experience the real world and what the "lost" are going through. This way you can see what has to be done in using the special talent(s) God has given you. There are some VERY strange people in this world, and they were all at Mardi Gras!

"You see about everything in one place, condensed down to several blocks. There was NO political agenda. We were all Americans (mostly) and having fun—some more than others, and more than what needed to be. You can still have fun without the drinking, drugs, and getting drunk or high, and letting your inhibitions get the best of you."

Ephesians 5:18
Do not get drunk on wine, which leads to debauchery.
Instead, be filled with the Spirit,

I don't have to agree with any of it, I certainly don't condone it, but it's not my place to judge it, either. You must witness the behavior of others to really appreciate what an enormous blessing it is, being a Child of the Living God. How does anyone live without the hope of Grace? Thank you, Lord, that I don't have to live this life without you.

Romans 12:2
Do not conform to the pattern of this world,
but be transformed by the renewing of your mind.
Then you will be able to test and approve what God's will is
—his good, pleasing and perfect will.

Thank you, Lord that I am a saved and redeemed child of God. That we are who we are, in Your world instead of The world. Thank you again for your hedge of protection.

MARCH 1

We only had a short drive on I-10 East, to US 90 east into Mississippi today. We took our time packing this morning, and finally pulled out of the campground around 10am. As we passed through the tornado-ravaged area again, I once again prayed for those with so much work ahead of them. The streets were busy today, with trucks and cars parked everywhere. Now that Mardi Gras was over, work in New Orleans was back to regularly-scheduled business.

The drive today reinforced two things: that we are getting closer to the east coast, and Spring has officially arrived. The deciduous trees were in various shades of "spring" green, some bearing flowers of white. The left side of a stretch of highway was totally lined with tall pine trees, just like back in South Carolina. Azaleas were blooming in all colors and I saw my first vines of purple wisteria today. The air smells like spring!

When we arrived in Waveland, Mississippi, we stopped at their Rest Area / Visitor Center. The women who worked there were quite hospitable, and one offered me a cup of fresh coffee as I approached the counter. Larry and I collected information on points of interest that we could visit in the next six days.

The trip from the Visitor Center to Buccaneer State Park Campground was only a few miles. Frankie told us where to turn, but we saw only a high chain-link fence gate with signs stating, "Do Not Enter" and "Private Property." Even though we could clearly see the campground through the fence, we drove on down the road, expecting a public entrance.

Frankie was taking us in a large circle around the State Park. Alarmed by the narrow, and in some places unpaved roads, Larry told me to put the destination into Frack, as well. They both told us the same thing, to go around the lake and back to the same gates. Each turn we took put us on a skinnier road than before. One even had a

Dead-End sign on it, but the road took a hidden turn to the left, anyway.

We arrived back at the same fence and gate. The left half of the large gate was wide open. I got out, opened the right gate, and allowed Larry to drive the rig through it. There were no alarms, no lights, or sirens. No blue lights arrived, wither. We drove a few hundred feet and I spotted a couple riding their bikes. I told Larry to stop the rig. I got out to ask directions to the check-in. In minutes, we arrived.

I politely complained to the clerk that both navigation programs had brought us in the service gate, and she commiserated with us. She told me that it seemed to happen a lot and apologized. Site 12 was great, and we discovered that we even had full utilities, which was a pleasant surprise for a state park, which Larry rated an 8. One edge of the campground faces the beach on the Gulf of Mexico, and in season, it even has a water park and wave pool.

After we set up, I vacuumed and cleaned, started some laundry, and sat down to write. Larry busied himself with FOX News. Neither of us had been able to watch President Trump's first State of the Union address, so it was interesting to hear the wide variety of opinions of it.

Larry wanted to explore a little yet today, so we hopped in the car and drove through Waveland, MS to nearby Bay St. Louis, MS. He had read that this had been Ground Zero for Hurricane Katrina in August 2005, which hit at 174 mph, and brought a storm surge of 27.8 feet. The area is beautiful now. Everything looks new. We marveled at the well-maintained stretch of the Gulf shore. Beach Boulevard went on for miles, the beach of white sand and dunes to our right, the two-way bike trail, and the sidewalks all added to its beauty.

We decided on Cuz's Oyster Bar & Grill for supper and we were not disappointed. Everyone already there seemed to be enjoying the crayfish, so we ordered some, too. The pepper in crab boil makes me sneeze, and my mouth was burning by the time I finished. I asked the waitress if they had anything sweet, and she showed me a list of about fifty different flavors of "popsicles" they offered. I chose a Very Berry Lemonade one, that tasted like tart lemonade, and contained fresh strawberries, blueberries, and blackberries. It was refreshingly delicious and exactly what my flaming taste buds needed. As always, we left a packet of seeds and a Motorhome Ministry brochure with our tip.

As we drove back toward the campground on the same road, this time it wasn't the Gulf shore that we admired, it was the "first row" of real estate that we noticed. Every home looked to be built since Katrina. They sat atop at least two stories of pillars. There was an outrageous number of For Sale signs all down the highway, mostly on vacant lots. You could easily tell where homes had once been, because the driveways were cut into the road. Some driveways led only to a concrete slab; others to rows of concrete pillars reaching into the sky. It was sad to imagine what destruction and loss these folks had suffered so long ago. Larry noticed an entire set of concrete steps that went to nowhere.

> Psalm 107:29
> He stilled the storm to a whisper; the waves of the sea were hushed.

Driving back from dinner, as it got dark, we could see an "island" of bright, flashing lights on the highway, past the campground, so we drove there to investigate. It was the Silver Slipper Casino we had heard about. We went inside for a little while, played a couple of slot machines, and decided to go home. We had to admit we were still bushed from our day at Mardi Gras. The thunderstorms that were supposed to come through passed north of us, and it rained only a short while.

We watched an episode of *Alaskan Bush People*, and Larry went on to bed. I wanted to finish my journaling for these past few days, while the details were still fresh in my mind. What an amazing adventure New Orleans offered us; one I will never forget.

MARCH 2

We awoke to a sunny but much cooler day. The storms that rushed through the area yesterday must have taken our temperatures with it. We will certainly have to run the heat pumps tonight. Larry told me he'd found a Sam's Club in Gulfport, Mississippi, about an hour's drive away. The ride was pleasant, the sun shining the entire way.

We hadn't been to a Sam's Club in a while, so we picked up a case of this, and a couple of boxes of that, and we hadn't had those in a while. The cart was overflowing with stuff that will last us for weeks! The first challenge was to get it all in the car, because we keep a lot of stuff in that poor car all the time: both collapsible bikes, a large cooler, the gas grill, the satellite dish, and crates that hold the tow dolly straps.

You can't get everything on your list at Sam's, though, and I asked him to drive next to a nearby Walmart. He stayed in the car, and I headed inside with my list. I found everything quickly, except the box of stuffing mix that I needed for a recipe, which I did finally locate. The cashier was pleasant, and I returned to the car. And, by the grace of God, we managed to get all the food in there, as well. But the biggest challenge will be finding places for everything when we get back to the motorhome!

There was a Mexican restaurant right there in the same parking lot, so we went in to eat. We were there at Aztecas way before the supper crowd showed up and nearly had the place to ourselves. We ordered fajitas with chicken, beef, and shrimp, and it came with lots of vegetables and sides. Once again, the portion was so large, that the two of us couldn't eat it all. Yum. As always, we left seeds and a Motorhome Ministry brochure. We can only pray that the seeds will be planted literally and spiritually, but God will know for sure. We always try to leave a card or brochure to everyone we meet. It's our way of leaving God's calling card.

The ride back with the car and our tummies full was enjoyable, until the Low Tire Pressure light came on in the car. At the very moment it chimed, we were passing a gas station. Larry jerked the car into the lot and we proceeded to fill the tires with air. The rear tire on the driver's side was down to twenty pounds. The poor car needed new tires, but our lease is up this month, and we're just going to turn it in anyway. Quickly, we were back on the road. We hadn't traveled another fifteen minutes before it chimed again. This must be bad. All the tire centers I Googled along the route were already closed (it was 6pm), but I found Walmart Tire Center eight miles away. We held our breath as the miles passed.

Check in for service was a bit clumsy, so I left Larry to handle things, and I went to wander the store. Long story short, the tech eventually got to our car and discovered a large screw had pierced the tire. He had it plugged in no time, and we were back on our way home. We were so grateful that the Escape has such technology; in the old days, we would have just wound up on the side of the road with a flat tire. It would have taken us thirty minutes just to unload the car, much less get to the spare tire!

Finally, back at the motorhome, we hauled everything inside, and started stuffing things into our little refrigerator and freezer; the dry and canned goods could wait. We doubted that everything would fit in the freezer, but surprisingly, it did. We caught the end of Bill O'Reilly and Larry headed off to bed.

I proceeded to put everything else in its proper places before I started writing. In no time, a mosquito announced his delight in my ear, and quickly got to work by biting me twice on the back of my neck and once on my left arm. They itched like crazy and quickly began to swell. I had to wake up poor Larry to ask him to smear them with cortisone cream.

Larry doesn't wake up easily, and when he wakes, he's often confused or disoriented. He sat up abruptly and yelled, "What snake?" I laughingly explained there was no snake. "Are you all right? Did the snake bit you? Is it poisonous?" It took a while for him to understand there was no snake, the problems were mosquito bites. It was quite funny, but he was finally coherent enough to apply the cortisone to the back of my neck, where I couldn't reach. When I asked, he said the swellings were bigger than quarters. I took a Benadryl and knew I'd be sleeping late in the morning. By then, Larry was already back in LaLaLand.

What a day of excitement and adventure. But God had given us a beautiful, amazing sunset to encourage us the eight miles to Walmart. I took it as a sign that everything was going to be okay, and it was. Every day is just fine, because God and his hedge of protection is there with us.

Psalm 50:11
I know every bird in the mountains,
and the insects in the fields are mine.

MARCH 3

I had to sleep off the double dose of Benadryl I took last night for the mosquito bites, so I got a late start today. Larry had been up for hours, as always, and he asked me to sit down so that he could show me the adventure we will take next.

Let me say first that, by the time we arrive back home in South Carolina in a few weeks, we will have visited 30 states—including Alaska—2 cities in Mexico, the Baja, as well as the Canadian

Provinces of British Columbia, Yukon, and Alberta. He showed me the next leg of the trip, which will include 19 more states and the Provinces of Nova Scotia, Prince Edward Isle, New Brunswick, Quebec, and Ontario, Canada. Wow.

Yes, that totals only 49 states, and we didn't actually take the motorhome to Alaska, we used planes, trains, and busses instead. We visited Hawaii in April 1986 over Bobby's first missed birthday. Although it was a great visit, I don't think we need to go back there again. I can't wait to begin this next leg of the trip. I know it will hold as many amazing discoveries as this one.

Yesterday, they had King Cakes on clearance at Walmart, for only $3.50. I had seen them earlier in the week, for nearly $14, so I bought this one cheap. Larry decided to open the box this morning, to taste it. Some King Cakes have filling in them, but I knew this one didn't. "…the King Cake is an oval-shaped braided cake similar to a coffee cake which has cinnamon within the braids and is decorated with icing and sugar the colors of gold (God's power), green (faith in Christ), and purple (Justice of God)—and contains a tiny plastic baby symbolic of the Baby Jesus usually baked within but sometimes placed within the cake after it has been baked."[5]

Our King Cake wasn't braided, and the box contained a small, clear bag that enclosed three small necklaces of beads and the tiny plastic baby figure. The cake was delicious and big enough that it should last us quite some time. I froze some of it for later.

Larry napped part of the afternoon, and I took the opportunity to write. I also called my best friend, Deb. We first met in third grade, and sang together in high school choir, but didn't get to be besties until after we were both married and raising kids. She is my bestest friend

---

[5] https://kingkingcakes.com/history-king-cakes-mardi-gras/

and I love her bunches. I thank God for her; she is my go-to angel here on earth.

We like to try local fare wherever we travel, but only occasionally do I attempt to prepare local fare. I did tonight, but I really cheated. I purchased a can of Shrimp Creole base at the store, added frozen shrimp, and fixed white rice on the side. It was terrific! I told Larry that I'll have to stock up on the base before we leave this area. I would definitely do that again.

I've been doing laundry all day, even getting the opportunity to wash the throw rugs. After supper, Larry was surfing the satellite feed and found the movie *Windtalkers*, about the Navajo Code Talkers in World War II, starring Nicholas Cage. What amazing things those brave men accomplished for the war effort. I believe I read recently that only one of the original Code Talkers is still living. We also appreciated the end of the movie, where the hero goes home to his Reservation. We had seen that scenery before, near Antelope Canyon and Lake Powell. I remembered fondly our Canyon guide, BooBoo, who was native Navajo.

We just had to catch Jesse Watters on FOX TV, before Larry went to bed. I stayed up in the quiet motorhome to continue writing. It has indeed been another peaceful day.

MARCH 4

Today was a quiet day, spent inside. Both of us spent the morning at our respective computers. I was writing a book, and Larry was searching for a way that we could afford to see a Broadway play during our visit to New York later this year. He found some matinee tickets for like $85, but then there were fees, on top of fees, on top of fees. The most expensive tickets he stumbled upon were over $4,000—EACH. Most were $600 - $800 for the play *Hamilton*, the "hot ticket" in Broadway at the moment.

Larry learned that a lot of theaters have daily lotteries for low prices on tickets the day of the show. The only way we had been able to afford a show in Las Vegas was stepping up to a last-minute sales booth on the sidewalk. Donnie and Marie were great. I'd much rather re-watch the animated version of *Lion King* than ever pay $300-$500 for a couple of hours of entertainment. Not for me.

He was also busy planning the details our next leg of the trip beginning in May, which will take us north along the east coast, up to Nova Scotia, then West through Canada. God will lead us where He wants us to go.

Numbers 14:8
If the LORD is pleased with us, he will lead us into that land, a land flowing with milk and honey, and will give it to us.

MARCH 5

We had always been dependable church attenders, even more so in recent years. Participating in organized worship has always been very important to me. But this past year of travel has not provided us with abundant opportunities to attend church, and I have sorely missed the fellowship, music, and learning.

I had searched on Google yesterday for a local Baptist church and decided on First Baptist Church of Bay St. Louis. We got up and got ready, then took our time enjoying the scenery as we drove the ten miles to get there. There was a historic marker in the front, dating the brick and pillared church back to the mid-1800's, but ended in the fact that it had to be rebuilt after Hurricane Katrina.

The inside reminded me of our church at home, albeit smaller. The walls were painted a pleasing mint green, and the carpet matched perfectly. With lots of folks still chatting away, the pianist began to play Pachelbel's *Canon in D*, and the choir joined in with a beautiful song, *Seek Ye First*. It was beautiful! The praise band was small, but did a good job. I love to sing, but was disappointed that I didn't recognize any of these modern songs.

The youth pastor had the privilege to baptizing a student and his dad today. Baptism is always a joy to observe; dead to the old life, born in a new life with the Spirit.

The pastor stood up to introduce their guest speaker for today, whose name I recognized: It was Jerry Rankin. He told stories of when he and his wife were missionaries in Southeast Asia for twenty-three years, then his seventeen years as president of the Southern Baptist International Board. But the main emphasis of his lesson was all about God's grace. It was a great message, indeed. At the very end, the youth pastor took the pulpit and thanked everyone for all they had done this past week for his family, who had suffered the death of their son. He was standing nearby when we were dismissed, and I walked straight up to him.

I offered my condolences and explained that we had also lost a son. I asked how old his son was. "He lived about two and a half hours." He went on to explain that they had been aware since October that he would not live, but did as God led them to do, and carried him to full term. I quietly asked his name. "Oliver." And then he quickly added that, "Oliver suffered the same fate as his sister, Alexandria." I held his hand, and looked straight into the eyes of this young minister: "By your suffering these losses, God is preparing you to better serve others. I know this because He prepared me the same way." God bless them in their grief.

When it had been time for the offering, Larry discovered that he'd left his wallet at the motorhome, so I would be driving us home. We stopped at a Popeye's and enjoyed chicken and shrimp for lunch. Walmart was right around the corner, so we stopped to get Larry two new iPhone charger cords. I'd bet this makes ten cords we've bought since the first of the year. This is getting old.

My old Sunday routine was Sunday School, church, lunch, then a nice, long nap. We didn't get to Sunday School, but ditto for the rest of today. It was wonderful.

> Acts 20:28
> Keep watch over yourselves and all the flock of
> which the Holy Spirit has made you overseers.
> Be shepherds of the church of God,
> which he bought with his own blood

As I wrote later that afternoon, I noticed a strange ritual going on outside of the motorhome windows. There are perhaps two dozen male robins outside, right here on our campsite. Although I don't see any females, the males appear to be doing some kind of ritual dance. They all stand very still, staring ahead. One or two moved a few steps forward. Then several others moved a few steps forward. This went on and on. It was really quite odd. I don't see a female among them. It sure is spring, here on the Gulf coast.

We enjoyed Stouffers for dinner and tried to watch *I, Robot*, now that the DVR has been replaced. But when it recorded, the audio didn't sync with the video; there's no way I could watch this for the next couple of hours! We decided instead to watch the classic *A League of Their Own*, which is loaded with stars. Larry went to bed, and I managed three more hours of writing. It had been a wonderful day, praise the Lord. His day.

MARCH 6

Larry secured more south Florida campgrounds for the winter of 2018. We still can't manage to get into any in the Florida Keys, but at least we have confirmed reservations from January 2 through February 20. He's still up at 6am every morning, to search for available sites with an open reservations window. It is near to impossible to be the first computer of probably tens of thousands to win your choice of campground, in the split second it becomes available. But, he did get another one today. Yay! He will continue to lock in more for the rest of February, then for March. I am so grateful to be allowed to sleep past 6am. Thank you, honey.

The sun peeked through the clouds a few times today, but the cloudiness bringing in tomorrow's rain certainly won. We took turns working and napping. Larry took advantage of today's weather to do some routine maintenance: oil and coolant checks, lubricating the slide-out gaskets and the levelers, check the battery water levels, tire inflation checks—you know, all the guy things. In the quiet, I enjoyed writing. I again saw the male robins doing their dance, while I enjoyed hearing the songs of other birds in nearby trees. There was a beautiful male cardinal on this site when we arrived, but that was his only guest appearance.

For supper, we enjoyed a delicious Shepherd's Pie that we had picked up at Sam's. It's amazing how tasty prepared foods are nowadays. I know, I know, they're probably chock-full of salt and preservatives, but when you live with a tiny kitchen, they are a Godsend.

My niece, Jana sent back my second submission for my first book. I was excited at first, but it quickly became evident that I had sent her a version of my writing that was not my final. So, I spent the entire evening comparing her edited version to my final. It was more than one evening's work and I'll try to get back to it again tomorrow. Writing a book is certainly not a simple task. But hey, if it was easy, I suppose everybody would be doing it.

Being an author is really hard work, and involves countless details of writing, grammar, punctuation, edits, even the research. Who knew? Then there's the publishing and marketing. I could never estimate the hours spent on these books, in the simple hope that it will sell. My biggest hope is that it will bless someone beyond imagination. Perhaps I'll even get some great reviews.

> Proverbs 22:9
> The generous will themselves be blessed,
> for they share their food with the poor.

MARCH 7

Today was supposed to be simple. We got up early to drive to Gulfport to have blood drawn for lab tests, in advance of our doctor visits next month back home in Myrtle Beach. We would come back to the campground and I would write all day. Simple.

Frankie encouraged us to take the I-10 into Gulfport, but Larry refused and took US 90, to follow the Gulf shore all the way. The scenery was better, the traffic was much better, and we had such a treat on the way—an eagle sitting on the seashore. It was splendidly regal and unmoving, majestic. He almost looked like a statue. On this overcast, full day, this creature seemed to bring a glimmer of sunshine through the clouds. It's a great thing that the majestic and powerful eagle represents America.

We accomplished our first task by 9am. Taking the same scenic route back to the campground in Waveland, we treated ourselves to Waffle House, because neither of us had been allowed to eat breakfast. Back on the road, Larry complained of a pesky mosquito buzzing around his face. He rolled his window down, to shoo him out. When the window got to the bottom, we both heard "thunk." Uh, oh. That can't be good. As he continued to drive, he repeatedly tried to get the window to rise again, to no avail. I quickly Googled the nearest Ford dealer as Larry made a U-turn to head back to Gulfport. At least Butch Oustalet Ford was nearby.

I quietly prayed that God would go there before us, so that the window could be quickly fixed. They were forecasting heavy rain and storms later tonight. He indeed answered that prayer, as they took the car right in. We walked to the waiting area, but Larry reminded me that we would be turning in our lease car in a few weeks, so why don't we take the time to go look at the new models and prices?

The next salesman on the line walked right up and introduced himself. I was explaining that we were from out of town, and just wanted to look at available options on a new Ford Escape. I was in mid-sentence to explain that we were on a special discount plan, because Larry's dad retired from Ford, when he interrupted. Another young man had walked into the area. Our original guy introduced us to him, mumbled something about leases and Z-plan, turned his back and walked out the door, leaving the three of us standing there. Awkward!

The new guy was puzzled, but never missed a beat. He introduced himself and asked how he could help. I started at the beginning, explaining that we would be turning in our lease next month, and we just wanted to look at the 2017 Escapes, while we were waiting for service. He was more than willing to spend the time with us, and encouraged us to test drive one, then another.

In the meantime, we received a phone call from Sherri in the Service Department. The window repair required a part, which they would have to order to make repairs tomorrow. The quote was over $350. I said, why don't you just hold that thought; we just might be leasing a new car today.

I apologized that I could not recall our salesman's name. He replied, "They just call me 'Preacher'", and explained that he pastors a church. We told him about Motorhome Ministry and gave him a brochure. Then we got to talking about Operation Christmas Child, which he had never heard of. Not only had God come before us for the repairs, He had come before us with our lease car. Preacher (aka Shaun) spent over four hours with us today and we couldn't have been happier. We left my old High Impact Blue Escape with the service department, and drove back in a new silver Ford Escape.

Just a question: do you name your vehicles? I have friends that call their cars "Myrtle" or "Betsy." Larry has always declined, saying it's silly, but he had named the voice on his GPS "Paris", after a rich and well-known dumb blonde. I've decided I'm going to name this car "Sylvia." She's silver, and it works for me. We'll see how long that lasts.

In all those hours at the dealership, we had missed lunch, so it was a good thing we'd eaten that big breakfast at Waffle House. It was now nearly suppertime, we stopped at el Agave in Gulfport to enjoy a delicious Mexican shrimp platter.

Waveland, Mississippi was Ground Zero for Hurricane Katrina. One thing I saw in Waveland, and even here in Biloxi, are how folks have turned storm-ravaged trees into works of art. I've seen large skeletons of trees turned into rows of dolphins. I saw a small, simple tree trunk turned into a huge eagle. One tree had large branches that were all different: one was carved into a mermaid, another a whale tail, another a bird. Each work of art is beautiful, and amazingly detailed. Resilient residents chose to turn tragedy into something stunning—priceless.

And I must say that the white-sand beaches here on the Mississippi coast are the cleanest beaches I have ever laid eyes on, and I have seen a lot of beaches. Even in this off-season, we watched multiple workers with an assortment of heavy equipment keeping the beaches beautiful. Keep up the good work.

Larry's been DVR'ing lots of movies lately from a free preview period from Dish., so tonight we watched *True Lies* with Arnold Schwarzenegger and Jamie Lee Curtis. We'd seen it multiple times before, but it had been a while. It was, once again, good for a few laughs!

MARCH 8

Today was a short travel day to The Davis Bayou Campground in Ocean Springs, Mississippi, which Larry rated a 6. Frankie couldn't find it but Frack did. He kept insisting that we take the I-10, but we took the scenic route on US 90 east that follows the Gulf shore. We enjoyed seeing a lot of waterfowl. There were countless blue herons, pelicans, egrets, osprey, seagulls, sandpipers, and other birds we couldn't name. Going along a low bridge on Hwy 90, there was one pelican flying beside us when he suddenly dove into the water below. I hope he caught a good supper or breakfast depending on what time he thought it was.!

It's not a very big campground, but it's very nice, located here on part of Gulf Islands National Seashore. Our handicapped site is double-wide blacktop, and our door opens right into a wooded area. In bright daylight, we can look through the woods to see the large bay and marsh nearby. I have heard all sorts of bird calls that I don't recognize.

We figured the first thing we should do is clean out the car. We have done this same dance so many times. We show up at a dealer with absolutely no intention of driving away in a new car. Then we do a deal, and have to stand right there in the dealer's parking lot to collect all the junk out of the car, and throw it all in the new one. How embarrassing. And, since we did it again, we had to totally unpack the new car and go through everything again.

We had only been out there a minute when the gnat attack occurred. Oh, my goodness, the gnats were terrible! I jumped inside to cover myself with bug spray. It helped a lot, but they still went for my eyes and nose. We were done with the chore in short order, and decided to head over to the Visitor Center.

I received three stamps in my Passport today. The Visitor Center was small, but nice. Larry went outside to take a trail down to the water while I stayed inside. The highlight of my visit was to watch the Park Ranger induct a boy into the Junior Ranger program. Right hand raised, repeat after me… The uniformed Park Ranger, in all seriousness, was enjoying this as much as the boy. It was a precious moment to witness.

We returned to the motorhome after driving every road in the park that we could find. I wrote some, then fixed a small supper.

It was another quiet evening in front of the TV. Thank you, Lord, for another beautiful and wonderful day.

MARCH 9

This morning we set out to tour Beauvoir, the Jefferson Davis Home and Presidential Library in Biloxi, MS. The House has a very complicated history, but "Ex-Confederate President, Jefferson Davis lived here at Beauvoir in his retirement life and wrote his memoirs of the Civil War, 'The Rise and Fall of the Confederate Government.'"[6] It cost us$10 each, and we wound up spending a couple of hours there, touring the house, grounds, and museum. It was like going back in time, seeing all sorts of artifacts, family portraits, art, and furniture.

We began with a 25-minute film that taught us a lot about the Confederate President. He was the first and last President of the Confederate States of America, who was never a US President, and because he was considered a traitor, he had been stripped of his citizenship, as well. This is the only Presidential library for a non-US President—the President of a lost cause. We did learn later, that President Jimmy Carter reinstated his citizenship in 1978.

Jefferson Finis Davis was born in Kentucky on June 3, 1807 or 1808, (historians are not absolutely sure), the tenth child of Samuel

---

[6] visitbeauvoir.org/about-beauvoir

and Jane Davis. His mother had her way in naming him, declaring his middle name to be "Finis," which many feel was her declaration that she was done having kids. Jefferson hated his middle name and stopped using it at an early age.

He was also a West Point Graduate, a Lieutenant in the US Army during the Mexican–American war, a US Secretary of War, a Statesman, and a Senator from Mississippi. Davis argued against secession but believed in state's rights and the right to secede if necessary. He was a Christian, an honorable, proud, and decent family man and, believe it or not, a patriot.

Growing up in the North, we were not taught much about the South as it pertains to the Civil War, it was pretty much a one-sided view of history by the North. Today, I learned a lot about the man who tried for twelve years to avoid a war, but led the South during our country's Civil War.

One of my friends from church, Jason, made a comment on my Facebook post about visiting here. "History is written by the victor. In this case, as in most, the other side has to be demonized in order to prove that the victory was achieved by righteous means. The truth is that the victor has the same blood on their hands." Well said.

After the film, we joined a small group for a guided tour of the home, accompanied by stories in great detail of the history of its owners, its furniture, its care and maintenance, and the damages from hurricanes over the years. It was all very fascinating. The house has been restored in all its glory as it was in the 1800's, down to the original paint colors.

The ceiling has ornate hand-painted murals with rounded corners and eves. You can even see the black smoke soot from candles and fireplaces in each room on the walls and ceilings. The smell was musty and old but not overbearing. I admit that all I ever knew about Jefferson Davis was what I'd learned by watching the mini-series *North & South* like twenty times, but that wasn't very much at all.

After the house tour, we walked through the museum, which contained all sorts of items from the Civil War. They have a large resource library there, as well. Their gift shop was filled with all sorts of Civil War and regional items, and the friendly ladies that worked there were dressed in period clothing. It was another fact-filled and interesting tour.

The preachers of the South during this time "defended slavery and took the Bible literally. They asked who could question the Word of God when it said, "slaves, obey your earthly masters with fear and trembling,"

Ephesians 6:5
You servants who are owned by someone must
obey your owners. Work for them as hard as you can.
Work for them the same as if you were working for Christ.

---

or "tell slaves to be submissive to their masters and to give satisfaction in every respect."

Titus 2:9
Those who are servants owned by someone must obey their owners and please them in everything. They must not argue.

Christians who wanted to preserve slavery had the words of the Bible to back them up. The preachers of the North had to be more creative, but they, too, argued God was on their side. Some emphasized that the Union had to be preserved so that the advance of liberty around the world would not be slowed or even stopped. One Boston preacher, Gilbert Haven, sermonized, "If America is lost, the world is lost."

"Julia Ward Howe wrote the lyrics to "The Battle Hymn of the Republic" after visiting a Union Army Camp on the Potomac River near Washington D.C. in December of 1861. Her ancestors were famous during The American Revolutionary War, and the rest is history:

Mine eyes have seen the glory of the coming of the lord,
He is trampling out the vintage where the grapes of wrath are stored,
He hath loosed the fateful lightning of His terrible swift sword,
His truth is marching on

Glory! Glory! Hallelujah! Glory! Glory! Hallelujah
Glory! Glory! Hallelujah! His truth is marching on.

I have seen Him in the watch fires of a hundred circling camps,
They have builded Him an altar in the evening dews and damps,
I can read his righteous sentence in the dim and flaring lamps,
His day is marching on.

Glory! Glory! Hallelujah! Glory! Glory! Hallelujah
Glory! Glory! Hallelujah! His truth is marching on"[7]

What I have learned over my years is that one cannot take bits and pieces of the Bible and use it for your own causes and beliefs without taking the whole Bible to understand His wisdom, His commandments, His love, and His wrath. President Abraham Lincoln offered the most constructive perspective on religious warfare, "My concern is not whether God is on our side," he said. "My greatest concern is to be on God's side." He was a wise man, indeed

---

[7] specialneedsinmusic.com/folk_song_pages/battle_hymn.html

I just don't know what to think about current demands to remove the rebel flag and the statues of brave men who fought in the Civil War. The flag started out solely as a battle flag to differentiate the Confederates from the North. Of course, the Ku Klux Klan's adoption of the flag ruined its sincere reputation forever. It's probably their use of the flag that has turned it into something it was never intended to be.

But the statues? Does the public believe that by removing these statues, one can forget that the War ever happened? I would think that we could look upon those things as constant reminders to never let such a thing happen again.

While we were out, Larry decided we would visit a couple of casinos today. He had chosen the Treasure Bay as our first stop. We signed up for Players Club cards and hit the slots floor. We each blew a $20 much too quickly, so we left there. When we received our cards, the ladies explained that since we were first-time players there, if we wound up losing today, we could bring back our cards tomorrow morning, and they will comp that amount back to our cards. We can't get it back in cash, but we can play that same couple of $20's again. Sounds more than fair to me!

I asked Larry to stop at a place called "Sharkheads," so that I could look inside. The owners had been customers of ours when we were manufacturing and wholesaling pearl gifts through our company Oyster & Pearls. The last time we had been in Biloxi was not long after Katrina had hit. Right on the oceanfront, Sharkheads had been completely destroyed and they had just begun rebuilding, bigger and better, they said.

Well, let me tell you, this place is fantastic! They have everything you could ever want or need for a vacation at the beach, and even more stuff you would want to take home. I treated us to a box of saltwater taffy, which ironically, had been made by the same company that now owns Oyster & Pearls, Forbes Candy company in Virginia Beach, VA. It's a small world.

From there, we drove straight to the Golden Nugget. Larry gave me a $20 and took another $20 out for himself. He said when we lost those, we were done. There are only a couple of slot machines that I'm familiar with, and I like to walk the entire floor first, just to see if the machines are there. I found my favorite machine and Larry found his. We split up and went to work.

He had used up all his cash, but I was still going strong. I played for another half-hour, and still cashed out with $10 in my hand. Not too bad for an hour of fun. As I've said before, you can be a Christian and still have fun. Just keep the wisdom of Him in its proper place. I don't play slots to win a fortune, I just play them to have fun. Kinda like old-fashioned pinball machines, or Pacman. To me, slots are a source of entertainment, like paying to go to the movies. I just love the lights and sounds of these machines as I play, especially the Howling Wolf. Some wise person once said, "Don't bet anything that you can't afford to lose." Absolutely. Always.

Hebrews 13:5
Keep your lives free from the love of money
and be content with what you have, because God has said,
"Never will I leave you; never will I forsake you."

Larry had picked up a 15% off coupon for a local BBQ place, so we drove back to the other end of the main drag and enjoyed a half-rack of ribs with sides at Slap Ya Momma. It was a rustic-looking place inside and out. Two of the walls were completely made of different colored, brightly-painted door panels. They had a creaky wooden floor, too. We ate our fill, paid the bill, and left a Motorhome Ministry brochure.

We were driving back to the campground when I asked to drive through McDonald's for one of their little ice cream sundaes. With a little hot fudge, I was filled. My sugars weren't too pleased, but it sure was yummy.

We finally parked the car in front of the motorhome, having been gone all day. Larry unlocked the front door while I gathered up all the stuff from the car, and stepped inside. He folded and put the bikes back in the car, because rain was forecast for tonight. When he came back in, he had a funny look on his face. He had finished with the bikes, and was walking back to the door when two possums waddled right out of the wooded area, a few feet away, right across his path. He said, "They scared the living daylights out of me! They acted like they didn't even see me." As blind as they're rumored to be, they probably didn't.

We settled in for one episode of *Alaskan Bush People* off the DVR. Larry headed to bed and I wrote for a while. It had been a perfectly beautiful and sunny 70-degree day. Rain in the forecast for tomorrow, but that's okay.

Thank you again, Lord. Thank you, so very much.

MARCH 10

What a frustrating morning it turned out to be! Larry first had difficulties getting into our online banking account, an account where we must change the password monthly. Then, we forget what the current password is, so the system locked him out. Then, he attempted to order a new banner for the book and the file just wouldn't download. For me, the frustration began when I meant to delete some useless email and wound up deleting my entire email folder. EEK! Larry did manage to bring it back to life, but now it has 2,200+ emails sitting in it, that I will have to go through...again. Needless to say, we needed to get out of the motorhome for a while.

We got in the car and drove back to Treasure Bay Casino; they're the ones that would credit us for whatever we lost on our first day. In a matter of minutes, I had $19 in credits to play and Larry's card had $17. I found a new game to play, played my credits and wound up with over $20 of my own cash. We were going to take that cash and leave, but Larry found a Wheel of Fortune game. I sat down with my cash and played the max. In no time, I was up to $45 of my own cash. We played another Wheel of Fortune game, and was up to $56 of my own cash. NOW it was time to walk away. We were $55 down at the end of our first time here, and now had recovered all of it. What a blessing.

A Facebook friend of mine, Denise had suggested I stop by McDonald's to get one of their seasonal shakes, with green chocolate mint on the top and chocolate on the bottom. It was delicious.

We stopped at Dollar General to pick up a few things on the way back to the campground. I had put chicken in the Crock Pot before I left. So, for supper we had delicious Hawaiian Chicken (recipe in the back of the book) on the grill with fresh corn on the cob.

The rest of the evening was spent watching every single *Alaskan Bush People* on the DVR. What a bunch of characters.

MARCH 11

Today will be a stay inside and work day. I have got to get some writing done! It's sunny and mid-sixties right now, but rain is forecast for later in the day. We've done so much running around already here, it's time for a slow day at home.

But before we settled in for the day, it was time to dump the tanks. After nearly a year on the road, we finally have this pack-up, set-up thing down pat. We quickly finishing the dump, and backed into the site. All is well—at least until the tanks fill again.

Looking out the windows as I write, I saw something I thought odd for spring: leaves are falling from the trees. The trees throughout the campground seem to be oak trees, but the leaves are very different from the oaks I grew up with in Ohio. Those oaks I knew held onto their brown leaves all winter, falling only when the new leaves are ready to emerge in the spring, and that's what these trees are doing. A review of photos online tells me they're a type of southern oak. An occasional wind gust sends those little leaves flying through the air and tumbling down the road. It's all very pretty.

Larry's been busy working on the book's cover design and marketing tools. I learned just a while ago that one of my high school friends, Kathy has preordered an autographed book! Hers will be the first signed copy I mail. This is really happening. It's still a little hard to believe. Wow.

I fixed my simple potato soup again and it really warmed our souls in this chilly weather. I'd never watched *Blue Bloods*, and picked up Season 1 at Walmart recently. I watched the first episode, but Larry went back to his computer work. I wound up watching 4 episodes by my bedtime--Donnie Wahlberg and Tom Selleck can make anything interesting. At least those who produce it can write crime stories about a multi-generation NYPD Catholic family, without the use of cuss words. They even pray at the supper table. I think I'm going to like this one.

MARCH 12

Today was a travel day to Pensacola, Florida, mostly on I-10 east. We have reservations at Big Lagoon State Park, which Larry rated a 3. It's a very small park with a 75-site campground. Our Site #1 was gravel, with wild brush on two sides, although random sites had concrete pads. The sand is a beautiful white here on the Panhandle of Florida.

With my friends in Cincinnati, Ohio, Myrtle Beach, South Carolina (really?), and Boston, Massachusetts all getting snow today, it's easy to look at the wild areas here and imagine that the white sand here is snow. We have only water and electric here, but our tanks are usually good for holding up to four days, so we should be fine. If not, we just have to pack the whole place and go to the dump early.

We both worked hard on our computers most of the day. I fixed a frozen bag of sweet and sour shrimp for supper.

Today we have reason to celebrate something new. I have complained repeatedly that our internet usage has been really high, as are, of course, our bills. We've had a 40G plan through Verizon that, as long as we kept our usage under the allowed 40G, we paid about $150 a month. Our problem was, we kept going over…waaaaaaay over, and some months would cost us $600+ in internet service.

It was with huge excitement that we discovered that Verizon finally offered an Unlimited Plan, and we were quick to hop on that train! We know they may slow down our speed rate if we use a bunch, but we'll take it. Now, we can enjoy Netflix, with or without local Wifi, without it costing us an arm and a leg—and a kidney.

MARCH 13

Today was another cloudy day of writing. I had a problem with my computer in the afternoon, and it really ticked me off, for some odd reason. I usually take such things in stride, reboot, and get over it. But today, I grabbed my car keys and told Larry that I needed a break from writing. The nearest Dollar General was less than 2 miles away, so there I went. Milk was the only thing I truly needed, but chocolate and sugar are always good staples to keep on hand. Chocolate, did I say Chocolate? A woman's aphrodisiac. And there I am, writing a book with no stash.

On my way back to the campground, I spotted a Fantastic Sam's. I've needed a haircut for a while, so I stopped in to see if they could take me now. Walking in the front door, I noticed a sign advertising Ladies' Nights on Monday, which knocked $5 off their regular price! Ann gave me a great cut, one that will last for a while, and the conversation was pleasant. God bless Ann.

We drove out to eat supper. The first place I'd picked out appeared to be more of a bar than grill, so I Googled for somewhere else nearby. We drove to a place named Hub Stacey's. The building was a wooden A-frame, and they had plastic curtains hung around the patio, so patrons could enjoy the outside without being too cold.

We agreed on a table indoors, then quietly took in our surroundings. There were dollar bills on every surface one could reach—and some places one couldn't! They were everywhere, stapled into the rough-hewn walls of the restaurant. We enjoyed a traditional French Dip on a toasted bun with Au Jus. I explained to the waiter that we would be sharing, and he was kind enough to bring us 2 baskets, with a half sandwich each, but I swear each basket had its own full order of onion rings.

Back at the rig, we watched some TV while the rain blew in. It was getting colder each day we were here, and tonight would be in the low 40's. We only have 30amp electric service here, so running both heat pumps is just not possible. Even if we only ran one of them, one mindless touch of the microwave or the coffee maker would blow everything, and one lucky soul would have to go outside to reset the box. To avoid confusion, we just used the propane furnace.

I received an email late in the evening, and my niece Editor Jana had more editing ready to go. I thought, "There is no way I'm going to start in on this so late." I went quickly to sleep, but awoke an hour later. I figured that I'd might as well put the awake time to good use, so I wound up editing until 3:30am. I sure did get a lot of work done tonight, after all!

MARCH 14

After staying up until nearly 4am, I slept in. I had left a note for Larry, so other than waking me up at 8am, asking me where the Jetpack wifi was, he did let me sleep.

Once up and ready, we went to National Naval Aviation Museum. "…the world's largest Naval Aviation museum and one of the most-visited museums in the state of Florida. Share the excitement of Naval Aviation's rich history and see more than 150 beautifully restored aircraft representing Navy, Marine Corps, and Coast Guard Aviation. These historic and one-of-a-kind aircraft are displayed both inside the Museum's nearly 350,000 square feet of exhibit space and outside on its 37-acre grounds."[8]

The world-famous Blue Angels are based at the Pensacola Naval Air Station. If we had come only a couple of weeks later, we would have had the opportunity to sit outside on bleachers and enjoy their practice show.

---

[8] www.navalaviationmuseum.org/

On another subject, when we ran our retail store, Pop 'N Stuff back in Myrtle Beach, I always encouraged tourists to ask the locals were to go to eat. I assured them that locals not only knew the best places with good food and reasonable prices, but they could steer you away from the bad ones. So, now that we're the tourists, I usually ask upon check-in, "I'm in town for only a few days. What's the absolute thing I must do before I leave town?" The park ranger was quick to answer, "Joe Patti's." We were going to go Sunday evening, but my Google app told me they were closed. So, we tried again today.

From the Museum, Joe Patti's was in the opposite direction from the campground. We entered the building to a tremendous fresh seafood market. There must have been 2 dozen people behind the counter waiting on customers. They were cutting and weighing out all kinds of fresh catch seafood: cod, flounder, shrimp, shark, mahi mahi, oysters, scallops, crab, lobster, salmon, and lots more.

Every type of fresh seafood you could imagine was on ice to the left, as far as you could see, and frozen seafood in glass-doored freezers on the right. Wow. I walked through an open break in the freezer wall and came to a large store area filled with spices, hot sauces, breading—anything you'd want to prepare your fresh catch.

Leviticus 11:9
Of all the creatures living in the water of the seas
and the streams
you may eat any that have fins and scales.

There was a deli counter, a sales counter, even another counter in the back that I never got to visit. When we took the Tabasco tour, we purchased a bottle of Tabasco Sweet & Spicy sauce and Larry loves it. We've looked for it at every place we've shopped, but no one has carried it. But Joe Patti's did! I bought him 2 bottles, so now I don't have worry for a while.

When I took my purchases to the counter, I told the cashier that someone had told me there was a great restaurant here, but I hadn't found it. She explained that it was in a separate building across the parking lot, but it closed at 4:30—it was 4:40. Dangit, we missed it again! And we're leaving tomorrow. Oh, well. At least we found the Tabasco sauce.

On the way out, a young lady offered me a coupon for beignets—buy an order, get an order free. I eagerly took the coupon and stepped over to the concession trailer, just a few steps away. I paid her, then watched her every step of the way as she pulled the dough, rolled it, cut it, fried it, then filled a few with raspberry and Bavarian crème. She smothered them in powdered sugar, put them in trays and bagged them. So, I paid for 6 and managed to get 13. Yum.

We were quickly back to the entry to the campground and still hadn't decided on a place to eat. For the sake of location, we chose Triggers, just a hop and skip from the park entrance. The online reviews were good. I ordered a small broiled dinner of shrimp and scallops with coleslaw and cheese grits. It was delicious, and both of us were filled. We left our Motorhome Ministry brochure and seed packet with the tip for our lovely waitress. May God bless her and her beautiful smile.

It was dark when we returned to the rig. We watched a recorded episode of *Alaskan Bush People*, and Larry went to bed. I stayed up to write in the quiet. It was another great day.

MARCH 15

Today started out as a simple travel day. As the crow flies, we were probably only about 10 miles from our destination. But there was a large span of water between here and there with no bridge over it, so it took us about an hour-and-a-half to make the trip. But let's do the math: we left a little after noon. We finally arrived about 4pm. Let me explain what else went down.

Well, before we even left, there was a holdup. Larry's mom was just fine when he called her Sunday afternoon, as he usually does. By yesterday, we'd heard from both of Larry's sisters telling us how sick she'd become, just since Monday. She did see the doctor on Tuesday, and he confirmed she had pneumonia. For someone 81 years old who's had a heart attack and struggles daily with COPD, this was very bad news.

They started her on powerful meds and sent her home, saying that the hospital was too full of the flu right now. She had another doctor's appointment scheduled for Thursday, but we got texts and phone calls this morning saying she was sicker than ever. We insisted they keep us informed, but wondered if we should be heading home.

We were still at Big Lagoon State Park at noon. We stopped at the dump station, checked out, then drove on the park service road until we could find a straight place to pull over and load the car onto the tow dolly. We have a system for this. I drive the car up onto the dolly, with Larry directing me. No problem there. Larry's job is to lay the strap assemblies over the tires and use the hooks and ratchets to secure the car onto the tow dolly. My job, while he's doing his job, is to put the tow lights onto the rear of the car and plug them into the electrical harness by the hitch.

I took the lights to the back of the car. I now put cloth underneath the strong magnetic bases, so they won't scratch the new car. I wind the long cord around the luggage rack, wrap it around the rear-view mirror, through the lawn chairs and reconnect the harness. But, it was then I noticed there were only 2 little prongs hanging out of the harness instead of 3. If I plugged this in, I knew that something was not going to work. Ahem. I'm smart that way.

I called Larry over to look at it, and after some time, we determined that the right turn signal wouldn't work properly. We would have to repair the harness as soon as possible. Lucky for us, there was a Walmart close by, right on the way.

We parked the rig way out in the parking lot, out of everyone's way. We quickly found the part he needed, and a couple other things on his list. I encouraged him to go pay for his stuff, go begin the repair, as I shopped for the rest of the items on my list. By the time I checked out, he nearly had it done, but with one little complication, which we soon worked out together. I nuked each of us something for lunch and we sat in the front seats to eat. I pointed directly across the street and said to Larry, "You see that Target over there, with the CVS sign?" Yes, he did. "Well, I told you yesterday that you have a prescription that has to be filled. While we're stopped here, how about we just go over there and get that done, too?"

He stayed in the motorhome while I went into Target, waited for the script, and walked the 201 steps back to the rig.

We were finally on our way! Our destination was Fort Pickens National Park, ironically still in Pensacola, Florida, which Larry rated a 6. The park is part of Gulf Islands National Seashore. Usually a drive is out on an Interstate, out in the open, with only scattered business exits. Today was completely through the developed city, so speed limits were slower and cluttered with traffic.

We basically took FL292 east then US98 south to Fort Pickens Road West. All along the beautiful Gulf. We got about 10 miles from the campground and lucked right into a dozen school busses pulling out of Santa Rosa Middle School at the end of the school day.

But we finally arrived at the park, and it's beautiful. A strip of white sand between the blue waters of the Gulf of Mexico and Pensacola Bay.

There was a huge nest in the campground, and we marveled at it. We eventually determined there was a pair of osprey in it, perhaps waiting for baby ospreys to hatch?

The park road that took us almost to the end of the peninsula has an amazing view of the Pensacola Bay to the right, and the Gulf of Mexico to the left. Nearly 80% of Fort Pickens National Park is underwater, which includes 30,000 acres of sovereign submerged lands protected as the Fort Pickens Aquatic Preserve.

Genesis 22:17
I will surely bless you and make your
descendants as numerous as the stars in the sky
and as the sand on the seashore.
Your descendants will take possession
of the cities of their enemies.

When I checked in, I picked up a bunch of park information, as I always do. One was a legal-sized sheet of paper, printed on both sides, listing all the amphibians, reptiles, and mammals that have been observed on the land and in the water of Gulf Islands National Seashore. I didn't sit and count them, because there were so many, but I'd bet there are over 125 species listed. One bird in particular, rated its own glossy card.

The rangers take pride in doing all they can to protect all wildlife, but especially endangered shorebirds. For that reason, you can only go 25 mph on the main road. The card explains: "Each spring, shorebirds like Least Terns, fly thousands of miles from South America to nest and raise their young on the beaches of Gulf Islands National Seashore. Some of these shorebirds, like the Snowy Plover, are threatened or endangered. Snowy Plover adults and chicks frequent the road and shoulders to feed on insects. Least Terns have been hit while flying low over the road while attempting to defend their nests."[9]

It continued to explain just how bad the situation is: "Gulf Islands National Seashore and research partners study the survival rates of shorebirds in the park. In 2016, Snowy Plovers laid 70 nests in the Fort Pickens and Santa Rosa Areas of the Park. These nests produced 78 chicks, but only 9 survived long enough to fly away from the park. Of the 69 chicks killed, 11 were hit by vehicles traveling on the road."[10] They even have another card for the Santa Rosa Beach Mouse, which is found only on Perdido Key, nearly next door.

We quickly set up, and settled in for the evening. Even though we have sufficient electric, it's going down to 39 degrees tonight, so we didn't even bother with the heat pumps, we went right to the propane furnaces. It's a nice warm heat, and the only way to warm this place when it gets this cold. I thawed out a pork syrup patty that I'd bought back in Avery Island and Larry took it outside to grill. We had leftover onion rings from our huge meal at Hub Stacey's, and I ask him to put them on the grill, too. A can of baked beans finished out the meal. Everything was delicious, and our bellies were full.

We watched one episode of *Alaskan Bush People* that I knew we'd seen already, and Larry watched a Showtime series available on Netflix. I won't even name it, because I don't like it at all. We watched the first one and I didn't like it. I agreed to a second one, just to see if it would pick up. I didn't. It's depressing, and I don't like to watch depressing stuff. Give me happy any and every day!

Larry's mom called us herself to explain what was going on at the hospital. Every bed in the hospital is full. They want to admit her,

---

[9] nps.gov/GulfIslands

[10] nps.gov/GulfIslands

but they have nowhere to put her. So, she's still in the ER, but at least she's lying down in a bed, being taken care of. Praise the Lord.

I wrote until nearly midnight. I prayed desperately for mom.

MARCH 16

The sun is shining and it's the first day of the warmup. Lots of folks wouldn't consider a high of 57 degrees today a warmup, but tonight's only going down to 47, then tomorrow night will be 55—most definitely a warmup! By Sunday, we'll see 73 for a high. That's much, much better. It is Florida, after all.

I have the window next to my computer table open. There's a slow, cool breeze coming in, and the sounds and sights are ever-changing. Seeing a beautiful but unusual bird, I Googled it to find it was an Eastern Bluebird. I watched as a family of 5 walked by in the direction of the beach, all of them carrying fishing poles. I'm hearing another bird close by, caw-cawing like a crow. Every few minutes, someone on a bicycle goes pedaling by. As crowded as the campground is, it's wonderfully quiet.

In addition, we're still close enough to the Pensacola Naval Air Station to have some of the jets go screaming high overhead, as well as smaller aircraft from Pensacola International Airport.

We enjoyed hot tomato soup for lunch. Yum. And just about the time I'd written about how wonderfully quiet it was here in the campground, a ranger decides to load pea gravel into his little bulldozer and repair all the mudholes around our campsite. Dump, turn around, back up to drag the plow to level the gravel, pull back up over gravel, drive over gravel to pack it down, drive away to go get more gravel, repeat. And he just had to pick our site and 6 others right next to us. Geesh.

By the end of the noisy afternoon, I was ready to get outside for a while. Larry drove us out to the end of the peninsula to see Fort Pickens itself. The fort was completed in 1834 and remained in use until 1947. It was built in a pentagonal shape, as was common at that time, and was named after Revolutionary War hero Andrew Pickens.

I walked first into the Visitor Center and stamped my Passport. The rangers at the counter were busy, so we walked on; we would get it at the end. It was fascinating to walk the historic fort, attempting to determine what each of the primitive-looking areas had been used for. The first numbered site we came across had the number 12 on it. Then, the more we walked, the lower the numbers became, ending with number 1. Back to where we began, I could see through the glass door that the rangers in the Visitor Center were no longer busy. I walked in and said, "Now that you're not busy and now that we've taken the entire tour backwards, may we have a printed tour guide?" They both laughed and offered me a map with a smile, as I stamped my Passport. It had been an interesting tour and it was free.

We drove back to the campground and I started supper. I grilled some shrimp, basted it with sweet and sour sauce, and served it with fried rice. It was mighty tasty indeed.

After a couple hours of FOX News, Larry watched another episode of the depressing Netflix show. I asked him politely to find something else to watch. We agreed to check out *Quantico*, and I found the first episode to be quite interesting. It's about a fresh FBI agent who's being set up for a New York City Terminal bombing. We'll see if it's worth watching.

MARCH 17

We were very worried about mom. We decided early that it was time to start heading home.

We hopped on I-10 east from Fort Pickens Road, and put the pedal to the metal. We had at least 11 driving hours ahead of us, 726 miles. We stayed on the I-10 until we headed north on I-95. North of Jacksonville, Florida, we arrived at the Pilot Travel Center in St. Mary's Georgia to refuel. We knew we had to stop and rest. We could go the rest of the way tomorrow. Despite the comings and goings of massive trucks all around, we slept deeply.

MARCH 18

We were up early, anxious to get home. We continued up I-95 north to Route 378 east to US501 south to US17 north. We were home.

* * * * *

APRIL 25, 2017—5 weeks later

It's late as I feel the need to sit down to write this evening. Early in the morning, day after tomorrow, we will set off for Odyssey 2, which will be from late April to November. It's another amazing quest, set for all New England and parts of Canada. There should be much excitement in the air.

But, I sit here tonight, I'm unsettled. We've been "home" for weeks now, and it's been a whirlwind of events. My heart is sad. We took care of a few doctors' appointments, but planned to help Diana with a lot of projects at her house, which never happened.

We had come home about 10 days earlier than planned, because Larry's mom became ill and was taken to the hospital. She spent 9 long days in there, fighting pneumonia. For an 81-year-old, that's tough. Then one afternoon, the handsome PT guy came to walk her around on the ward floor, and she did great. I walked with them, and Mom was amazed! No oxygen, hardly no breathlessness at all.

She had made an amazing recovery in those past 24 hours, while we were speeding home. They sent her home the very next afternoon.

She managed 2 days at home, but when Larry checked on her on the following Monday morning, she was nearly unresponsive, with an oxygen level of only 83. He managed to get her in the car and took her straight back to the same hospital, only a few miles away. Although they'd discharged her only 3 days before, her pneumonia was still present, so they restarted her on antibiotics and steroids.

She did recover some, but then they discovered a UTI, and began treating her for that, as well. A few days later, as she laid in bed, she began moaning in pain. I would have to say that her nurse Joseph was on top of things, but the doctor didn't manage to see her until late in the evening, when she decided that Mom be moved quickly to the ICU step-down unit (with a smaller nurse-patient ratio), which was a step-up for her. It quickly became obvious to them that the pain she was feeling was coming from deep in her belly. A surgeon was called. They took her in for emergency surgery at 2am, when a nurse called us at the rig, and we rushed to the hospital.

According to the surgeon, it had started with diverticulitis, which could have begun days or even weeks earlier. Undiagnosed, it had led to a perforated bowel, which turned septic very quickly. Her final diagnosis was c.diff. She was very, very sick and kept in ICU after the surgery, given constant care. Larry's sister Sherri and her husband, Ron, flew in from Cincinnati the next morning, and we left mom long enough to pick them up. I'm so glad they could spend those days with her, because by Wednesday, it was clear that mom was losing the battle.

Skipping the rest of the details, she just couldn't find the strength to rebound from the surgery. She had whispered to Larry, "I want to die." It was the last thing she said to him, her dying wish.

Several times during what would be her final evening, I witnessed her eyes pop open, her eyes fixed at something high and faraway. I knew in my heart she could see the angels who had come for her. I hugely regret not asking her about them. She did that 3 times that evening, then she became still. We quietly left her, planning on seeing her again in a few hours, but that was not to be. Sherri, Lisa, and Ron arrived minutes after our departure, and she died just before midnight on Wednesday, April 5, on what would have been our son Bobby's 38th birthday.

Larry read this at his Mother's Funeral:

> Revelation 21:4
> He will wipe every tear from their eyes.
> There will be no more death or mourning or crying or pain,
> for the old order of things has passed away."

Larry told those attending that "This generation has passed. He is now the Patriarch of the family, the oldest of his generation. It's a very strange feeling."

Mom was always a stickler for details and paperwork, and Sherri quickly discovered 3 sets (one for each of the kids) of 8-page, single-spaced instructions on how things were to be handled after her death. She had written her obituary, and where she wanted it published. She left specific instructions for her funeral and flowers. She even labeled a page that was to be read at her memorial service.

My brother-in-law Ron is an ordained minister, and that's exactly what he did the next Tuesday evening, before 100 people at her home church in South Carolina, Chapel by the Sea in Cherry Grove. He asked them, "How many of you know someone who preached their own funeral?"

Wednesday was another day of frenzy, trying to help Sherri plow through stuff at mom's condo. Thursday was an early jet flight to Cincinnati for all of us, where the service at the cemetery in Milford would be held Saturday afternoon.

That Saturday was a beautiful, sunny day. We enjoyed the hugs and kind words of dozens of extended family members and friends, some of whom we hadn't seen for decades. Some were once friends in Epsilon Sigma Alpha, a philanthropic women's sorority of which Mom, Sherri, and I had been members. Dear friends, nieces and nephews and their spouses, an aunt, some cousins, and cousins brought grandchildren that we had never met.

I had purchased bundles of plastic flowers to put on my family graves. Both of their copper vases have been lost over the years to nature or thievery, so I stuck my parents' flowers into the hole in the ground, where the vase had been. I was disappointed to discover that Bobby's marker had been pulled up in order to bury Mom next to Larry's dad, Charlie. My best friend, Deb was with me, so I asked her if she would bring Bobby's flowers back at a later time. As her mom and dad are also buried nearby, I knew that she would. She's been putting flowers on all their graves for decades.

| Revelation 14:13 |
| Then I heard a voice from heaven say, "Write this: |
| Blessed are the dead who die in the Lord from now on." |
| "Yes," says the Spirit, "they will rest from their labor, |
| for their deeds will follow them." |

But many other, happier events occurred during this time at home in Myrtle Beach. We showed up at one Sunday School class and my friend, John walked up to me, gave me a big bear hug, and asked if I would do him a favor. I had no clue what he might ask, but I answered, "Sure." He was just a-grinnin' when he pulled my book from behind his back and asked me to sign it. I was dumbstruck. It was real. It was the first book I'd ever laid my hands on! I was speechless. I thumbed through the pages, recognizing the words on them. I was in awe. I nearly cried. God is so good! Of course, I'd sign his book! He and his wife Teni invited us to lunch afterward, which we thoroughly enjoyed.

Although we went there only on special occasions, I have always loved the Copper Kettle in downtown Conway, South Carolina. They offer a wonderful, home-cooked buffet brunch on Sundays, and the best Southern-fried chicken ever. We took our time, catching up on each other's lives. I had known these wonderful folks for over a decade now. Over dessert, I asked, "Why haven't we done this more often?" None of us could answer that.

While my beloved Pastor Barry was at Langston Baptist Church, he once explained the acronym that BUFFET stands for: Big Ugly Fat Folks Eating Together. Ha ha. How true that can be.

It wasn't until weeks later that my case of books arrived! Larry and I had placed an order for 50 books, and finally received them just a few days ago. When folks order them online to be signed by the author, I now have them readily available.

APRIL 26

It was our last day at "home." I stayed busy washing and preparing for the trip, and picked up some last-minute stuff from the grocery. We invited Diana over to the motorhome for supper, and we enjoyed some of those white bratwursts that we Cincinnatians love. What a treat. I gave Zoe a new bone and she was as content as we were. There were lots of hugs and sweet things shared. I didn't want to leave.

> Isaiah 40:3
> A voice of one calling: In the wilderness
> prepare the way for the LORD·
> make straight in the desert a highway for our God.

APRIL 27

Six am came early. I had an 8am doctor's appointment nearby and Larry had a 9:40 doctor's appointment about 15 miles away, so we split up. He would finish packing up the motorhome, then meet at the grocery store near his doctor's office, where they had a big parking lot in which to park the rig.

My appointment with the neurosurgeon who wired together my fractured C-2 went well. He told me the x-rays confirmed that all my hardware was exactly as it was when he installed it. I had complained that I'd begun to have pain over the past few months where there'd been no pain before, so he had sent me for a CT scan.

He began today's visit by asking me to specifically show him where the pain was, and when it hurt. I showed him where, he laid hands on the right side of my neck, then backed away. I was telling him how even looking up would sometimes cause pain. To illustrate, I looked up toward the ceiling and I heard this huge "crack." My eyes met his—which were as large as saucers—and I asked, "Did you hear that?" "Oh, yes, I did!" He asked if that was the first time, and I confirmed that it happened all the time.

His solution: take out the hardware. "It's done its duty, so if it gets bothersome, we can always take it out." I laughed, crossed my forefingers in front of me as if to ward off evil spirits, and said, "Not in this lifetime!" We both understood that I would have to live with this bit of pain. I was just delighted to hear that nothing was wrong!

I drove to where Larry was waiting in the motorhome. When I arrived, he was sitting in the reading room, and when it was time to flush, the fresh tank water wouldn't pump. Great. We're not even out of town yet, and something's messed up. Well, we didn't have time to investigate right now. He hopped in the car and I dropped him off for his appointment.

I quickly headed to nearby downtown Conway, to the Baptist Association where I used to work. My co-worker Diane still works there, and she had been one of the first to review the beginning of my book. I figured I owed her one. I arrived quickly, only to find a note on the door, "Running errands. Be back at 10am." That was 20 minutes away! I returned to my car and began writing her a note: "Of all the times you chose to run errands..." And, at the very moment I finished it, here she comes, back into the parking lot. Thank you, Lord, for such blessings!

She didn't recognize my new car, but she quickly realized who was in it and came running toward me. We're both "huggers" and the hug she offered up was great (though I'd forgotten just how short my friend is). She thought I had already left town, so it was quite a surprise. We stood right there in the parking lot to squeeze in a brief visit, before I had to leave to go pick up Larry. We hugged several more times and made a promise to see each other, to share an evening when we came home for the holidays. Deal.

I will stop here to explain something in life that's very special to me. I call them "smiles of recognition", and I think they are the greatest of compliments. Imagine that you see your friend before they see you. Then, that instant when they realize it's you, their eyes light up and they get that beautiful smile from ear to ear. Not one of those, "Oh, my goodness, I can't stand her, I hope she didn't see me, I'll bolt the other way..." kind of looks. Smiles of recognition. Smiles of love and acceptance. Smiles of delight. They truly bless my heart.

When I returned to the doctor's office, Larry had been waiting just a few minutes. When we returned to the grocery store, we quickly dollied the car. I returned to the motorhome, but stopped at the door. I laid my right hand on the door and prayed that God would bless that goofy water pump, so that we could be on our way without further delay. I went back to the control panel, turned the pump back on and lo and behold, it worked! Thank you, Lord again for more blessings!

We were on our way. Today's destination was north of Raleigh, NC, because we had matters to attend to there.

It wasn't long before we entered the mainstream of traffic on I-95, north. I really don't like I-95 at all. It's outdated and insufficient, heavily traveled, and folks drive like idiots. The cars and pickups drive like racecar drivers, and the truckers are all running against the clock. And it's a known fact that drug traffickers frequent the I-95. But the skies were a brilliant blue with big, white, puffy clouds. Yet another silent prayer for God to keep that hedge of protection around us.

The Master Tow dolly we'd purchased last year has one grease fitting that has never accepted grease, and by this time, it was becoming a deep concern of Larry's. If it locked up suddenly, the results would be terrible, so he decided to have the manufacturers check it on the way.

As we continued our drive to Fayetteville, NC where the Master Tow manufacturer is located, we were eventually blessed with twisting, winding roads that took us through lots of farmland.

We saw acres of what I think was winter wheat, and lots of corn coming up already—one field was already knee-high! To my Ohio farmer friends, corn is usually "Knee high by the Fourth of July." Yet other fields were sad, either waiting to be prepped for late plantings or simply abandoned, I couldn't tell. There were plenty of cows and horses about, and we even spotted a few donkeys.

The most noteworthy thing I saw today was a church sign that encouraged all to have a "Blest Easter." Really? I can't make this stuff up!

We took an exit for Bethune Drive in Carvers Creek, then drove to Slocomb Road.

We finally arrived at Master Tow in Fayetteville, and even unannounced, they were more than happy to take the dolly into the shop. They quickly replaced the fitting, then greased them all, as well. Kuddos that they repaired it at no charge, considering it had never worked at all.

Well, that went well.

We picked up I-295 north in Fayetteville, then US401 at Ramsey Street. Back on I-95 north, then I-40 west. Then it was a jumble of other routes, I-440 to NC50 to US70, I-440 west and took exit 7B. We followed NC50 north to Falls Lake State Recreation Area, in Wake Forest, North Carolina, which Larry rated a 5.

On the way, we noticed that the chassis air conditioning was not working when we put it in the max position. Larry figured it was a wire shorting out, under the motorhome. As soon as we were settled, he crawled under the rig to investigate. He did find a pinched wire that had begun to rub the metal chassis, but since it acts up continuously, there must be something else messed up, too. No more max AC until he has the opportunity and the good luck to find the short. He compared it to finding a needle in a haystack.

We wanted to meet up with one of Larry's cousins and his family, who live in Raleigh, and we hadn't seen them in 5-6 years. We'd hoped to see them this evening, but as we texted them during the drive, we learned that something had come up. We would have to try again tomorrow.

There was also someone else we wanted terribly to see, who also lived in the area. Priscilla had been in high school when she came to work for us at Pop 'N Stuff back in Gatlinburg, Tennessee. She was a delightful young lady, in the same class as Diana in high school. God love her, she was one of the clumsiest people ever! Remember the old series *Alice?* Remember the opening theme when clumsy Vera spilled an entire box of straws, and they flew everywhere, like the box had exploded? That was our sweet Priscilla.

Larry and I had enjoyed some of the silliest conversations with those 2 girls! Her family's last visit to Myrtle Beach had been long before their youngest was born, and she was now 5. Priscilla and I texted back and forth and by the time we arrived at Rolling View Campground at Falls Lake Recreation Area, we had finalized arrangements for her and her home-schooled children—Noelle, Garrett, Giana, and Amelia—to have a field trip to the state park the very next day.

AND, we would meet Larry's cousin's family for dinner tomorrow evening. Perfect!

APRIL 28

My heart is so full that it just may explode as I write tonight. Today had been a hot, sweaty, but wonderful day! Priscilla showed up promptly (she is usually late) at 11am, with her 4 beautiful and talented children, and enough food to feed an army. We threw a tablecloth on the picnic table outside and we all dug in.

Between bites, we were asking all sorts of questions to get acquainted with the kids, and they were good at shooting questions right back at us. They understood that we lived in our motorhome. How do you wash your clothes? Where do you stay? Do the steps come in when you drive? We showed them how the extensions come in and go out. They thought the canopy was fantastic and they all thought the closed-system potty was "really cool." Weird, but cool.

They had brought a fishing pole and Giana and Amelia really wanted to fish. So, Larry took them down to the lake and showed them how it's done. The lake was flooded and murky from recent rains, so they didn't catch a thing, but they sure had fun. The rest of us eventually joined them and Priscilla took lots of selfies of the group. We were even treated to a visit from a tiny lavender moth who landed on each and every one of us. Sweet.

They are tremendously talented kids, but if I tried to list their credentials, I'd just mess it up, because all of them are smarter than I am. Priscilla and her husband Adam are doing a wonderful job of raising God-loving, independent, caring, loving, talented children. Oh, if only all parents would invest such time in their kids!

I cried when they pulled away, my heart was so filled with love and hugs. We had just enough time left to freshen up and drive to meet the Sander Family for dinner.

John 15:12-15

My command is this: Love each other as I have loved you.
[13] Greater love has no one than this: to lay down one's life for one's friends.
[14] You are my friends if you do what I command.
[15] I no longer call you servants,
because a servant does not know his master's business.
Instead, I have called you friends,
for everything that I learned from my Father I have made known to you.

We had arranged to meet at Fujisan Steakhouse, a Japanese hibachi restaurant in Northwest Raleigh. We met now-teenage daughter Sarah, daughter Victoria (who was barely toddling when we saw her last) and son Landon, whom we had never met. We sat close to Dale and his wife, Regina so we could chat. The entertainment was good; the food was fantastic. I ordered scallops and filet, which I shared with Larry, of course. He always tells me, "I can't eat much." I jokingly threaten to charge him a quarter every time he says that.

It was the first time I'd seen fried noodles prepared on the hibachi along with fried rice. Everything was absolutely delicious.

The hostess recognized the Sanders and generously allowed us to tie up the table for a while. They too, have talented and busy kids. It was a wonderful evening.

That's one thing I really miss when we're on the road: friends. We're always in the company of only each other and strangers. Sometimes, that just feels lonely. But days like this will keep me content for a while. After all, we only have to wait until July to see Diana again, August for a date with the Kirbys, then back home to the beach in early November to see all of our friends.

Today was an absolutely wonderful day.

Psalm 127:3-5
Children are a heritage from the LORD,
offspring a reward from him.
[4] Like arrows in the hands of a warrior
are children born in one's youth.
[5] Blessed is the man whose quiver is full of them.
They will not be put to shame
when they contend with their opponents in court.

APRIL 29

We took our time getting ready this morning. We probably shouldn't have, because by the end of the day, the trip turned out to be much longer than we'd anticipated.

Our destination before nightfall was Shenandoah National Park, Virginia. Frankie determined that today's route would be up I-85, and I did enjoy it much more than I-95. Our route was 2 lanes northbound, with an 18-mile stretch under construction in North Carolina. Once in Virginia, most of the time it was a beautiful drive, 2 lanes northbound, framed for miles by heavy foliage on both sides. You couldn't even see the southbound lanes! There were all types of evergreen and deciduous trees crowded in, with a scattering of dogwoods and other trees, some of which were a lovely purple.

We stopped in the Virginia Welcome Center and collected lots of information about local places of interest to visit. We returned to the motorhome, cranked up the generator and prepared a lunch of White Castles and Hot Pockets to tide us over until supper.

The further and further we drove, the skinnier and curvier the routes became. It was a beautiful ride and Larry did a terrific job of keeping that huge motorhome between the painted lines. The reasonably flat land became higher and hillier. The route took us through many miles of beautiful lands, some grazelands, some farmlands, even some wineries on the way. Many acres of the grazelands were covered in small, bright yellow flowers. I don't think they were dandelions, but they were that same, brilliant color. There were small cozy houses and large, perfectly-manicured mansions. Parts of the route reminded me of Lexington, Kentucky, where perfect white or brown fencing surrounded the large horse farms. It was all simply beautiful.

On today's drive, up I-85 north to I-95 north to Richmond, Virginia, then I-64 northwest to US15 north and US33 north. Country roads and change of elevation had taken us from full-bloom spring to barely out of winter. Many of the trees in the park had no leaves at all. There were some princess trees that had flowers on them (which Smoky Mountain rangers consider weeds), and a few of those with purple blooms. There was only a rare Dogwood and not a single azalea or mountain laurel that I could see.

The last part of the trek found us climbing from a 500-foot altitude to well over 2,500 at the summit, then back down again. The 6-hour trip had been mostly enjoyable until Frankie announced that we had arrived at our destination. The address I had found online was not the address of the campground, but the National Park Office. We were in the wrong place!

We were hot and tired and ready to park. Larry found the correct address, which we'd passed about 6 miles back, so we made a U-turn and headed back up the mountain. We pulled in, only to be told that all the campgrounds in the National Park were either filled or closed. The ranger allowed us to enter the Park to turn the rig around, and I was on my phone, searching for somewhere to camp nearby.

I found a Yogi Bear Jellystone Park, in Luray, Virginia, which Larry rated it a 6, only short distance away, and we went back down the mountain on US211. They had plenty of room AND they had full utilities. Maybe this wasn't such a bad thing after all, as the current heat wave will take us to 90 degrees again tomorrow. There were plenty of kids in the park and we put the banner and the kids packets out, but not one packet was taken. We were a little disappointed in that but knew God is in control.

So, by the time I wrote this, we've escaped the 90-degree weather outside, enjoyed a nice meal, a nice shower, nice air conditioning, and plenty of electric to work on the book. I've already done 2 loads of laundry. We are here, safe and sound. As usual, not without some sort of frustration, but we'll be here for a couple of days.

With the hot temperature outside our main refrigerator will not keep up with keeping the foods at 40 degrees. The best it can do is a 30-degree drop in temperature, so all the foods are at 60 degrees. It was time to plug in the electric small fridge to get the dairy and most perishable foods into it. Out west, we found this to be the case when it got really hot.

I stop here for just a moment to say I wish every time I see a photo op, I could freeze time in that second, take the shot, then be on our way. It's amazing what you catch glimpses of, while speeding down the road. In one small town we drove through today, I spotted a guy working on his pickup truck. Not so special, right? But, he wasn't just standing there with the hood up, or underneath it—he was stretched completely flat ABOVE the engine, with his head deep inside and his legs sticking straight out the front. I've never in my life seen such a sight! If I only had pics of all the crazy things I've seen.

I've watched a wide band of terrible storms cross the US earlier today. I will be saying more prayers for the friends I have in Ohio, Indiana, Kentucky, and Tennessee. Lord, I pray they are all safe. I praise God that we are.

> Isaiah 4:6
> It will be a shelter and shade from the heat of the day,
> and a refuge and hiding place from the storm and rain.

APRIL 30

Today was a Sunday, and Larry's taking this Sunday pretty hard. It had become his practice to call his mom every Sunday afternoon, when we could. Now the notion hits him, and he realizes once again that she's gone from this green earth.

But we have peace in knowing that she is safely with the Lord, enjoying an existence that we can only begin to imagine. Grief affects Christians, as well, no doubt about it. I do find it confusing at times. We live our lives as Christians, knowing that a better and pain-free eternity awaits us. Yet, when we lose someone to that eternity, we cry for them. We complain that it was such a shame that she died.

As I explained repeatedly when Bobby died, my tears were not for my son. Bobby was just fine—in the presence of Jesus. The tears were for me. I missed him terribly.

I tried to reassure Larry the best I could, because he already knows these things. This must become our "new normal."

> Matthew 5:4
> Blessed are those who mourn, for they will be comforted.

The only thing on the agenda today was to drive through the Shenandoah National Park on Skyline drive, the main park road. And the drive was indeed beautiful.

Again, this area was just beginning to come out of winter, because of the elevation. It was hazy when we set out, so the few pictures we took in the morning were not very good. As the day progressed, and we could better enjoy the amazing views from the overlooks in the park. One of the overlooks we pulled into had several swarms of bees that had settled into one of the short stone walls that edge the parking lot. I even warned some foreign tourists who were walking too close for my comfort. Even though most of nature was still asleep, the dandelions were in full bloom everywhere! Nothing hardier than a dandelion plant, for sure.

As we traveled Skyline Drive, we decided to stop at Skyland Inn and have lunch. This scenic rustic lodge in the National Park is set on 16 acres overlooking the Shenandoah Valley and a 5-minute walk from the Appalachian Trail. We visited the gift shop first, where I splurged and purchased a 45-cent postcard of the Park in the spring. In the rustic dining room, we enjoyed the panoramic view along with a club sandwich and a side salad with blackberry vinaigrette dressing.

When the club arrived, we were amazed at its size! It may have been only 3 slices of bread, but they were the biggest slices I'd ever seen—like 6-7 inches' square! Larry doesn't care for ham, which I love, so we swapped. He had a turkey-bacon club and I enjoyed a ham-bacon club. There was absolutely no way to eat it all.

We continued to the Visitors Center, where we viewed the displays and stamped my passport.

There we learned about how the Civilian Conservation Corps (CCC) was responsible for the Shenandoah National Park that we see today. "They built the roads, walls, buildings, trails—even planted the trees and shrubs. It was a public work relief program that operated from 1933 to 1942 in the United States for unemployed, unmarried men from relief families. They were a group of young men in their teens and twenties and paid very little. But they were housed and fed.

"The Civilian Conservation Corps was one of the most successful New Deal programs of the Great Depression from the new President, Franklin Delano Roosevelt. In his first 100 days in office, President Roosevelt approved several measures as part of his "New Deal," including the Emergency Conservation Work Act (ECW), better known as the Civilian Conservation Corps (CCC).

"With that action, he brought together the nation's young men and the land in an effort to save them both. Roosevelt proposed to recruit thousands of unemployed young men, enlist them in a peacetime army, and send them to battle the erosion and destruction of the nation's natural resources. More than any other New Deal agency, the CCC is considered to be an extension of Roosevelt's personal philosophy. It existed for fewer than 10 years, but left a legacy of strong, handsome roads, bridges, and buildings throughout the United States. Between 1933 and 1942, more than 3,000,000 men served in the CCC.[11]

My daddy had taught me about the CCC when I was young. Columbia Parkway was the most common way to get from the eastern suburbs where we lived into downtown Cincinnati. Spanning for many miles, there is a massive concrete wall that had been built during the Depression. It was determined years ago that the area above would inevitably, over decades, slide down onto Columbia Parkway, Eastern Avenue and into the nearby Ohio River. A collection of smaller communities, the city refers to them as East End communities, would also slide down with it. I can personally vouge that the wall they built stands tall yet today.

---

[11] u-s-history.com/pages/h1586.html

The sun was finally shining on us, as popcorn storms formed to the northeast. As we drove back down, everything looked different in the sunshine. Instead of a huge variety of trees, as we often see, the forest seemed comprised mostly of one type of tree, which I think might have been white oaks.

They are gnarly trees, and none of them yet had leaves—they were all buck naked. They were all faded in color, many covered in some type of moss. They were the types of creepy-looking trees you see in spooky movies, with long bending branches, and odd faces on them. Even the rocks had the appearance of big bugs or turtles. It was indeed an adventure.

Numbers 24:6
Like valleys they spread out, like gardens beside a river,
like aloes planted by the LORD, like cedars beside the waters.

After leaving the park, we drove back down the mountain and west on US211 again into the small historic town of Luray, VA. A quaint little town with small rural homes along a main street. A stone tower welcomes you to the town.

"The Belle Brown Northcott Memorial Tower is more commonly known as Luray's Singing Tower. The carillon was erected in 1937 in memory of Belle Brown Northcott who was the wife of T. C. Northcott the former president of Luray Cavern Corporation.

"The singing tower stands 117-feet tall and contains a carillon of 47-bells. The largest bell is six feet wide and weighs a total of 7,640 pounds, while the smallest bell weighs in at 12 ½ pounds.

During the summer, regularly scheduled recitals are held on the grounds located in a small park directly across from Luray Caverns."[12]

"Luray is known as the gateway to the Shenandoah National Park connecting nature lovers and sightseers to the Skyline Drive which extends eastward along the Blue Ridge Mountains."[13] We had seen signs for the Luray Caverns, but we did not stop there. We have already enjoyed such amazing caverns at Mammoth and Carlsbad Caverns National Parks; there just seemed to be no point. The historic town is well-maintained, but considering it was Sunday, most everything was closed. God bless the small town.

We drove back to the campground, and put the car back up on the dolly, in preparation of leaving in the morning. I put some chicken on the stove to cook, hung a load of laundry, then started another load. I treated myself to a 40-minute nap, to rest my neck from all the side-to-side sightseeing I'd done that day. The cool was delightful! After supper, Larry found a series we'd never seen on Netflix called *Night Shift*. It was pretty interesting, so we watched 3 episodes before Larry went to bed. That was my opportunity to write.

Tomorrow, we'll be heading toward a campground in Maryland, outside of DC but within the beltway, where we will stay for probably 5 days. No water, sewer, or electric. It will be interesting, going back on the battery grid after being on full utilities for a bit. But thank God that He is going before us. The highs will begin to drop tomorrow, and should be more seasonal by tomorrow night. The older I get, the more these heat waves just kill me. But thank you, Lord, that the weather overall is not bad at all.

---

[12] waymarking.com/waymarks/WM9K7Y

[13] townofluray.com/tourist-information.html

And thank you for another day of enjoying your beautiful creations. From the mountains to the city tomorrow: keep us safe.

MAY 1

We started out on US211 east then US29 north, I-66 east and I-495 north to MD201 south to Kenilworth Ave in Greenbelt, MD. There is definitely more traffic in the concrete jungle of our Nation's capital, Washington, DC.

We purposely delayed departure this morning to make sure the morning commuters were out of the way. While we were driving out of the Shenandoah National Park, it was the first time I'd noticed there are no evergreens in this forest. Well, maybe some were out there somewhere, but there were none where I was. It looked so different, considering how many months we've traveled through forests that were supremely conifer.

We passed through small towns, with small businesses, many still waiting for the tourist season to arrive. Just an hour on the road, we saw lots of evergreen—not so much pine but lots and lots of cedar. I also saw a wildflower that was new to me: a mustard-colored flower, with fronds hanging from the stalk. Very nice.

We're passing the exit for Dulles, and the roadway is in great shape. Much better than we've seen recently. The traffic is light, and we're convinced that it's simply because of the time of day. We sure need to be off the roads before school lets out.

Washington has plenty of HOV lanes on their interstate highways. I can understand that local governments want people to carpool, which would result in less cars during busy hours, so they give them an incentive. Okay. One sign explains that HOV is for High Occupancy Vehicles, with more than one occupant. But then, it states that motorcycles can use the lane at any time. Motorcycles? Really? I certainly wouldn't consider them a high occupancy vehicle!

Larry was nervous with this big rig on the DC expressways. He was like this in LA, too. There were just so many vehicles speeding, changing lanes, no signals, exit only lanes, bumper to bumper traffic.

I had to laugh when we crossed over into Maryland. Frankie loudly stated there is a "border crossing ahead." Yes, Frankie, we are entering a new country, DC. I do notice, once in Maryland, that I'm seeing a lot of what I call Princess Trees, or paulownia tomentosa.[14]

I learned long ago from the park rangers at Smoky Mountain National Park that they're considered weeds in the pristine park forests, because they throw so many gazillions of seeds, that they can easily overtake other naturally-occurring vegetation.

Once in Maryland, we found very little construction and no potholes along our route. There are little bumps getting off and on bridges, but that's nothing. Good job, Maryland!

We pulled into Greenbelt National Park, a day early, which Larry rated a 4. There was no one there to check us in. Reading the instructions, we went back to the campsite we'd been assigned for the rest of the week, and no one was checked in for tonight. We filled out the paperwork, paid for the extra night, then deposited the envelope at the entrance.

The campground is near empty. I began to wonder if people even know there is a campground only 12 miles from our Nation's Capital within the Beltway. We unloaded the car, stowed the tow

---

[14] nps.gov/grsm/learn/nature/trees-shrubs-list.htm

dolly, and backed in the rig. With no utilities to hook up, it was time to explore!

We planned to ride the Metro, which would take us into downtown Washington, D.C. I pulled up the site on my iPhone, only to discover an alert, which explained that Greenbelt and College Park stations were both closed this week—the two closest stations to us! We would have to make other plans.

But we were in a rush to see downtown, so Larry drove the car. It took a while because of the heavy traffic, but we finally made it. Then it took a while to find a place to park that didn't cost us a bloody fortune.

We were blessed to find a parking spot right on the Capital Mall on the main circle road. Once parked, we walked several blocks to arrive at the Smithsonian Museum of Natural History, and we went inside. I posted a pic on Facebook, to ask where the pic was taken. It was a view of the Rotunda information center. The mammoth was made famous by the movie, *"Night at the Museum."* starring Ben Stiller. The Museum was enjoyable, and spent a couple of hours there.

The museum has just about anything in it regarding nature from animals, earthquakes, weather, volcanos, rocks, sea life, butterflies, even mummies. It was all so amazing—we could have spent days in there.

When coming to a place like this, I leave with more questions than I arrived with. I read all this information about things that occurred to Earth millions of years ago. Yet the Bible leads me to conclude that He created the earth about 6,000 years ago. It was authored by the Creator and is without error. You can make your own assumptions from that statement.

Genesis 1:1
In the beginning, God created the heavens and the earth.

> Genesis 2:7
> Then the LORD God formed a man from the dust of
> the ground and breathed into his nostrils the breath of life,
> and the man became a living being.

"The most amazing sight in this museum is the Hope Diamond. The Hope Diamond is one of the most famous jewels in the world, with ownership records dating back almost four centuries. Its much-admired rare blue color is due to trace amounts of boron atoms. Weighing 45.52 carats, its exceptional size has revealed new findings about the formation of gemstones."[15]

It is currently said to be worth about $3,500,000. It is so beautiful sparkling in the light. Its rays are mesmerizing.

We finally made the drive back to Greenbelt and decided to eat at T.G.I.F.'s. They had a note on the door that said they were short of help, Strike 1, and there would not be Endless Apps tonight, despite being advertised nationally. Strike 2. I ordered a bowl of French Onion Soup, only for the waitress to return and tell us that they didn't have any. Strike 3... Otherwise, our waitress was great and the food we wound up with was good, but the restaurant was not.

We'd been monitoring a huge band of severe storms crossing from the Midwest today, but they fizzled out just as the rain arrived. Since we had no electric, we ran the generator until bedtime. We went to bed early, since there wasn't anything else to do. And because we needed to build up some strength for the next 4 days of running all over Washington, D.C.

---

[15] en.wikipedia.org/wiki/Hope_Diamond

MAY 2

I discovered this morning that I had failed to lay out one of my prescription meds these past few days. There was no backup to be found. I was truly feeling the effects of its absence, so a trip to CVS was in order asap!

Considering that the two closest Metro stations were closed, we set Frack to take us to the Prince George station. Well, now that we have the new car, when you plug your iPhone into the system, it converts your navigation into Apple Navigation and puts it up on the screen in the car. I don't particularly care for Apple maps, so my phone is plugged into the car and I set Larry's phone to Google maps, just as a backup.

At one point—with heavy traffic and construction—Larry was getting a bit frazzled, because I couldn't tell him which way to turn at the intersection ahead. I put the 2 displays side by side to show him: Frack said turn left and Alice (the Apple) said turn right. Geesh! I suggested left, but he chose right. Wrong guess! But after some aggravation and navigation, we finally arrived at the Metro, none the worse for wear.

Larry blamed it on operator error. Pfft. We both have since learned that that Prince George's Plaza is different from Prince George's Station. I set one map to the plaza and the other to the station when it came up in Google. The Plaza was a mall of shopping to the right, the station was the train station for the metro to the left. All right, I'm wrong not Frack! Frack forgive me, but you and Alice need to get your acts together.

The Metro here didn't have an unlimited daily pass, as we have seen in other areas. You buy a card and put money on it. You scan your card to get into the Metro, then you scan again when you exit. It immediately computes and deducts your fare—depending on how far you went and whether you rode during peak or non-peak hours. I didn't like that at all. Over the next 4 days, we were constantly computing in our heads the balance that was left on our passes.

As we entered the Metro for the first time, there was an attendant working in a nearby closed kiosk. I went up to ask her about buying the cards. She gave me a little map not designed for old eyes (emphasize "little") and pointed me toward the card dispensers. For a professional card-user, I guess they're quite simple. For a newbie, they were terribly confusing.

The machines to buy a card were massive with all sorts of buttons and instructions. We are just looking for a simple buy button. While Larry and I muddled our choices, she had mercy on us, got out of her kiosk and walked the distance to help us. She showed us how to get our cards, then helped us plan our first trip, including how to transfer from the green to the red line, to get to our destination. Those few minutes of kindness really made a difference! Never pass up the opportunity to make somebody's day better. She sure blessed the rest of our day!

Larry's iPhone also took this opportunity to shut down completely. Again. We were in the middle of navigating somewhere and—blip—shutdown. There have been other minor blips over the past few weeks, but this was shutting down like 3 times in a half-hour. My personal goal today would include finding a Verizon store in D.C.

Once on the metro, we settled in on the train with the commuters. No one makes eye contact or speaks. It was eerie, to say the least. The train runs along tracks above- and below-ground. Armed with the Metro lady's great instructions, we quickly transferred from the green line to the red line. We got out of the train at the Federal Triangle station and headed up the escalators. Now, we had to get our bearings as to which direction to head down the street. Google, where are you?

iPhone Input: Ford's theater, and Frack immediately tells us where to go. How did we ever find our way around anywhere before Google maps? After several blocks going down 'F" street and passing 10th street, we arrived. We should have known something important was here because there were all sorts of food trailers and souvenir booths on the roadside.

Ford's Theater, where President Lincoln was assassinated, is maintained by the National Park Service. The tickets were free for the asking, and also included touring the house where he died, right across the street. The Ford Theater still offers live theater most evenings. It's a cozy little place, compared to most modern theaters.

"Abraham Lincoln, the 16th president of the United States, was assassinated in Ford's Theatre on April 14, 1865. The mortally-wounded, but still breathing president was carried across the street to Petersen's boarding house, where he remained unconscious through the night. On April 15, 1865, President Lincoln died in the Petersen House. First opened to the public in 1968, Ford's Theatre National Historic Site protects the Theatre and Petersen House, houses a museum about the assassination, and is a working theater."[16]

Our emotions were raw as we toured the museum and theater, trying to imagine what had taken place here. Thoughts go back to the time of the civil war, with tensions high across this bruised nation. This area was swimming with different viewpoints regarding slavery and states' rights. The war had just ended and then this, the President of the United States had been shot.

The museum tells the story well, first showing us the actual seating balcony box where Lincoln and his party sat in the theater. They explained how John Wilkes Booth shot Lincoln from behind

---

[16] nps.gov

then jumped from the box onto the main floor, breaking his leg. The painful broken leg slowed his escape and eventually led to his arrest.

Across the street, we toured the Petersen House, where the gravely wounded President was taken. He died the next day in a small bedroom in the back of the house. We saw the adjoining rooms where Mary Todd Lincoln, the first Lady, waited for news about her husband. The rooms were all beautifully wallpapered and decorated. Everyone on the tour spoke in quiet whispers, in respect for all that had happened here.

They had an exhibit of the railway car containing Lincoln's coffin. The train which took him from DC to burial in Springfield, Illinois stopped many times along the way, allowing mourners to show their respect for the slain president.

I'm sure Booth yearned to become a national hero for his acts. I always wondered how he was given such close access to the President. Today I learned that Booth was "one of the most famous actors in the country when he shot Lincoln..."[17] Everyone at the theater knew him and was given access without a second thought. I never learned such detail in history class. As I have said before, a parent should take their kids across country like we are doing as a home school program for them. They would learn so much by seeing first hand everything that is taught in books in a classroom.

> Exodus 20:13
> You shall not murder.

Though, as I go back to research for the book, one thing does make me shake my head: Google Maps shows that the Historic Ford's

---

[17] history.com/this-day-in-history/lincoln-assassin-john-wilkes-booth-dies

Theater is now located between a JCrew store and the Hard Rock Café. Really? When and how did that happen?

We had lunch around the corner at Qdoba, a popular Mexican fast food restaurant. My feet, legs, and back were killing me. I chose a threesome of fancy tacos, but they were a bit too spicy for both of us. We picked at the food and tarried, enjoying the opportunity to sit.

We finally walked the few blocks to arrive at a Verizon store to replace Larry's phone. It had finally died. We all depend on so many electronics on a daily basis, even old folks like us. And especially my OCD husband. It took us about a half-hour to get the essential information downloaded, then we were out the door. The rest will load as wifi becomes available.

We were determined to visit the Bureau of Engraving and Printing today. Google says, several blocks again, 22-minute walk (perhaps for young people) straight down 14th street. Their motto is "The buck starts here." And it sure does.

When we arrived, we learned that the next tour was filled. Security was tight and they wouldn't allow us to wait inside, so we sat on the traffic wall nearby to enjoy the breeze, and waited for 5pm to come. After we went inside, we watched a short film, then began the tour. It all boils down to 4 printing machines that make our nation's currency.

In the 40-minute tour of the process we watched literally millions of dollars being printed in steps, cut, stacked, and wrapped. They keep the layered printing process complicated, and not easily duplicated by forgers. Even the engravers are special. It takes ten years of training to become an engraver.

The backs of our bills are printed first, in green ink. The ink rests to set into the paper. The fronts of our bills are printed next, in black, then rested again. Then they go through another printer, that prints serial numbers on them in sequence.

A little FYI: Have you even seen a serial number on a bill that ended with a *? That is a very special bill indeed. It's not worth any more than its face value, but "...when an imperfect sheet is detected during the manufacturing process after the serial number has been overprinted, it must be replaced with a new sheet. A "star" sheet is used to replace the imperfect sheet. Reusing an exact serial number to replace an imperfect note is costly and time consuming. A "star" note has its own special serial number followed by a star in place of a suffix letter."[18] Check out their website at moneyfactory.gov for lots of other interesting facts about cash money.

Seeing all that cash, stacked on pallets and tightly shrink-wrapped was definitely a WOW moment. This printed paper doesn't become currency until it is checked into the vaults at the Federal Reserve, just down the hall.

> 1 Timothy 6-10
> For the love of money is a root of all kinds of evil.
> Some people, eager for money, have wandered from
> the faith and pierced themselves with many griefs.

We were done sightseeing for the day, but had another few blocks to walk back to the Metro station at the Smithsonian. They seemed to be the longest blocks ever! Standing in lines today had taken its toll, and I had to resort to the back brace the last half of walking to the Metro. My Health app told me that I'd walked 7,673 steps today—over 2 ½ miles of walking. And that gave no credit to time standing. Vindication for how I felt at that moment!

We were pros at riding the subway now, and before we knew it, we were back at Prince George's Station. On the way back to the campground, we decided on dinner at Outback.

---

[18] moneyfactory.gov/resources/serialnumbers.html

It was nearly 8:30pm when we arrived back at the rig. Needless to say, we both slept well.

MAY 3

The same attendant was working at the kiosk again this morning. As I approached, she smiled, remembering this white-haired woman she helped yesterday. I thanked her profusely for helping us, telling her that those few minutes of instruction had really helped us along the way. I wished her a blessed day and bid her goodbye. I hope my small act of kindness gave her a smile to wear all day.

We headed back on the Metro train to Union station. When Larry got tickets for the White House months ago, he had to go through South Carolina Senator Tim Scott's office. The coordinator who set up our tickets also scheduled a meeting with the Senator as before the Capital tour. Again, getting the right direction to go with Google and after a several-block walk, we arrived at the Senate offices at 113 Hart Street.

We met with the senator and had our pictures taken with him. I also had the pleasure of giving him a signed copy of my first book. Larry told him what we do on the road for Him. After our meeting, an aide took us on a personal tour through the Capital building, its history, and stories of its inner workings. We even listened in on a Senate hearing from the balcony.

The majestic ambience of this building, the grandeur, is so awesome. We marveled at its history and the thought of the men and women who have walked these very halls in the steps we're taking today. There were thousands of kids here on field trips. It was loud to say the least! There were kids everywhere, going in all directions. Where were the adults in charge?

After lunch, with the sun and blue skies overhead, we were able to get some great pictures of the Capital building and grounds. Then began the walk of a lifetime.

As we were coming past the Capital, we watched the staging of a motorcade. Would the President or Vice-President arrive soon? There was a black SUV—could that be the vehicle the Secret Service has named the "Beast"? I'm sure the men and women in suits were armed but none more than the guy with the automatic machine gun over his shoulder. There were police on motorcycles, police in cars. Yep, there was something cooking. We stood and watched a few minutes, then became tired of waiting. We moved on.

We set off to find Dorothy's ruby red slippers from the *Wizard of Oz*. Really. Diana wanted a picture. It was a long walk and my biggest questions was, "Why isn't there any place to sit and rest?"

Remember required reading of George Orwell's book *1984* in high school? For a book published in 1949, he was spot on. Big Brother is indeed watching. For obvious reasons, there are cameras everywhere in this place of power, not even counting all the cameras you *can't* see.

We continued our long walk down to the Smithsonian Castle, that odd-looking red building, built like a castle. When we finally arrived, we discovered it was closed, the building empty of life.

We put Google to work again, which informed us that the ruby red slippers were at the American History Museum. It was further down and across the mall. We walked a lot more. Winded, we finally arrived at a massive stone contemporary building, right next door to the Natural History Museum we had visited before.

But wait. There was a sign on the door stating, "Sorry. We are closed." What! Why? Who made this decision without warning? We wondered aloud how many more folks would be disappointed today?

Tired and frustrated, we called it quits. We took the closest entrance to the Metro. We would take the orange line and transfer back to the green line. Even though it was long before rush hour, the train was packed.

We picked up the car at the parking lot and spotted a Boston Market on the way back to the campground. We had never eaten at one, so we decide to give it a try.

We ordered the chicken pot pie with some potatoes and vegetables. When it arrived, it sure looked good, but it was cold—very cold. Again, Strike 1. When we complained to the manager, he said, "We can give you another one, but we have to cook it, and you would have to wait another 15 minutes.", Strike, 2. Well, we sure couldn't eat this one!

We not-so-patiently waited another 40 minutes and finally asked where our food was. Another manager was on duty now and replied, "Oh, that was yours? No one told me!" Strike, 3. We finally got to eat a hot and delicious chicken pot pie. The food was great, but for a first-time customer, we were not impressed.

MAY 4

We were up early. The birds were singing and the sunshine breaking through the dense trees. There were also sirens in the distance. It was difficult to process that we were inside the busy Beltway of Washington, DC, in this primitive campground with wildlife and trees all around us.

We knew the drill when we hit the Metro this morning. We decided to continue our mission to find the ruby red slippers. At the appointed stop, we walked to the museum and it was open! Unfortunately, the masses who couldn't see it yesterday were all here today. There was an hour-long line to get through the security checkpoint. They manually checked every single bag before they allowed anyone to enter the building. They even went through purses! They did more extensive checks than at the airports.

Kids on field trips were everywhere. You could think that every school in the nation was here today. There were buses unloading in front of every museum and the kids were running and yelling like they were on the playground. Again, where are the adults here? This is not how you act in public.

Once we were inside, I just had to sit and rest, as I was nearly sick with the pain of standing in line for an hour. Then the search was on: where indeed were Dorothy's ruby red slippers?

We covered the first floor that contained all the film and TV exhibits. We saw Archie and Edith's chairs from the TV show *All in the Family*. We smiled at Kermit the Frog and others in the pop culture exhibit. Larry admired Farrah Faucet's red swimsuit from the famous posters every man in America had admired. I was personally impressed by Harrison Ford's hat and whip from *Raiders of the Lost Ark* series.

The museum had everything from yesteryears. Machinery in industry from our wars as a nation, appliances used in kitchens, all sorts of things we remembered our moms using when we were kids. There was even a whole house built inside the museum with cutaway views as to how it was built.

This place was totally awesome.

"Music, sports and, entertainment play major roles in American life, shaping our national memory and often defining what is American to the nation and to the world. The infinite variety of popular culture offers a democracy of choices. The memorable objects and ideas in this exhibition were a sampling of more than a century of collecting at the Smithsonian."[19]

We had covered the entire museum and still no ruby red slippers. I finally inquired at an information desk. The worker said, "Oh, they've been removed for restoration and should be back on display next year." Larry joked, "The ruby red slippers had to be returned to Oz, so the wizard could resew them and bring them back to life for all to see. The Wicked Witch of the West must have put a spell on us and those darn slippers. She knew we were coming."

We were walking outside when we spotted the Pavilion Café at the Sculpture Garden. It was a quiet, little place and not busy, so we decided to have lunch there. We sat outside in the sunshine and watched the masses of field trips from afar, as we enjoyed our pizza. It was time to call it a day and take the Metro back to the campground. Hopefully, it won't be as crowded as it was yesterday.

It had been a wonderful day of appreciating this time and place that God had chosen for us to live. Thank you, Lord.

MAY 5

Today we were ready at 9am, all dressed up for a special day. Several months ago, Larry had procured tickets from Senator Tim Scott's office for tickets to the White House. We again drove to Prince George's Station and you got it, took the Metro's green line to transfer to the redline to the Federal Triangle Station. Once we got our bearings and Google up and running, we began our walk to the White House visitors center.

------

[19]americanhistory.si.edu/exhibitions/national-treasures-popular-culture

"The White House is the official residence and workplace of the President of the United States, located at 1600 Pennsylvania Avenue NW in Washington, D.C. It has been the residence of every U.S. president since John Adams in 1800. The house is now the home of Donald J. Trump, the 45th president of the United States of America. The term *White House* is often used to refer to actions of the president and his advisers, as in "The White House announced that...".[20]

Even being observant, we probably had no idea as to the height and width of the security surrounding the White House. We could plainly see the Secret Service agents armed with guns and automatic rifles. We could see the obvious cameras homed in from all directions. There were K9 dogs that sniffed for all sorts of things as we passed through checkpoints to finally enter through the east gates.

I tried to leave a signed copy of my book, *His Road Trip* for the President with a Secret Service agent, but he told me no, I would have to mail it to the White House.

Upon entering the east wing, you wished these walls could talk. What stories could they tell about the men and women who have walked these floors. We have all seen pictures of event held in this ball room. My mind's eye was disappointed to see that the room wasn't all as big as I'd imagined.

In the quiet respect of the tour, my thoughts wandered to past Presidents who have been in these exact rooms with their families in my lifetime: Dwight Eisenhower and Mamie. JFK and wife Jackie, with children Caroline and John. LBJ and Lady Bird, who saw daughter Lynda married in the East Room. Richard Nixon and wife Pat, who witnessed their daughter Tricia married in the Rose Garden.

---

[20]en.wikipedia.org/wiki/White_House

There was Gerald Ford and Pat, Jimmy Carter and wife Rosalyn with daughter Amy. Bush 41 and Barbara. Bill Clinton and Hillary with daughter Chelsea. Bush 43 and Laura. Barack Obama— with Michelle, Malia and Sasha.

Entertainment history was made in this wing when Princess Diana and John Travolta danced impromptu in November 1985.

Then we thought of the crises that took place and the decisions that were made over in the west wing of this place. All the wars being fought, the first atomic bomb dropped. Truman made the decision to kill millions to save millions more. There was JFK and the Cuban Missile Crisis, then the aftermath of the JFK assassination.

Watergate. Monica's blue dress and other goings on behind closed doors. Bush 43 on September 11, 2001. The world changed forever on that day. I can't begin to imagine what this House was like on that day.

From this White House, men and women have determined the course of history.

And I was standing right here in it.

Despite the high ceilings and exorbitant décor, this House could indeed be someone's home. We passed through comfortable rooms designed by Jackie Kennedy nearly 50 years ago, that no one has dared to change. The Red Room, the Blue Room, the Green Room, all named for obvious color schemes. There were pictures showing past Presidents and historic moments in them. It was all overwhelmingly breathtaking.

I stood for a moment in a hallway, preparing to point my camera toward the beautiful landscape outside. A security guard rushed up to protest my taking the pic through the rain-spotted window. He took some keys from his pocket and unlocked the door, allowing me a perfect, unhindered shot of the gardens. He didn't need to do that, but I certainly appreciated the fact that he did. He really blessed my day.

The carpets were all rolled up so that the unending stream of visitors won't ruin them. The views of the immaculately-maintained grounds from the windows of this East Wing are breathtaking. Who has enjoyed these same scenes?

And then there were the protestors. Today they were protesting circumcision. I certainly admire their desire to make their opinions known, but why protest the White House over such a matter as this? The Bible has already covered this subject. What hot water would Trump be thrown into if he were to rule on this topic?

Ropes at the doorway of the China Room kept us far away from the details of the various china designs used over time and history. Oh, if only these walls could talk!

All throughout the tour, I continued to approach Secret Service personnel to give my book to the President, but no deal. I will just have to mail it. When I do, the envelope will include the following letter to our great President.

Dear Mr. President;

Our home state is South Carolina, for the last 22 years. But, we have been on the road in America for over a year, so far, **30 states**, **16,300** miles and another 2 years to go. We travel the country teaching kids the Bible. Our society is breaking at the seams because parents are not teaching the basic principles of the Bible. Plus, the fact that 28 million kids in America have never set foot into a church. We try to reach both the kids and parents.

Our reason to writing you is that while traveling there are several issues I would like to address with you.

1. The "**homelessness**" of our country is staggering, including South Carolina. We go into cities all across our nation and I have

never in my sixty plus years seen the situation as bad as it is now. The disintegration of the middle class is apparent. People begging in the streets and in front of stores. People living in tents along river beds, under overpasses, in parks and along road ditches. Some laying down on the sidewalks in financial districts of major cities. People going to the bathroom right in front of anyone watching them or walking by-- including in front of children. Los Angeles and San Francisco are the worst, the problem is America's problem. **What has happened to America?**

2. Our **infrastructure**, the roads are in terrible shape. Traveling in a motor-home we are bumped up and down like a yo-yo. The potholes, uneven roads, the bridges are ridiculous. The worst states are CA, AZ and LA, but most others are not far behind, including SC. Not only highways but local streets and interstates. **What has happened to America?**

3. The amount of **litter** and trash on our roads is sickening. The trash especially in our cities makes us look like a third world country. Some states do better than others, but it seems CA and LA are the worst. SC is not as bad as those, but you have probably seen it as well. Even the trash in our National Parks is on the rise but not as depraved as on our roads. Major cities and urban areas like in New Orleans, are so dirty with so much poverty and are run down it makes you ask" **"What has happened to America? "**

4. The **drugs and crime** are out of control as seen on the news daily in every city. But, the disrespect of the law is unbelievable. We traveled to most of our National Parks, and witness the use of Marijuana right out in the open is outrageous. Most cities you can smell it when you are walking the streets. People so high they are just laying around on the sidewalks. We just visited Mardi Gras, in New Orleans and right out in the open several people smoking away, sharing joints with each other. Overdoses on the news each night in each of the places we visit. Even while we were back in our home

state and city, Myrtle Beach, SC. there were 8 murders during Easter spring break—a major family vacation resort destination. **What has happened to America?**

5. **Healthcare** while on the road has been a challenge. We both have health care, but my wife can only use it in our state of SC. Even then we can't see our doctor of choice. When we travel our SC healthcare coverage does not go with us to other states. We tried to get other coverage that goes with us as we travel, but we were denied because of pre-existing conditions. What gives? Obama care has cheated the American health care system! What do we do when we are sick or need care while on the road? **We want your insurance available to us! What has happened to America?**

6. The amount of **disrespect** for our **laws** is concerning to us, from legal residents to illegal ones. Laws are being broken and ignored at a staggering rate. The deportation of illegals has taken away the bread earner of the family and left the rest of the family including children to fend for themselves. The issue is not sending back the "illegals" has we have believed in the past. But, seeing mothers begging for food for her kids has put a deeper meaning into the issue. It is a problem with many layers, more than the surface problem. **What has happened to America?**

At this time, we know you have only been in office about 100 days. These problems have been rising in America over several years. We did vote for you, to **Make America Great Again.** I hope you can address these issues with real solutions. We have seen these first hand. The media is **NOT** reporting any of this. They just keep attacking you and your administration. **What has happened to America?**

We have written about these issues and our trip in a new book called "His Road Trip." We hope you have the opportunity to read it. We hope it opens everyone's eyes to what is happening in America. **An Aspiring Adventure Across America!**

Sincerely, Larry and Lugene Hammond

Maybe one day I will find out if he read my book. But, it feels good that I sent him one in the hopes that he would. After all, I did vote for him. The least he could do is read a free book, right?

We left out the main door of the north lawn taking plenty of pictures and noticing the secret service agents on the roof standing guard watching our every move with rifles. Trying not to stare, we just continued walking down the driveway through the north gates.

We both were hungry; it was well past time for a bite to eat. Googling the closest restaurant, we found on the corner of 17th NW and H street--Au Bon Pain. We shared a French Dip. I was so hungry, we ate every last crumb.

As we were leaving, there were sirens and security and police running everywhere. We had no idea what was going on. The security agents yelled at us to get behind the barriers of yellow ribbon tape they had just roped off. The streets quickly emptied of cars and people as everyone was rerouted. The streets became eerily quiet, the only presence being the bike-riding police with guns drawn. We were in a city block lockdown. Several minutes passed and it was all over. We had no idea what had happened to initiate those measures being taken.

We continued our walk south down 17th street to the south lawn and back to the visitor center. We had made a complete circle around the White House, the administration building, and both the west and east wings. Several layers of fences and barricades line the streets to protect the White House and the President. All with well-armed security guards, German shepherds, and check points. They all are constantly watching you and your every move.

After taking a bathroom break back at the visitor center, we rode the Metro back, in reverse of the way we came. One thing I wished the day would have been blue skies for our pictures, but it was an overcast day. The White House just doesn't look the same without blue skies and the sun shining.

We enjoyed a quiet evening and a restful night at the campground until... We were awakened at 1am to a bunch of young folks setting up tents nearby. They raced their car engines, played music, ran their flashlights over the area, and yelled loudly. They paid no mind to the rest of us who were trying to sleep. They came and went, making plenty of noise through 3am. Even they had to sleep eventually. Where were the rangers when you needed them? Why can't people be respectful of others?

MAY 6

We were up and ready to pull out by 9am. Our destination today is the Harpers Ferry National Historic Park in Harper Ferry, West Virginia, which Larry rated a 6. I was so excited—it has full hookups!

It would be a short drive, a little over an hour. We took I-495 North, then I-270 north, then picked up US340 west. Once in Harpers Ferry, we followed the signs to the National Historic Park.

We are trying to make sure we hit this state while it is close, so we can put a sticker on the map on the motorhome. I have a great number of friends who grew up in West Virginia. Let me take this opportunity to say that they are, every one of them, good people.

According to the NPS website, "The history of Harpers Ferry has few parallels in the American drama. It is more than one event, one date, or one individual. It is multi-layered - involving a diverse number of people and events that influenced the course of our nation's history. Harpers Ferry witnessed the first successful application of interchangeable manufacture, the arrival of the first successful American railroad, John Brown's attack on slavery, the largest surrender of Federal troops during the Civil War, and the education of former slaves in one of the earliest integrated schools in the United States."[21]

They had 10 stamps in their Visitors Center, and I stamped every one. After exploring the Center, we took the shuttle down to the old town. It's a peaceful little place now, where the Potomac and Shenandoah Rivers meet. We took our time, stopping in some of the concessionaires there, who had all sorts of curious things for sale. Since I used to be a candy maker/seller, I'm always drawn toward folks who sell candies.

In True Treats, I had the pleasure of meeting owner Susan Benjamin, who's written a book, "Sweet as Sin: The Unwrapped Story of How Candy Became America's Favorite Pleasure." She personally explained to me how the shop is set up in chronological order, displaying the treats in the order they were conceived.

She did indeed have some amazing sweet offerings. There were roots and barks that have been around forever, then period candies beginning in the 1500's. She had hard tack displayed, which I have read about in books but had no clue what it looked like. Penny candy from the 1800's was plentiful and colorful. Most of the stuff from the 1900's was familiar to me, as we sold lots of nostalgia candies in our stores.

The one item I truly coveted was a small bag of sassafras root. Oh, my goodness, how long it had been since I'd enjoyed its sweet fragrance? Have you ever enjoyed tea made from this boiled root? It is so sweet and smells so good! My daddy used to dig me up root whenever he could, but that hasn't been for a very long time now. But back to the present. As much as I wanted it, I was not about to pay $12.95 for the small packet offered. I just couldn't bring myself to spend the money. I have since looked at true root prices online, and

---

[21] nps.gov/hafe/learn/historyculture/index.htm

it seems the price she was selling it for was accurate. I will just have to let my memories suffice.

It was spitting rain, so we decided to eat lunch. We picked out a small BBQ place called Hannah's Train Depot and went inside. It was a small, plain place and the shrimp basket we ordered was good. The rain had stopped by the time we returned to the streets.

Although matters had been simmering for quite some time, it still difficult to imagine something as terrible as the Civil War had begun in this quiet little place. We learned a lot in the John Brown Museum, the Lewis and Clark Expedition display, and learned that the Appalachian Trail goes right through the town. There were other little shops scattered about, selling stuff from hot coffee, jewelry, clothing, to post cards.

Walking through town, up and down the hills wore us plum out. We'd enjoyed a big lunch, so supper was small. I was in bed by 7pm-dead on my feet from this active week. Good night.

> Matthew 24:6
> You will hear of wars and rumors of wars,
> but see to it that you are not alarmed.
> Such things must happen, but the end is still to come.

MAY 7

I had set my alarm for 7:30, just in case I was rested up by that time. Nope. I took my morning meds, and rolled over and went right back to sleep. It was only an hour's drive to Gettysburg, Pennsylvania, so there was no rush. Finally, by 9am, I was prepared to start the day.

Of course, we started out in West Virginia. In just a few minutes, we found ourselves back in Virginia. Not too long after that, we were cruising thru Maryland. Then, we zipped right into

Pennsylvania. All within that first 30-40 minutes, we covered 4 states. Wow, that was fast!

We left on US340 east to US15 north. The rolling hills were beautiful and there were trees blooming everywhere along it. The leaves on the trees in this area were still that bright spring green and looked so soft, unlike that dried-up crispy look they get after a brutally hot summer. Everything was new, fresh.

It's only in the 50's again today, but I don't really mind. I'd take 50's over 90's any day!

We came across a car accident in the median. It looked like it had just happened, a fender bender, and folks had already stopped to help. I'm so glad there was someone already there. At the rate of speed we were traveling, it would have taken us another half-mile to get the motorhome stopped.

After we maneuvered through some construction, we enjoyed cruising along a nice, 4-lane divided highway, then took some winding, narrow local roads to arrive at Gettysburg Battlefield RV Park, Gettysburg, Pennsylvania, which Larry rated a 7. Once we were set up, we drove to Gettysburg National Military Park.

Run by the National Park Service, the visitor center was something to behold. "The National Park Service Museum and Visitor Center is the place to begin your visit to Gettysburg National Military Park. Here visitors will find information on how to visit the park and what to see around Gettysburg.

"The GETTYSBURG MUSEUM OF THE CIVIL WAR, with 22,000 square feet of exhibit space, features relics of the Battle of Gettysburg and personalities who served in the Civil War, inter-active exhibits, and multi-media presentations that cover the conflict from beginning to end as well as describe the Battle of Gettysburg and its terrible aftermath...

"The center also hosts the film, "A New Birth of Freedom", narrated by award-winning actor Morgan Freeman and the restored Gettysburg Cyclorama, which depicts the final fury of Gettysburg-"Pickett's Charge".

"Cycloramas were a very popular form of entertainment in the late 1800's, both in America and Europe. These massive, oil-on-canvas paintings were displayed in special auditoriums and enhanced with landscaped foregrounds sometimes featuring trees, grasses, fences and even life-sized figures. The result was a three-dimensional effect that surrounded viewers who stood on a central platform, literally placing them in the center of the great historic scene. Most cycloramas depicted dramatic events such as great battles, religious epics, or scenes from great works of literature…

"The "Battle of Gettysburg" Cyclorama at Gettysburg National Military Park is one that has survived. This fantastic painting brings the fury of the final Confederate assault on July 3, 1863 to life, providing the viewer with a sense of what occurred at the battle long touted as the turning point of the Civil War." [22]

To learn more about the Cyclorama at Gettysburg, go to the web address in the footnote below.

The area is breathtaking. As we traveled the roads, there were many monuments which explained the battles that took place there, when they occurred, and where the men who fought the battles were from. There were canons lined up between the monuments. There were graves marked with stones. It was a beautiful place with a horrific history. We spent hours there, in that solemn place. Everyone should visit here, at least once. I would certainly like to go back again.

---

[22] nps.gov/gett/learn/historyculture/gettysburg-cyclorama.htm

We took a trip to Walmart to get a few things. We dined on Italian at a nice little place called La Bella Italia, where my iPhone decided to die. I was convinced it was a goner.

Before we returned to the campground, we stopped so that Larry could climb an observation tower. I took one look at the 7 stories of steps and politely declined. I can take perfectly good sunset photos from down here on the ground.

Larry: *My heart was beating so fast, after climbing those 7 stories. My Myositis screamed loudly, too, but it was not going to stop me from the steep climb. From atop the tower, the view was incredible! I gazed at the battlegrounds in every direction and watched as God's Fingers touched downwards, toward the setting sun. The photos I took were priceless.*

He did take some amazing pics from up there, but I took some pretty good ones, too.

Psalm 19:1
The heavens declare the glory of God; the skies
proclaim the work of his hands.

MAY 8

Today started out to be a wasted day. By 2pm, we had accomplished nothing, save a few reservations for the month ahead. The camera has been acting stupid lately, changing aspects or programs at will. In between reservations, Larry's been looking for the software CD and can't find it anywhere!

Then my phone wasn't on iCloud. Another crisis.

We were cleaning up from the CD search, and when Larry picked up one last pile of stuff to put away, lo and behold, the disc had been on top of the printer all along—stuck in between paperwork.

Hallelujah! Problem solved.

We drove 45 minutes on US30 west to Chambersburg, to break bread with a dear friend, Sue. We first met her and her husband, Dave at Shepherd of the Sea Lutheran Church we attended when we first moved to Myrtle Beach. Sue came to work the counter with us at Pop 'N Stuff, and eventually Dave came to help make our popcorn and candies.

Sue was a typical redhead, in that if you really made her mad, her hair might as well be on fire. She worked with us for about a decade, and was the hardest-working employee I had. Despite she was the oldest of all of us (except her husband), she could run circles around us all. We nicknamed her The Energizer Bunny. Dave passed away several years ago and she returned to her home of many years, to be close to family. I did miss her so.

When we arrived at the Lone Star restaurant, we were surprised that Sue's sister, Betsy, Betsy's husband, Bob and her granddaughter Kiely were there, too! We had a wonderful supper altogether, and conversation came easily.

When it was time to go, I gave my friend *His Road Trip* as a gift. We exchanged lots of hugs, because I just don't know if fate will enable another visit in this lifetime. When we walked to our cars, Sue said something about the blankets that she's been making for a long time being in the back seat. I rolled my eyes upward and said, "You mean those beautiful blankets that I've coveted for so long?" She handed me one right over. Hugs again.

The blanket is large and warm, the designs made with yarn run through the weave. When I was young, I wove cotton thread into hucktoweling in the very same way, to decorate kitchen towels. I could most certainly appreciate the amount of work that went into my gift. I'm sure to use it in cold weather, and lovingly think of Sue.

It was a long drive back to the campground in Gettysburg. It was still chilly, but the sky was blue and bright. It had turned out to be a great day after all.

MAY 9

We started our day off by driving on PA116 east to nearby Hanover, Pennsylvania to tour the Snyder's pretzel factory. It was totally amazing! According to their website, "The story of the pretzel begins about 1500 years ago in a monastery; it is believed, in Southern France or Northern Italy. There, the monk whose task it was to bake bread found he always scraps of dough left over when he'd shape the loaves.

"Being as imaginative as he was frugal, he formed these scraps into dough-ropes which he twisted into the now-familiar shape. Someone soon noticed how this shape resembled that of a child's arms folded in prayer, and since the demand had almost instantly outstripped the supply, our friend decided to call them "Pretiola"– "little rewards" in Latin – and saved them for the children who learned their prayers well."[23]

We were part of a small group that was personally directed through a viewing hall, high above the working machinery below. Our young guide explained each part of the process, explaining that they produce about 1.2 million pretzels an *hour*. I can't remember all the details, but she explained how much flour and salt they use and it's phenomenal. It was a fascinating tour.

Despite their massive production, their warehouse inventory turns over every 6 days. The place runs 24/7 except for Thanksgiving and Christmas Days.

---

[23] snydersofhanover.com/our-story

When the tour was complete, we were taken back to their store, and grabbed up lots of great bargains. We walked away with 4 full shopping bags and only spent $32. That should last us for a while.

We drove to the ChickFilA nearby to enjoy lunch. I love ChickFilA for many reasons. The company as a whole operates on Christian principles. They hire a special type of worker, treat those workers well and they, in turn, treat their customers well. My niece, Maria works for them. Their food is great and they still close on Sundays, so their staff can attend church. Well done.

"Chick-fil-A, Inc., Founder S. Truett Cathy died Sept. 8, 2014, at age 93. Cathy started the business in 1946, when he and his brother, Ben, opened an Atlanta diner known as The Dwarf Grill (later renamed The Dwarf House®). Through the years, that restaurant prospered and led Cathy to further the success of his business. In 1967, Cathy founded and opened the first Chick-fil-A restaurant in Atlanta's Greenbriar Shopping Center. Today, Chick-fil-A has the highest same-store sales and is the largest quick-service chicken restaurant chain in the US based on annual system-wide sales.

"Cathy was the author of six books and was a committed philanthropist dedicated to making a difference in the lives of youth. He was the recipient of countless awards over the years, both for his business acumen and for his charity. With his wife of 65 years, Jeannette McNeil Cathy, he led a life that was centered on biblical principles and family, and is survived by his sons Dan T. and Don "Bubba" Cathy; daughter Trudy Cathy White; 12 grandchildren and 23 great-grandchildren."[24]

And their food is terrific, too.

---

[24] chick-fil-a.com/About/History

We drove on to the other factory tour in town, Utz. This was a self-guided tour, so you could take as much time at each viewing station as you cared to. It's highly automated, although there are workers everywhere, keeping a close eye on the machinery. To see the raw potatoes go through the cleansing process, peeling, slicing, oil bath, deep frying, seasoning, cooling…right into bags, then into boxes, onto pallets into the warehouse. It was amazing. A few seemed bored, but others smiled and waved at us folks in the tours.

We even learned that the potatoes are sorted and prepared by size. If a batch is going to be packaged into small bags, they use smaller potatoes. Larger bags get the larger potatoes. Who knew?

Their warehouse inventory is dispensed daily. Let that sink in: everything that's in this gigantic warehouse today, will be out of here tomorrow, on their way to stores everywhere. Wow!

According to the company's website, "The Utz Story begins in a small-town kitchen in 1921. William and Salie Utz began producing Hanover Home Brand Potato Chips in Hanover, PA, in their summer kitchen, cooking about 50 pounds of chips an hour. Today, Utz is the largest independent, privately held snack brand in the United States, producing over 3.3 million pounds of snacks per week (about half of which are potato chips) while operating over 900 company-owned routes."[25]

The Utz store was filled with lots more goodies and we spent another $23. We won't have to buy snacks for months!

We took our time on the beautiful drive back to the campground, stopping at the National Cemetery. It was a solemn place. As you look out over the small, white tombstones that mark the soldiers' graves, you know you can't even begin to imagine what

---

[25] utzsnacks.com/timeline.html

their lives were like in the days, hours, and minutes leading up to their deaths. It was a place of pondering, reverence, grief.

There were all sorts of monuments scattered throughout the battlefield. Markers have been erected by quite a few states, commemorating their citizens who fought and died here. They were all shapes and sizes, made of stone and bronze.

And America is about to have another civil war, fighting about the first Civil War. It's as though we didn't learn a darn thing from the first one. Bringing up old wounds from this era, I feel, accomplishes little. I believe we should keep those statues and flags handy as constant reminders to remind us not to make the same mistakes again. The past is the past, let's learn from it and move on. Let's work on making this United States the land of milk and honey, in peace with each other. Our sins are the same, our skins may be different in color, but we are all made in the image of our creator.

Psalm 18:39
You armed me with strength for battle;
you humbled my adversaries before me.

Then we saw the place where President Lincoln made his Gettysburg Address. The beautiful large monument lists every battalion who fought in the battle there. It's a large monument, dedicated in 1910, long after Lincoln had spoken those infamous words there. "Four Score and Seven years ago...

"Four score and seven years ago our fathers brought forth on this continent, a new nation, conceived in Liberty, and dedicated to the proposition that all men are created equal.

"Now we are engaged in a great civil war, testing whether that nation, or any nation so conceived and so dedicated, can long endure. We are met on a great battle-field of that war. We have come to dedicate a portion of that field, as a final resting place for those who here gave their lives that that nation might live. It is altogether fitting and proper that we should do this.

"But, in a larger sense, we cannot dedicate -- we cannot consecrate -- we cannot hallow -- this ground. The brave men, living and dead, who struggled here, have consecrated it, far above our poor power to add or detract. The world will little note, nor long remember what we say here, but it can never forget what they did here. It is for us the living, rather, to be dedicated here to the unfinished work which they who fought here have thus far so nobly advanced. It is rather for us to be here dedicated to the great task remaining before us -- that from these honored dead we take increased devotion to that cause for which they gave the last full measure of devotion -- that we here highly resolve that these dead shall not have died in vain -- that this nation, under God, shall have a new birth of freedom -- and that government of the people, by the people, for the people, shall not perish from the earth."

We stood right where Lincoln is believed to have stood (there is great debate regarding this) as he spoke those now infamous words. We saw what he saw—at least the stench of the dead has long passed. The new admiration we have for those who gave their all cannot be taught from a book.

Larry and I were shocked at the busloads of field trip kids that came and went during our time there. We can only conclude that the adults in charge hadn't explained that tens of thousands of men had died right here, on this hallowed ground. They ran playfully up the stairs to yell names from atop of the tower. It was all fun and games to them. What's the point of taking kids on a field trip to such a historic place, where they aren't even taught to respect the dead. I found it very, very sad. And very disrespectful.

If you're a teacher reading this book please take the time to teach your students to be respectful of others, dead or alive. There is so much to learn on a field trip. I do give kudos to the teachers who had given them questions to answer and specific tasks to complete. But I have more often seen in the National parks, Presidential libraries, and other historical places we have visited, that the children on these field trips are just left to run and play.

Leviticus 19:32
Stand up in the presence of the aged,
show respect for the elderly and
revere your God. I am the LORD.

After a quick ice pack to my aching, craning neck, I popped in a quick dinner. We'd discovered a series called *Night Shift,* which has been quite interesting. It's fast-paced and full of lots of medical information, as well. We watched several episodes on Netflix, then Larry headed to bed. I chose to write a few words, then hit the hay myself. It's been a low-keyed day. I think it made it to a whole 66 degrees today, and the sun was bright. It was a great day.

MAY 10

We left Gettysburg this morning after spending a couple of hours taking care of business, and making some telephone calls. I needed to speak to someone at the South Carolina Department of Motor Vehicles about still yet another problem in transferring my license plates to my new car. I was surprised to get a recording, telling me that the office was closed today, due to a South Carolina holiday.

I immediately Googled, and quickly learned that May 10 is recognized in six southern states as Confederate Memorial Day. I lived full-time in that state for 22 years and never knew that. I wonder if that's something new.

Tasks complete, we hit the road around noon. We began on Lincoln Way west, then US30 east. We took PA340/Old Philadelphia

Pike and headed east, route T521 to Lynch and route T944 in Salisbury Township.

We even went through the small town of Intercourse, Pennsylvania. What were they thinking? I went to their official website and learned a great deal. "It's okay, you can giggle! We know our name gets us lots of attention, but we're proud that who we are keeps folks coming back again and again. So how did we get our name? There are a few theories.

"First our town used to sit at the edge of a race course, right where visitors would enter the racing festivities. The entrance was coined "Entercourse" and may have evolved into Intercourse.

"Or, the name may have come from the Intersection of two major roads, or courses. The Old Kings Highway which traveled from Pittsburg to Philadelphia and the route from Wilmington, Delaware to Erie, Pennsylvania. One final theory suggests the town was named after a phrase commonly used at the time of the town's founding. In early English, Intercourse was used to refer to fellowship and social interaction shared in a community of faith, a description still relevant to our town today.

"Whichever theory holds true, we're happy with our name. It's the perfect conversation starter!"[26]

We finally arrived at Spring Gulch Resort Campground in New Holland, Pennsylvania, which Larry rated a 2.

There aren't many campers here, and it feels like we have this entire grassy section of the campground to ourselves. The campground was older, with grassy sites and rusty utility poles. Larry

---

[26] villageofintercourse.com

hesitated for a few moments before plugging in, considering all the electric problems we've already had. We surely didn't need more.

This was the first time we had used our RPI membership for special rates on campgrounds. We thought we would get it for $10 a night, but it turned out this specific place was at the Encore rate of $20. $20 for water and 30amp electric was a stretch, but if we upgraded to 50amp electric, water with sewer and cable, it would have been $40 a night. It was most certainly overpriced for this older campground.

We had spent $2,000 for the initial membership with Coast to Coast, plus the Good Sam annual dues of nearly $500. This RPI membership was a "bonus." In this case, we should have just skipped the membership and paid the regular rate.

Recently, this copilot—me—has been having a lot of trouble staying ahead of the game with Frankie. Now that we have an unlimited data plan, Larry suggested that I use the iPad instead of his iPhone. Boy, did those few extra inches of screen make a huge difference! Now I can keep the iPad open at all times and easily look ahead for route changes, which I just couldn't see that well before.

These eyes are now nearly 63 years old and can't quite read the fine print like they used to! It was an uneventful trip, once again, right up until the end. Those last few miles somehow always convince Larry that we're way off the beaten path and will end up at a dead end somewhere, and he always gets so wound up and upset.

Except for the couple of miles on Snake Lane (aptly named), all turned out well, and we wound up exactly where we should have. But this road shouldn't have been considered a Truck Route. It went up and down hills with tight turns, and the paving was in grave disrepair. It was like riding in a bouncy house.

We set up quickly. The day was sunny and mid-60's. My neck was giving me trouble again, so I iced it down for a half-hour.

Feeling better, Larry suggested we go out driving, and find someplace nice to eat. It's beautiful here in Lancaster County--blue skies, warming sun, and beautiful rolling farm lands. We'd been here once before, but it was a rushed detour during a business trip, probably twenty years ago. We were here in the fall and enjoyed watching the farmers and their horse teams out harvesting. Now in May, we were blessed with watching some farmers till the ground, others were planting, a few harvesting hay.

Of course, we spotted many folks in their horse and buggies, going quickly about their business. It was also laundry day for many. Those long lines are very organized, beginning with the biggest pants and dresses down to the smallest of underwear.

> Hebrews 6:7
> Land that drinks in the rain often falling on it and
> that produces a crop useful to those for whom it is farmed
> receives the blessing of God.

We had the opportunity to see many family members all out working together. One young lady drove a tractor while a man picked up the hay coming out of the baler and stacked it on the wagon behind them. We saw one young boy (maybe 10) commanding a SIX-horse team, tilling the entire field alone, all while standing on a wagon. We spotted one man steering a horse that was pulling a gas-powered bush hog, hastily mowing his large yard. Amish and Mennonite and Regular Joe were all doing their own things. Everyone getting along despite their great measures of diversity.

Of course, we traveled through miles of grazing farm animals, beautifully manicured gardens, spots of colorful iris, pink dogwood trees, and barns and silos covering the hills and valleys of this beautiful area. Sure, you smell the cows and horses in the air, but the land here seemed fresher, cleaner, more colorful than most anywhere I've ever been. We even spied a hot air balloon, high and aloft, miles from where we were. I hadn't seen one of those since we left the International Hot Air Balloon Festival in Albuquerque last October.

We finally arrived at Miller's Smorgasbord, where we enjoyed dinner. Their website explained, "Lancaster PA's Original Buffet & Restaurant. 88 years ago, Anna Miller served chicken & waffles to truckers as her husband repaired their rigs. It was a simple dish, but it was always served up with a smile…"[27] I've never had such a thing, so I had to order it. My plate came with 3 sweet, tender waffles (each about the size of a biscuit), covered in gravy and shreds of chicken that had been "cooked to death", as my mother would have said. It was delicious!

I wanted to check out the quilt shop at Miller's, but sadly it was already closed for the day. Peeking through the large windows, I could see all sorts of beautiful handmade things inside. Perhaps Larry will bring me back another time, before we leave.

We had never before seen what we learned is called a Kick Bike. "Amish scooter sizes approach that of a bike and because of the similarity, they are sometimes called a kick bike or foot bike. Riding one is similar to riding a bike, except that the rider stands on a low floorboard, rather than perched on a high seat, and propels it by kicking instead of pedaling."[28] They have a front hand brake and a rear stomp brake. I never did see an Amish ride a regular-style bicycle in this area, but we sure saw lots of these!

We took our time driving back to the campground, while the sun was still high in the sky. We saw lots of folks still hard at work in their fields. I'm sure they know that rain is on the way tomorrow and they're rushing to get the fields prepared. We parked the car in

---

[27] millerssmorgasbord.com

[28] cottagecraftworks.com/amish-push-scooter-bikes-kick-bikes

the grass by the motorhome, satiated by good food and the peace of the area.

We tried to stream some more *Night Shift* on Netflix, but for every 2 minutes it played, it took another 4 minutes to spool the next 2 minutes. Larry gave up, but I stuck it out to the end of the episode.

Diana's been texting this evening, proud of the fact that she's bought another bookcase, put it together, and unpacked more big boxes of DVD's and VHS tapes. Maybe she'll have it all unpacked when we make it back home at Thanksgiving. We can only hope!

Deuteronomy 28:12
The LORD will open the heavens,
the storehouse of his bounty,
to send rain on your land in season and to bless
all the work of your hands.
You will lend to many nations but will borrow from none.

Tonight, we're in the Amish Country of Pennsylvania. Right before I sat down to write, I walked outside to take a picture of the rising moon. It's completely full, rising above the nearby tree line. There are thin, wispy clouds stretched in front of it, perhaps an indication of the rain we'll see tomorrow. It's quiet. It's peaceful. All is well with the world. I feel at peace.

MAY 11

I was feeling punky when my alarm went off this morning. Another couple of hours' sleep helped a bit, but not much. By noon, the rain was coming down. It wasn't a bad rainfall, but it was just steady enough to make you want to stay inside, instead of roaming around this beautiful Amish landscape surrounding the campground.

I spent the entire afternoon in front of the computer writing, watching the rain out the window. I put a small roast in the crock pot and we enjoyed it along with a pile of mashed potatoes for supper.

We watched Netflix long enough to finish the season of *Night Shift,* and I was sorry to see it end. We watched a couple of *NCIS,* which we always enjoy. The rain finished about sunset, and Larry went to bed. It was indeed a day of rest. And for all those farmers I witnessed plowing yesterday, God blessed them with a nice, soaking rainfall. Thank you, Lord.

MAY 12

We pulled the rig out of the campground about 10am, with our sights set in the direction of Philadelphia, Pennsylvania. We headed out on Lynch Road/T944 and took PA897 south. We picked up PA41 south/Gap Newport Pike to US1 north, PA52 south and Kennett Pike to 9th Street in Wilmington.

After a while on the backroads, admiring once again the most beautifully-kept collection of farms like anywhere, we found our way back to I-295 north. We quickly sped through Delaware and on into Pennsylvania.

We stopped at the PA Welcome Center and Larry allowed me to take a quick nap while he ate lunch. Big difference! Shortly afterward, we arrived at Timberlane Campground in Clarksboro, New Jersey, which Larry rated a 5. It was another gloomy day, and we decided to stay in and take care of our never-ending list of unfinished business.

We leased our new Escape in Gulfport, Mississippi and have spent the last 2 months trying to get our license plate transferred to the new car. Geesh! Anyway, I called SCDMV to discuss a letter I'd received about the latest problem, and got the rudest woman ever!

All she would do was repeatedly tell me what couldn't be done. What couldn't be done over the phone. What couldn't be done from out of state. Enough already! I insincerely thanked her for her time, bid her goodbye and hung up.

There are some days I really miss having an old-fashioned land line—it felt so great to SLAM a receiver down at the end of a frustrating phone call! You just can't risk it with a cell phone.

Anyway, I reviewed the letter again and decided to handle it by snail mail, another option pointed out in the letter. I made copies of everything and made out yet another check. Envelope, stamp, done.

The only other thing in the world more aggravating than calling the DMV is calling the IRS. Really long story cut short, but the next hour was spent on the phone. Once again, my luck connected me with a brusque representative. The words she said were apparently to help me, but the tone of her voice was so condescending and rude. My daddy would have called her uncouth. She probably didn't even realize how rude she was being to me.

After making note of her complicated instructions, I decided to call back with another plan in mind. The woman I had the blessing to speak with this time really made my day. She paid close attention to my situation, answered my questions politely, and we freely discussed options and ideas. By the time I hung up the phone with her, I was blessing her for her kind and wonderful assistance. Same day, same me, same situation, very different representative, very different outcome.

Anyway, this campground is the first in a while to have cable, so guess what background noise is behind all of this? Fox News, of course. They've gone and fired everyone we really liked, so now I get to listen to a crew of others I never really liked in the first place.

We spent the evening watching Netflix again, waiting for the rain to begin anew. We were planning to ride the train into

Philadelphia in the morning and be tourists all day, but the weather forecast is sad: 100% change of heavy rain all day long. We surfed to find quite a few theaters in the area, so we'll decide on a movie tomorrow. We can always be tourists on Sunday. We will have to try a real Philly Cheesesteak when we get there!

MAY 13

It poured rain all night long, just as predicted. When my alarm went off, I immediately knew there was absolutely no point in rolling out of bed. I laid there for a good long time, enjoying the sound of the pounding rain on the roof of the rig. It was pleasant, soothing.

When I finally did get up, I wrote on the book for a couple of hours. Larry had chosen a movie and used his trusty iPhone to plan the route. Little did he realize that this trip would take us deep into the heart of downtown Philadelphia in this torrential downpour. First, it ticked him off that we had to pay a $5 toll to cross the Walt Whitman Bridge, then we were surprised to be driving downtown, straight into the University of Pennsylvania campus.

Then, there was no place to park. We drove around the block and finally found the entrance to a parking garage that boasted prices of $11 for the first hour. What! But what other choice did we have? We finally found an unrestricted space on level 3 (we were now late for the movie), and thankfully signs that Cinemark customers could get their ticket validated and pay only $3 for a 4-hour park. Well, that's a whole lot better.

We rush up to the ticket counter and Larry tells the young lady that we wanted 2 tickets for *The Circle*. Oh, she says, we're not showing that movie here. At that news, Larry is about to explode. He's looking it up on his iPhone, planning to prove her wrong. I looked at the marquis above her, and said, "We'll take 2 senior tickets for the 3-D *King Arthur*." Larry gives me that "What?" look and I told him that we're here, we paid to get here, and that's the only movie that's starting right now!" We purchased his popcorn and soda and we were in. It certainly wasn't what we'd planned to see, but I did enjoy the movie.

It was still raining when we walked back to the car. We were almost back to the campground when I suggested a little Chinese restaurant I'd found on Google, the "Dragon Nest." I drank plenty of hot tea, and we each ordered wonton soup to take off the chill. We thoroughly enjoyed the seafood main dish. It was great, as was the service. My fortune cookie read, "See life through the eyes of a child, then you become truly wise." Very, very true.

Matthew 18:2-6
He called a little child to him, and placed the child among them. ³And he said: "Truly I tell you,
unless you change and become like little children,
you will never enter the kingdom of heaven.
⁴Therefore, whoever takes the lowly position
of this child is the greatest in the kingdom of heaven.
⁵And whoever welcomes one such child in my name
welcomes me.
⁶"If anyone causes one of these little ones
—those who believe in me—to stumble,
it would be better for them to have a large millstone hung
around their neck and to be drowned in the depths of the sea."

We tiptoed through the muddy puddles to get back into the motorhome. Both of us worked on our computers for an hour or so, then watched 2 episodes of *Colony*, another series we found on Netflix. With it still raining, Larry went off to bed, and I wasn't far behind. What a crazy day.

MAY 14

Today was Mother's Day. Diana texted me before she headed out to work—a wish for a happy day and a collection of little flowers on the screen. Some moms wouldn't care for that at all, but they were plenty enough for me. I have absolutely no doubt she loves me. But she's in South Carolina and I'm in New Jersey. She couldn't take me to dinner, flowers would be expensive and difficult, considering we're moving every three days, and presents aren't necessary.

Just knowing that she loves me is all I need. And, although every momma loves getting the day off from cooking, most moms would admit this exact same thing. A child's love is all they really, really need. Larry and I were both missing our moms today.

> Proverbs 31:28
> Her children arise and call her blessed;
> her husband also, and he praises her.

We set out in the car for the nearest PATCO rail station, Woodcrest. The Port Authority Transit Corporation runs between Philadelphia and Camden County, New Jersey. Unlike our bad luck in Washington, DC, we found the station easily. Being a Sunday, there were plenty of places to park free—and I do love free. It was a short walk to the lobby and the machines made it simply to purchase a round trip to downtown Philly. The seats were comfortable, the cars relatively new and well-maintained. We chose to get off at 8th and Market, the closest stop to the Independence Visitor Center.

Larry always studies up before we arrive at a new place. And he's very good at remembering everything he reads. He knew that we would need tickets to go inside Independence Hall, so we headed to the Visitors Center to get them first. It was a good thing we did, because it was only 11:30, but the first available tickets were for 2pm. After we collected our free tickets, I stamped my Passport with ten different stamps, then watched 2 videos about this historic place.

Back out on the street, we went to see the Liberty Bell. We had been to Philadelphia on a business trip quite a few years ago, but everything has changed. We had to go through another security line to see the beloved Liberty Bell. One thing is for sure, the world changed after 9/11. Before, it was displayed out in a wide open grassy area, and anyone could walk right up to it, enclosed in a clear protective room. Now the entire display is enclosed in a building with much more to see, all under heavy security.

Once again, we were surprised at how many Oriental people were visiting—they were everywhere! And plenty of folks speaking other languages, as well. They are generally quiet and respectful, so I'm not complaining about them in any way. But I fail to understand why they come by the busload to check out America's birthplace and so many National Parks. I guess I don't imagine myself going to another country and wanting to see where they formed their first government. I dunno, I guess it's just my mind wandering.

We decided to eat before our tour, so we sat outside on this beautiful, finally warm and sunny day, under a large umbrella at the Independence Hall Café. We ordered a classic Philly Cheesesteak and chips. They even granted me a free icy cold lemonade, because it was Mother's Day. The Cheesesteak was delicious, and we ate every bite.

Anyway, during our tour, I did learn that our nation completed the Declaration of Independence on July 2. Our National Park Volunteer taught us in great detail that the colonies had everything drawn up to vote on July 2. There were 4 states who would not agree, so discussion continued through July 3.

But, it all boiled down to the vote of one very sick man who rode 80 miles on horseback, on a terrible night of thunderstorms to make his vote count to make it unanimous. Google Caesar Rodney—who is shown riding his horse on the back of the Delaware commemorative quarter—and learn some more about the stuff they never taught us in school. Your independence and freedom were determined by this one man. Who knew?

We walked around a bit more, delighted by horse-drawn carriages on the streets as we walked. Then it was back in the direction of the PATCO station. I was determined to enjoy a pretzel from a street vendor, but I could find only one vendor out today. I was so excited, but sadly, it wasn't very good. Maybe I'll find a better one in New York City. The ride was as smooth and uneventful as our trip in. It's been a great day.

Thank you, Lord for this time and place in which You chose for me to live.

> Galatians 5:13
> You, my brothers and sisters, were called to be free.
> But do not use your freedom to indulge the flesh,
> rather, serve one another humbly in love.

MAY 15

Today was another amazing day. We left Philadelphia to head for the unequaled busyness of New York City! Remember those old salsa commercials? "New York City!" We traveled there today. And it was a nail-biter of a trip!

We set out this morning all charged up and ready for excitement. It would be a couple of hours before we arrived at our destination, but today we would walk the streets of New York City! We have been to NYC once before, but we have a LOT planned for these next three days. And what we managed to squeeze in today was pretty crazy.

We started out on I-295 north to US130 north. We took the New Jersey Turnpike (that Simon and Garfunkel sing about), then I-95 to Christopher Columbus Drive north in Jersey City, New Jersey.

There were a few other quick route changes, but we finally wound up on Marin Boulevard.

After paying a $32 toll for traveling the New Jersey Turnpike, and following quite a bit of drama brought on by Frankie, my dear Frack saved the day by taking us right to where we needed to be. The GPS coordinates furnished by the Allstays app were dead wrong. Frankie took us to Liberty State Park, a mile from the campground. But I had taken the liberty to set Frack with the street address in Google and he led us the correct way. You should have seen us! The motorhome, tow dolly and car, all wandering the skinny streets of Jersey City.

By the time we arrived, Larry was a nervous wreck! He was, after all, navigating this 56-foot traveling circus into the dense and busy city. Our destination was just across the Hudson River from Manhattan. Traffic was heavy and since the city is old, there were a lot of low clearances we had to avoid. There were tolls to pay, tunnels, bridges, tight lanes, tight turns, low tree branches, detours…one wrong turn would spell disaster. He had to keep a close eye not only on the right and left, but to the up and down, as well.

We arrived at the Liberty Harbor RV Park, which Larry rated a 2. Larry breathed a deep sigh of relief when we pulled in.

This campground folks, is a lesson in supply and demand. This place is literally a parking lot, and not even a nice one. The sites are chipped rock and the aisles are well-worn asphalt. There is 50amp electric and pressurized water, but no sewer and no dump station. There's construction on a high-rise office building not 25 feet from the back of our site. And, with only one other motorhome in between, there's a large path where boats are put in and pulled out of the bay on the other. For this, we pay $95 per night plus 7% sales tax. Youza!

On the plus side, we had a decent view of the Statue of Liberty from that parking lot. At night, she was all lit up and beautiful. We could walk to 2 different ferries or ride bikes to the PATH subway into NYC.

And there's not another campground for 20 miles in any direction. See? Supply and demand. Could we go to Central Park and pitch a tent? Nope. Well, not without getting an expensive ticket, that's for sure. The owners of this park could make this campground/marina into something magnificent and charge two or three times as much. They need to spend some money on improvements and upgrades. Take note and visit Las Vegas Motorhome RV Resort.

Anyway, we arrived about 2pm and after a bit of confusion about where we were supposed to park, we quickly set up. The only plan Larry had originally made for this afternoon was to take the subway in to see the World Trade Center Memorial. But in the process of killing a little time, he registered in a sort of lottery for discounted Broadway tickets.

By 3:05pm, they had selected the "winners" and we were among those named! I personally believe they're avoiding empty seats by allowing all the unsold tickets to go cheap hours before the show. We were going to see *CATS*, on Broadway! Well, put the shorts and t-shirts away and get out some decent clothes, because we were going uptown!

Not knowing exactly how far it was to the PATH, we chose to drive there. We won't do that again. In addition to the frustration and confusion, we had to pay $18 to park. Ouch. We'll probably take the ferry in tomorrow.

At least you can purchase unlimited tickets for the NYC Subway, and that's just what we did. No more tallying fares in your head; just be sure not to lose the cards. (Grove Street Station, Red line to World Trade Center (WTC)). We quickly arrived at the World Trade Center Subway Station. This Chambers Street / WTC Station is absolutely remarkable. It's humungous and white and full of light and shapes and angles that are impossible to describe in words. It's multi-story and full of escalators and retail stores.

Our gaping mouths gave us away as tourists, for sure. We finally found our way outside and quickly located the 2 pools at the WTC Memorial. It was awesome enough in the broad daylight, but I sure wish we could have also seen the memorial at night.

"The nearly 3,000 names of the men, women and children killed in the attacks of September 11, 2001 and February 26, 1993 are inscribed on bronze parapets surrounding the twin Memorial pools.

"The display of these names is the very heart of the Memorial. The design of the names parapet provides a direct relationship between the visitor, the names and the water, allowing for a feeling of quiet reverence between the visitor and the Memorial.

"Names are stencil-cut into the parapets, allowing visitors to create paper impressions or rubbings of individual names. At night, light shines up through the voids created by each letter of a name."[29]

We saw yellow rose buds tucked into some of the names. We learned that they were indicative of that person's birthday today. What a sad but important tribute to those lives lost.

We happened to stand close to Todd Beamer's name, one of those who dared confront the terrorists of Flight 93. "Let's roll." There were 2 unborn babies listed. There were FDNY departments and battalions listed, with the name of each crew member lost. I wondered which name was that of the first man we witnessed leap to his death?

The disaster was massive. Sobering. Inconceivable.

---

[29] 911memorial.org/names-memorial

It was time to leave the Memorial and head to Times Square. The police officers nearby could tell we were momentarily misplaced. They walked over to offer assistance and were quite helpful. We took the Yellow line to 42nd Street station, Times Square.

We had arrived in plenty of time, so we decided to have an early supper at Red Lobster. The food and service were great, and as always, we left a card and brochure on the table.

Between the subway tunnels and the walk-through Times Square, we passed a circus' worth of characters. A man playing a guitar, a man playing bucket drums. Three fellows performing acrobatics on the sidewalk. Wonder Woman, the Statue of Liberty, Ernie, Batman, Mickey Mouse, and plenty more. They wanted you to request a photo with them, and they would ask for tips in return.

One young man approached us to sell his poetry and music CD. Larry politely told him, "No, thank you." He responded by loudly calling him a racist. It was a racist thing not to buy; he needed to eat, too.

What in the world made that encounter all about racism?

Time Square was a busy, busy place. There were taxis everywhere, and they do love to blow their horns. Sirens. Retail and food carts were scattered about. A group of Chinese monks were giving out "love bracelets" for donations. One tried to put it on my wrist before I could even decline. I pulled away and told him, "No, thank you."

We were there on a beautiful Monday evening. Was this really just a regular night in Manhattan?

We slowly walked toward the theater. I called it Uptown, because the street numbers were getting bigger, but was it really? Or was it Downtown?

We passed on any souvenirs from the theater. $20 for a coffee mug, $40 for a t-shirt—I guess I'm getting old and cheap! I nearly choked when forced to pay $5 for a 20oz bottle of water!

Cats, precision, lights, effects—they all made you feel they were cats the way they acted on stage. The music—the hit song—*Memory*--often incorrectly called *Memories*, is a show tune from the 1981 musical Cats.

"*Cats* is a musical composed by Andrew Lloyd Webber, based on *Old Possum's Book of Practical Cats* by T. S. Eliot, and produced by Cameron Mackintosh.

"As of 2016, *Cats* is the fourth-longest running show in Broadway history and was the longest running Broadway show in history from 1997 to 2006 when it was surpassed by *The Phantom of the Opera*…It has been performed around the world many times and has been translated into more than 20 languages. In 1998, *Cats* was turned into a made-for-television film.[30]

The production was enjoyable, but the small, hard seats not so much. We had a 3-minute walk on stiff legs and 2 subway rides later--50th street station downtown to WTC, by way of the E Blue Train then to the red path and Grove Street station to get "home."

We were throwing off our shoes right before midnight. What an amazing, astounding day. And we had just arrived!

> Hebrews 11:10
> For he was looking forward to the city with foundations,
> whose architect and builder is God.

---

[30] https://en.wikipedia.org/wiki/Cats_(musical)
en.wikipedia.org/wiki/Kennelly%E2%80%93Heaviside_layer#Cultural_impact

MAY 16

When we awoke this morning, the day's plans only consisted of 9am tickets to the Statue of Liberty. But these tickets were special, because they granted us access to the Pedestal of Lady Liberty. Larry tried yesterday to obtain tickets for the crown, but the first available ticket was for—get this—mid-September! We considered ourselves blessed to have gotten these.

We drove to nearby Liberty State Park, parked for only $7, and walked the beautiful riverfront to the National Park Service security checkpoint to board the Miss New Jersey ferry, which would take us to Liberty Island and the Ellis Island Immigration Museum.

It was a glorious day to be walking outside! The skies were blue with little wispy clouds brushed all over the sky. The temperature was perfect, at around 80 degrees. As we stood outside waiting for the Ferry to arrive, we couldn't help but notice that we, besides the hordes of school kids on field trips, were once again the minority in today's crowd of foreigners.

The ride across the water brought to mind the day we learned that Captain Chesley Sullenberger had successfully landed his damaged USAir flight in the frigid waters of the Hudson River with 155 souls on board. If you haven't seen the movie *Sully* with Tom Hanks, be sure to see it. The movie explains in great detail the Captain's feelings about being a "hero," and the FAA investigation that ensued. How close to that spot are we now? What might that have been like to see?

We could also see the beautiful new building One World Trade Center. Again, we try to imagine what it would have been like to stand in this particular place and watch those towers' fate. I cannot truly imagine, in any way, shape, or form what that must have been like. Those live images are burned into my brain—the disbelief of the first plane, wondering if it was pilot error? Then, the moments before the second plane, the smoke, the fire, the debris, the ash, everyone running, scared, and hurting. I know that my life changed forever that day, and I "only" watched it on TV.

The Statue of Liberty was every bit as beautiful as it had been before, but standing on the Pedestal gave you a completely different point of view, for sure! Seeing her profile from any point of view is the same, just a different size. Looking up at her height from beneath her skirts was the first time I began to fathom just how huge she really is. We spent a good amount of time on and in the Pedestal; I was so grateful that Larry had obtained these special tickets.

As we looked down on Ellis Island, it seemed small in comparison. I thought about Nevada Barr's book, *Liberty Falling*. She's written so many fictional stories based on real National Parks, and I have read them all, I think. She writes in such detail, and now I have seen these places with my own eyes. I'm going to be sure to pack all her books when we leave for a restful winter in Florida. I'm going to reread every one.

After several hours of discovery, we took the ferry back to the rig. I laid down for a bit, while I texted back and forth with Keshia, one of our employees from our shop in Myrtle Beach, who lives and works nearby. We finally made plans to meet for supper that evening at the Brownstone Pancake Factory.

I met Keshia a long time ago, when she was in high school. Her mom escorted her through Broadway at the Beach one afternoon, to look for a job for the upcoming summer, and our dear Pop 'N Stuff, Inc. was one of her stops. I took her application and told her that I would be in touch. But, I was so impressed with her manners that I ran outside to catch up with her to give her the job on the spot. I grabbed her up before someone else could.

She was every bit the great person and worker that I'd pegged her to be, and she worked for me several years. There were times I helped her with homework. In time, her mom became ill and passed away. She watched over her younger brother while attending classes and after he graduated, he joined the military. Keshia moved away to attend college.

In due time, she finished college, worked for her law degree and was hired by a firm in New York City. I hadn't seen her for years, except on Facebook. It was such a God-thing that, in this small window of time, we were able to coordinate supper together.

Have you ever heard the phrase, "You can't get there from here?" That's exactly how I felt by the time we arrived in Edgewater, New Jersey. It was only a 10-mile drive from Jersey City, but it took us well over an hour to get there!

And we still beat Keshia there. It was so great to see what a beautiful, intelligent, and confident young woman she had grown to be. We talked about anything and everything. As friends, we could even talk peaceably about the fact that she would still love Larry despite him wearing his favorite red Trump hat, *"Make America Great Again."* Her opinions on many matters were different than ours, but that's because everyone sees life from his or her unique point of view. That doesn't mean I can't love her. And I will always love her. And we were delighted that she still loves us.

We had a wonderful 90-minute visit and great food. I was delighted to see that they offered potato pancakes, but stupidly ordered pigs in a blanket. I nearly cried when they arrived. The waitress was so very kind in taking them back. I ate the entire plate of potato pancakes with applesauce to prove my gratefulness.

> John 15:12-15
> My command is this: Love each other as I have loved you.
> [13] Greater love has no one than this:
> to lay down one's life for one's friends.
> [14] You are my friends if you do what I command.
> [15] I no longer call you servants, because a servant
> does not know his master's business. Instead, I have called
> you friends, for everything that I learned from my Father
> I have made known to you.

It was finally time to say goodbye. Our waitress was willing to take photos of us with each of our cell phones, and little sneak Keshia secretly paid the bill before we even had a chance to fight over it. What a blessing it was to have had this time together. It was an evening I will never forget.

With rush-hour long gone, it only took half the time to get back to Jersey City. Thank you, Lord for your hedge of protection in this busy place. Thank you, Lord for special friends.

MAY 17

You've heard of the movie, *Plains, Trains and Automobiles*? Well today was a day of Ferries, Buses, and Subways. It was a long, hot, sweaty, and adventurous day. Before 9am, we were dressed nicely and already walked to the ferry. We paid $6.50 each and the close-up view of the city from the water was amazing! It was a fast, bumpy ride, and we docked at Wall Street/Pier 11. The morning sun reflected blindingly off the skyscrapers. We would now have to find our way to the United Nations for our tour.

We walked up and over a few blocks from the ferry landing to catch the M15 bus, but in hindsight, I think we took the wrong M15 bus. We learned from other folks at the bus stop that we needed an extra "bus" trip on our Metro Cards, and the driver got upset when Larry walked right past him without giving him his ticket.

When the driver jumped out of his seat and charged after Larry, I held my hand up and quickly explained, "My husband is hard of hearing. This is our first time in riding the bus here in the city— just tell us what you need us to do." We showed him our purchased tickets and he backed off.

This driver was having a really bad day, or had been doing this job way too long. He picked up a lady along the route who didn't have change for the meter, and she didn't have a ticket. She asked every single person on the bus for change for a $20. He refused to move the bus until she paid. After several minutes, the driver shook his head dramatically, walked off of the bus, and stood talking to himself on the sidewalk. That bus was not moving until that woman paid her toll in full or disembarked. After much begging, someone finally opened their wallet and gave her change.

The bus we meant to take should have gone straight down First Street, and hit the UN about 40 minutes and 9 stops later. Somehow, this M15 bus we got on kept zigzagging off First and made at least twice that many stops. Fifty-five minutes later, but still way ahead of our 10:45 tour, we finally arrived at the UN. It was bright and sunny, and the view was majestic and breathtaking. We stared up in awe at the beautiful sight of all the member countries' flags, blowing in the brisk wind.

We walked up a set of steps and walked up to security, but they explained that security was actually across the street. Back down the steps, we waited for a traffic light and breezed through security. Another red light and back up the steps again to the same security, but this time with our credentials.

The walking tour took about an hour. Our tour guide was of oriental descent and I think English was her second language; Larry and I both had a lot of trouble understanding what she was saying. She was very educated and dressed in a very professional UN uniform. What we could understand, was very interesting.

"The United Nations is an international organization founded in 1945 after the Second World War by 51 countries committed to maintaining international peace and security, developing friendly relations among nations and promoting social progress, better living standards and human rights...

"The UN has 4 main purposes: to keep peace throughout the world, to develop friendly relations among nations, to help nations work together to improve the lives of poor people, to conquer hunger, disease and illiteracy, to encourage respect for each other's rights and freedoms, and to be a center for harmonizing the actions of nations to achieve these goals."[31]

We did get to sit in the big assembly dome, used primarily for the General Assembly of the UN in early September. There was plenty of room for leaders, the staff, and interpreters of the now 73-member countries. It boggled our minds to imagine this place, full of the delegates who represent their powerful countries.

> Genesis 11:7
> Come, let us go down and confuse their language
> so they will not understand each other."

Unfortunately, that confusion still exists today.

Once our tour was complete, it was time to leave the east side of town and head for the west side. We walked in the heat to catch the subway at Grand Central Station. Thankfully, the trip to Time Square was short.

---

[31] un.org/un70/en/content/history

We needed to find somewhere to eat, but didn't have much time. We should have just settled for a hot dog from one of the street vendors, but there was nowhere to sit. We found a little Italian Place right above the Planet Hollywood, called Buca di Beppo.

I told the waiter we had 30 minutes. I quickly ordered penne with marinara, a cup of zuppa soup for Larry and a Diet Coke. I drank 2 full glasses of ice water and gobbled down the penne. Paid and gone in 30 minutes. The only problem: the bill. The Penne was $8.95. Not bad at all. The small bowl of soup was $5.98 (I thought it was an add-on for the entrée) and $3.98 for the soda. Plus, a tip. Geesh. We should have just gone with the hot dog.

There were people crowded everywhere throughout Times Square, walking hurriedly in every direction. If you stopped, I believe folks would walk right over you and leave you broken and bloody on the street. There weren't many people strolling through, it seemed as if everyone was on a mission to get someplace else, fast and in a hurry. It was as noisy and busy as it had been before.

My back was killing me from the walking tour at the UN and we had to move quickly to make the 2pm Broadway show, *Get On Your Feet*, the story of Gloria and Emelio Estevez.

Our seats were wide and comfortable but in the very last row, underneath the balcony. But in the end, it didn't really matter. We had full view of the stage and the cast and crew were fantastic.

We learned that the Broadway show opened on November 5, 2015 with a cast that featured Ana Villafane as Gloria and Josh Segarra as Emilio. In July 2016, Puerto Rican singer and actor Ektor Rivera replaced Segarra. They certainly looked like the Estevez family and Ana Villafane looked, talked, and sang just like Gloria.

Larry was excited about seeing this. We lived in Indianapolis for a while, which was home for the Pan-American Games in August of 1987. A new group, The Miami Sound Machine, was the entertainment and they were great. The music, the dancing, the Latin rhythm and beat, was really something. We were sure on our feet for this performance. Hearing all of Gloria's hit songs was a treat and a trip down memory lane. Should I really admit that I enjoyed this production more than I liked *CATS*? Some would consider it shameful, but I did. The Marquis Theater had much more comfortable seats and lots more leg room. It was a great afternoon.

As an added note, after 34 preview shows and 746 performances, the show closed on August 20, 2017. I am so glad we were able to see it when we did.

Back on the hot streets, Larry wanted us to walk to enjoy the view from The Rock, the observation deck atop Rockefeller Center. On the way, we happened to pass the News Corporation Building. I peeked through one of the first-floor windows and called for Larry to join me. There sat Eric Boling at the center of a large desk, getting ready for The Specialists, as it was just before 5pm. The Five had been at 5pm for a while, but everything has recently been moved around. We had no idea if they could see us as we saw them, but Larry made sure they could see his Trump *Make America Great Again* hat.

I was beginning to fizzle in the heat and the back pain, but we made it. We couldn't ride the elevator up without tickets and you had to go to a completely different floor to buy those. We were greeted by a person at the door, but he redirected us to rows of machines from which we were to make our purchase. We choose the option for 2 tickets and it responds by telling us that the next available ticket was for 9:55pm—like 5 hours from now! No, thanks. I plan to be back in Jersey City, behind lock and key, sound asleep long before then! There would be no observation deck for us.

Back on the streets we were ready to call it a day. We found the subway under Rockefeller Center and headed for the signs to take us downtown by way of the F train on the orange line. We would then find the orange PATH trains to New Jersey.

There was this guy selling and showing everyone a new strapped-on head light that you wear. He went on and on how to use it and why everybody needed one. I didn't have the heart to tell him they have been around for like ten years. Ha! Only in New York. After just a couple of stops, we got off to switch trains to New Jersey.

Larry jumped on the first train that appeared and, of course, I quickly followed him, so as not to be separated. That would have been catastrophic! Well, apparently, they alternate the PATH trains on one rail, and he had managed to hop on the train that was going all the way out to Hoboken. Great, we get to the end of the line, and we're miles from where we wanted to be!

We stayed on the train, going back in the direction we came. On the long ride, I got up to take a closer look at the subway map, to figure out exactly what we needed to go. Once again, when we got off, they're running two different trains on the same tracks. Do not get back on the train to Hoboken! We want the one to Journal Square!

We had heard announcements that there was a problem with one of the trains, and they were running 5 minutes late. Well, when the first one not destined for Hoboken showed up, folks were packed in like sardines. The doors opened and not a soul could have forced their way in. Here comes Hoboken.

Then the next Journal Square, and they were squished in, too. Here comes another train. No, it says NO PAX—no passengers. Another Hoboken. Then, finally! The next Journal Square and Larry announced that we were getting on, so on we go, squished on with all the others. But then, another like 6 people get on behind us, nearly knocking us flat. The only thing that saved us was that the train was so crowded, there was no possible way to fall down!

Nobody talks on the subway, but Larry asks aloud if he started to lean, would everyone fall like "Dominos?" Everyone eyeballed him like, "Let's not try it." They were more likely thinking, "Stupid tourist." We were on our way to Journal Square and Grove Station, our stop. It seemed like it took a long time to get to that next station, and we gleefully escaped with a few other folks. Like herds of cattle, we all went up the stairs to the street. How do folks do this every day of the week?

We still had a long way to go to get to the campground. I saw a Krispy Kreme and bolted inside, before Larry could stop me. We could snack on a couple of them now, then eat them in the morning.

We were almost back to the rig when we decided to eat at the B18 Coffee Kitchen. It was an eclectic little place; the atmosphere and food were equally good. We enjoyed a tasty turkey club on toasted focaccia bread. We were done going into the city, but we still had another couple of days on our Metro passes. It would be a shame to waste them. I walked up to a man in the restaurant and asked if he rode public transportation every day. Yes, he did. I asked if he could get some use out of the balances on our passes. Sure. They're yours. Pay it forward.

While Larry unlocked the door to the rig, I stopped to take a final look at Lady Liberty out in the harbor. I turned around to enjoy one last look of the beautiful Manhattan skyline, close by and gloriously lit up. It was indeed a city that never sleeps. I took a quick shower and collapsed into bed, and Larry beat me to sleep.

I can honestly say that we were all New York'ed out. What a fantastic adventure it had been.

MAY 18

We started out early, because we had a 4-hour trip ahead of us. And, considering it had taken us over an hour to go 10 miles the other night, we were already worried they it might take us that long just to get out of the city. The sun was bright, and it was hot already.

Larry had a route in his head. A couple of small roads out of Jersey City to hop on I-95 north, then follow US1 along the coast of Rhode Island. Simple, right? But, Frankie had other plans.

Forgive me, as I've explained this before, but the reason Larry insists on using this Sygic truck program is that it's designed for use by truckers. The program has been told how much we weigh, how high we are, how wide we are, and how long we are with the tow vehicle. The program is designed to consider all those factors and direct us <u>only</u> to routes that will accommodate us. We originally named it Frank, but have recently resorted to calling it Frankie, because it does talk like a girl in an Australian voice.

To begin with, Frankie took us through miles of narrow, one-way residential streets. Folks were opening their car doors from parking spaces on curbs, only inches from the rig. Tree limbs hadn't been cut high enough for us, and they kept hitting the AC units and the satellite dish. The traffic lights and wires sure seemed low, too.

As good as Larry is at driving this rig, turns were tight, and he was already fretting about getting around in traffic this dense. He's constantly worried that he won't be able to change lanes or make an exit in time. He's petrified of getting stuck under an overpass, or hit hard by low trees. The absolute worst would be driving into a dead end. We can't back up with the tow dolly, and getting out would be time-consuming and frustrating. Each close turn wound him just a bit tighter. And when he's wound up, the volume of his voice increases accordingly.

The traffic getting out of Jersey City was stop-and-go for miles, and people were cutting across lanes and cutting us off whenever they could. Nobody understands "Yield" these days.

Larry was cranky already. He would only get worse from here.

We were finally aligned to cross the George Washington Bridge. We could see it straight ahead, but it took us well over another hour to get to the toll booth. While we were waiting, Larry entertained me with stories of the infamous "Bridgegate."

"The Fort Lee lane closure scandal, also known as the George Washington Bridge lane closure scandal, or Bridgegate, is a U.S. political scandal in which a staff member and political appointees of New Jersey Governor Chris Christie (R) colluded to create traffic jams in Fort Lee, New Jersey, by closing lanes at the main toll plaza for the upper level of the George Washington Bridge.

"The problems began on Monday, September 9, 2013, when two of three toll lanes for a local street entrance were closed during morning rush hour. Local officials, emergency services, and the public were not notified of the lane closures, which Fort Lee declared a threat to public safety. The resulting back-ups and gridlock on local streets ended only when the two lanes were reopened on Friday, September 13, 2013, by an order from Port Authority Executive Director Patrick Foye. He said that the "hasty and ill-informed decision" could have endangered lives and violated federal and state laws.

"It was later suggested that the lanes had been closed to intentionally cause the massive traffic problem for political reasons, and especially theorized that they were a retribution attack against Fort Lee's Mayor Mark Sokolich, a Democrat who did not support Christie as a candidate in the 2013 New Jersey gubernatorial election. The ensuing investigations centered on several of Christie's appointees and staff, including David Wildstein, who ordered the lanes closed, and Bill Baroni, who had told the New Jersey Assembly Transportation Committee that the closures were for a traffic study."[32]

I can't imagine traffic being any worse than it is today.

---

[32] https://en.wikipedia.org/wiki/Fort_Lee_lane_closure_scandal

Now, before I go on, I need to explain something here, about the highway signs controlling flow of traffic. There were lots of signs pointing directions for "cars" and "trucks." We are not a car and we are not a truck. It all depends on context.

At weigh stations, when they say that all trucks must exit, we are not a truck and do not exit. We know their context is regarding commercial carriers and weights. At rest stops, the signs say cars this way and trucks that way. We know, in that context, that we are not a car; as we require the oversized parking lanes for trucks.

Without fully understanding the context of the signs here, but knowing we were not a commercial truck, we chose a lane for cars. That turned out to be a big, big, BIG mistake. Now gridlocked in traffic, we looked like an elephant in a sea of zebras. We were the only RV in sight—was that a bad thing or just a coincidence?

It was finally our turn to pull up to the toll booth. Larry called out, "How much?" to the toll worker. "$84." "What?!" Larry yelled in a high, squeaky voice. "*How* much?" "$84—in cash." The toll guy explained that the motorhome alone was $64, and the dolly and car added 2 axels and $20 more.

Larry threw a fit right there, on the spot. I felt sorry for the toll collector. I had only half that much in my wallet, so I was trying to get Larry's attention as well as his wallet. I hoped I would not have to dig out the lockbox for additional cash. Finally, through much loud hollering, we paid the fee and requested a receipt.

The bridge isn't even a mile long, but it is the world's busiest bridge. Once we were through the toll booth, we flew! We were off the bridge in minutes. As we drove on the beautifully-maintained Henry Hudson Parkway, I listened to my husband carry on about that toll. Larry must have hollered "Eighty-four dollars!" in that loud, mocking voice 50 times before the next catastrophe quickly struck.

We heard a loud explosion. What in the world was that? Directly in front of us, a truck was zig zagging out of control, leaving behind it dust and the smell of hot brakes. He finally managed to pull over in the grass, but had left behind a blown truck tire in the road.

Larry was going too fast to miss it! He managed to drive the rig safely over it, but hit it with the tow dolly. We rocked for a moment, then all was good. He checked the mirrors and could see the traffic behind us swerving to miss the debris. As there was no place for us to pull over, we would have to wait until later to check for damages. Our nerves were shot!

We thought we were home free and finally on our way, but the excitement has just begun. We now saw the bold NO TRUCKS ALLOWED signs overhead. Uh-oh. What was the context here?

Our question was quickly answered, as we approached the first overpass: it was a low clearance—marked 12 feet at the sides, and we made it through. The second one was a bit lower, and Larry slowed the rig to a crawl.

Here was finally the context! There were no trucks allowed, because the clearances on the Parkway were too low! Couldn't they have just put that on the signs in New Jersey? We had to get off this thing before we got to another overpass!

We charged down the next exit and it was just in time. We could see the next overpass, and it was marked 10.5-foot clearance. The only way we could have traveled under that was sideways!

But now we had even more problems: where were we and how do we get to the interstate from here? Larry was beside himself, winding through these narrow residential roads in Inwood, New York. I begged him to stop the rig, and he yelled back that there was nowhere to stop. Okay. Point taken.

He was making turns faster than I could get a route into any of the navigational tools. Frankie's running out of juice on the iPad about this time, too. Oh, that's just great! We were moving the entire time. The rig moves forward, Frankie barks another route change, then another, trying to get us back on the HHP. She was adamant. "Make a U-turn, turn left, go 650 feet and turn right, make a U-turn…" Larry was talking louder than Frankie, wanting me to find an alternate route. There was just no place to pull over on the city streets.

You get the picture. On information overload, ,y brain chose that exact moment to squarely shut down. Help me, Lord!

Psalm 57:1
Have mercy on me, my God, have mercy on me,
for in you I take refuge.
I will take refuge in the shadow of your wings
until the disaster has passed.

So, by the time Frankie told us we were in Yonkers, God provided a way. In this crowded town, I looked ahead and spotted about 6 empty parking spaces, all in a row.

"Pull over, Larry," I nearly screamed above the electronics. "Pull right over there. Pull over. PULL OVER! Pull the brake, shut down this rig. Just stop!"

Thankfully, he did. Without saying another word, I got up from my seat and calmly prepared fresh Diet Cokes for both of us. I quietly requested that he crank the generator. I fixed him a couple of White Castles and nuked a little DiGiorno pizza for me. The iPad was dead, so we each picked up our iPhones and while we ate, quietly planned our escape route from this place named Yonkers.

I found out later that Yonkers is the fourth most populous city in the U.S. state of New York according to Google, just a few miles north of Manhattan. An urban jungle for sure! There were cars, truckers, buses and people everywhere.

Larry felt rushed to get out of those parking spaces, but I did not. As busy as the city was, God had provided them—all in a row— and I knew there would be no one to make us move. I searched Frack's options and there was absolutely, positively no direct route across the area to I-87 or I-95. None. You just couldn't get there from here! It's times like these you start to question why we put all trust into electronics, and don't carry an old-fashioned giant Atlas for times like these. At that moment, I sure wished we had one. All calmed now, we took our time and finally agreed on a route to the Interstate.

There were still a few residential streets to cover, that barely had room for us, horizontally or vertically, but we stuck to the plan. We took Yonkers Avenue to I-87, then I-287, which soon took us to I-95 north, further away from New York City. We basically followed a bus, then a semi to get out of the mess—we concluded that if *they* could make it, so could we! Thank you both, whoever you were. I typically despise I-95, but today I was so happy to see it!

Finally, free of the bonds of the city, we changed routes frequently through New York, Connecticut, and Rhode Island: Route 287E, I-95 north, RI2, RI78, US1 east and RI108.

As I wrote all this later, I can now say the rest of the day was enjoyable. Upon arrival in Narragansett, Rhode Island, we set up at Fishermen's Memorial State Park, which Larry rated a 7. We took an hour to do some general housecleaning, which was long overdue, and I started some laundry.

After a quick icepack on the neck, we hopped in the car to explore. The State Park is on the water, although we don't have a view from our camp site. The Park is tidy, well-maintained, and I'd guess about half-full. It was already hot when we left Jersey City this morning, but it's cooler here. Spring is just sprouting. We've enjoyed several springs since we saw the first one back in Louisiana in February. We have only 30amp electric and can't run both air conditioners, so the weather is perfect.

Larry announced that crab cakes were "invented" here, at Aunt Carrie's Restaurant nearby, so we drove there to eat. There wasn't a soul in the parking lot. I walked to the door to read a sign that announced they're only open on weekends right now. I think we'll check them out for lunch tomorrow, on Friday.

We drove into town looking for another highly-rated place named Champlin's Seafood. Right on the water, the view during dinner was fantastic. We agreed on crab cakes, with red potatoes and coleslaw. When I returned to the service counter to pick up our food, I was amazed to see a ginormous lobster sitting on the next tray. I couldn't wait to tell Larry about it when I returned to the table with our food. I held my hands about fifteen inches apart and told him about the huge lobster. Uh, huh. Yeah, right. I don't think he believed me at all.

We dove into the biggest and fattest crab cakes we've ever had, and they were done to perfection. While we ate, we watched fishermen and pleasure craft; we even saw the large Block Island Ferry come in, filled with passengers returning from Block Island, about 14 miles offshore. Late in the meal, it dawned on me that we hadn't received our coleslaw. I stood up, turned around and just 2 tables from us was THE lobster!

I called back to Larry and told him to turn around and look. We learned from the man that he had purchased the fresh lobster from their fresh market downstairs and brought it up for them to prepare for a $5 fee. I asked him how much it weighed. He proudly announced that it was a 5-pounder and cost him $45, which he considered a great deal, considering what you'd pay in a fancy restaurant for 5- or 6-ounce tail.

The tail alone was truly a foot long! If you stretched him out, from antennae to tip, it must have been 2-feet long. Larry asked if he could take a pic, and the guy's like, "Sure!" Our new pal, Tony explained that the crustacean was probably every bit of 30 years old. See, Larry, I wasn't exaggerating. Tony, here is your name in print— *His Road Trip 3*—as promised, as well as the tale of "Tony's Lobster." We're so glad you enjoyed it, all by yourself!

After supper, we drove on to Shaw's to go grocery shopping. I had a list and stuck to it, while Larry stayed in the car. The drive back to the motorhome was without incident and the smell of campfires greeted us home.

God is good. He took us safely through all that traffic, over a bridge, atop a blown tire, and under close clearances. Those angels providing that hedge of protection sure were busy today! Thank you, Lord for every grace.

Though today's events are now chronicled, I still have so much to say.

While writing this, I did a bit of research online. Without going into mega nerd data mode, the Port Authority of NY and NJ (www.panynj.gov) reported that, in the month of March 2017, there were a total of 4,062,892 vehicles that paid a toll on the GW Bridge. If every car paid $15 and every bus or truck paid the $84 that we paid, (what if they pay more?) they would have collected $85,079,636.16 in March alone. Wow. Them are some serious toll dollars.

I wonder where that money is going? It sure isn't going to fixing roads. The roads in PA, NJ, NY, and CT are in terrible shape with patch work from over the years and zillions of pot holes. The roads have been let go for so long that it is going to take a lot more than money to fix them. Granted, there are some short reprieves, but the majority of the roads are a mess. What will they do with the traffic while they expand these routes?

We also learned on the news that exactly 24 hours after we had hastily eaten Italian in Times Square—in exactly the same *place* where we had walked—an intoxicated man purposely drove his car into a crowd, killing one young woman and injuring 20 more. He told the police he was trying to kill them all. It was sobering to know that we could have been in that crowd, as we had been just the day before.

What a wonderful evening. After such a crazy day, I was blessed with a cool breeze coming through the window as I wrote. Our tummies were full of crab cakes; the smell of campfires was delightful.

God is good. All the time.

MAY 19

One thing about back trouble—you can't escape it. If you bind it up so it doesn't hurt at the moment, or medicate it, it's still gonna make you pay for pushing it in the first place.

These past few days in NYC, I have pushed my arthritic lower back and hips to the max. I now realize clearly that when I put my back brace on, my back does feel better, but it transfers the stress down to my hips. And this morning, my hips are killing me.

I took my prescription meds as directed, and stayed in the bed. I opened the window above my head and enjoyed the cool breeze coming off the water, listening to the birds chirping in the trees. I spent much more time than usual on Facebook, catching up on other people's lives. It would have been delightful, if I hadn't hurt so bad.

When I did get up, I was gimping around like an old woman. It reminded me of a joke I saw on Facebook just yesterday: How do you know if other people consider you an "old lady"? It went on to suggest falling down in front of a group of people. If no one pays attention to you, they think you're young. But if they come running over to help, then yeah, you're old! Ha ha. Yeah, I'm old.

Larry was on my computer, researching details for the book, so I got dressed and drove to the local CVS to refill prescriptions. It was a pleasant drive indeed. The road from here to nearby Kingstown is nicely paved and trees are everywhere. I figure that this is the fourth "spring" we've seen this year, and my seasonal allergies will concur.

The dogwoods are barely flowering and although some trees have leaved, others are barely budding. But one thing that we see here in prime form are the cherry blossoms. They're everywhere and they're so beautiful! I was so sorry that we'd missed them in DC, but now I can totally imagine how much their beauty decorates that city.

It was the largest CVS Pharmacy I had ever seen. Probably the largest CVS, as well. They were wonderfully interactive and took care of my business quickly. When I was checking out, I commented to the clerk how large it was. She said they we're the second busiest pharmacy in the entire chain. I commented how Myrtle Beach Carolina Forest must be first, as they have like 9 workers in there all the time. She said nope, Las Vegas was the number one CVS pharmacy in the nation. All those old farts there to play the machines all day long do need their meds. I laugh as I write this because I too, have done exactly that.

It was much warmer in the city, at 86 degrees. When I pulled into the campground, it was only 70 degrees, cooled by the water nearby. With the breeze still coming in the windows, the day was perfect.

Larry had told me yesterday that crab cakes were invented here. He was sorta right and sorta wrong. He had the "cakes" part right, but it was CLAM cakes that were invented here in Narragansett, Rhode Island. And they were invented right up the road at Aunt Carrie's. That's where we ate supper tonight.

The young and lovely Elena greeted us prompted. She had the prettiest brown eyes and smiling face. When she returned with our drinks, I told her we needed some help deciding what to try. She tried to also explain to me the "Quahog" that was on the menu. Apparently, it's like someone in Myrtle Beach trying to describe a clam—you know exactly what it is but it's pretty hard to explain to someone who doesn't. More on that later.

We like to try assortments of things, so we agreed on the Seafood Platter Dinner. We enjoyed a mound of seafood, which included the following: strip clams, whole clams, shrimp, bay scallops, flounder, and a clam cake. It also came with clam chowder, coleslaw, a basket of homemade and sliced cinnamon bread and dessert, to be announced. Oh, my glory! We had one slice of the cinnamon bread between us. We ate the chowder and slaw. We managed to polish off the scallops and shrimp, but hardly made a dent in the rest.

We asked for a box. And a bag for the bread. Then wondered aloud what was included for dessert.

She giggled as she listed a dozen types of homemade pies, strawberry shortcake, and cheesecake. I went for the strawberry-rhubarb pie with vanilla bean ice cream on the side. Roll me outta here in a wheelbarrow! It was all so delish. We took home enough cinnamon bread for breakfast and then some. And enough seafood for supper tomorrow. Sunday, we go back on budget.

FYI: A quahog is a large hard-shell clam. Theirs were filled with clam stuffing and baked. Now I know: quahog.

MAY 20

This morning we would move the motorhome to another campground nearby. Checkout wasn't until 11am, so we took our time. Larry didn't bother to put the car on the dolly; I just followed him there. In short order, we arrived at the Charlestown Breachway State Park, which Larry rated a 2. It's not a fancy place at all, as Larry had warned. It's pretty much a sandy parking lot with big rocks with site numbers painted on them. We took our place at # 20.

Larry painstakingly maneuvered the rig back and forth in the parking spot to be sure we were straight. Not an easy task since there was a large rock in front of us and a row of pickups parked behind us. It was kinda like parallel parking a motorhome. We set the levelers and put out the extensions. All done! There was no electric to hook up, no water or sewer. All self-contained for 4 days.

It's very pretty here. As I type this, the view I have through the windshield is lovely. From here it appears to be a lake, but the map shows that the Breachway flows downstream out to the ocean. Larry walked down in the afternoon and says the water is beautifully clear. Obviously, there are no or very few muddy rivers flowing into this area of the ocean. There are folks taking boats in and out of the water here and lots of folks fishing.

Still trying to recover from all the activity in New York City, I wrote for a while (by the power of the inverter) and when my neck started to cramp, I treated myself to an ice pack and a nice nap. It's cool here by the water, and it was great to feel the cool breeze through the window as I snuggled up in my bestest buddy quilt.

I wrote all afternoon and when it was time to eat, I cranked up the generator and microwaved an ear of fresh corn, then preheated the convection oven to warm up last night's leftover fantastic seafood from Aunt Carrie's. I wrote the rest of the evening and watched a beautiful sunset, without even getting up from my computer.

We turned the propane furnaces on early, as it will be in the 40's later tonight. Thank you, Lord for a day of low-keyed activities. There's a line in the movie, *Six Days Seven Nights*, where Anne

Heche's character proclaims, "I've had just about as much vacation as I can stand."[33] Yep, that was me in NYC.

MAY 21

Another day of peace. All 3 of the campers around us left early this morning, and we now have an unobstructed view of the waterway. Larry's not feeling well this morning. He said his blood pressure was a bit high, so I took it again. It wasn't his blood pressure that caught my attention, it was all the extra heartbeats that the cuff was registering. His blood pressure had been doing so well, that he'd reduced one of his meds from twice a day to once in the morning. I gave him a second one of those and I gave him an hour to rest. It was much better when I checked it again. Thank you, Lord.

When he got up from his nap, he wanted to go for a drive. And not just any drive: he wanted to drive to 10 Bluff Road in nearby Waverly, Rhode Island, about ten miles away. Why, I'm sure you ask. What's so special about that address? That is Taylor Swift's $18 million estate.

This home at Watch Hill Point is a very exclusive neighborhood. The home sits atop the highest point in this entire area, and the highest bluff along the entire east coast. The gates were, of course, locked and there were all sorts of private property signs to say no stopping, no parking, no standing, no trespassing, and definitely no loitering of fans. We did stop, despite the signs, but only long enough to take a couple of pics. The nearby roads were very winding, and what little parking there was marked "by local permit only."

As we descended the hill, I remarked to Larry that I'd bet the locals threw a fit when they learned she'd bought this estate, built back

---

[33] imdb.com /title/tt0120828/trivia?tab=qt&ref_=tt_trv_qu

in the 1930's. Yes, he had to agree, they probably did. Paparazzi camped out all hours of day or night, helicopters circling overhead, deplorable gawkers like us driving around. It seems some of the locals were upset after she spent $1 million by adding rocks and boulders to "her" public beach to protect her property. The beach had been very public until she bought the estate.

But at least he got to see it. No one was home, of course, but he got to see where Taylor lives, at least some of the time. He is a fan of some of her early songs that she wrote and sang. He has a few albums of hers on his iPhone, right along with The Carpenters, Alabama, John Denver, Celine Dion, and Gloria Estefan.

Although it was only the middle of the afternoon, neither of us had eaten lunch, and I suggested we stop somewhere. We agreed on Charlestown Famous Pizza and set Frack to get us there. It was a little tiny place, with perhaps a half-dozen tables inside. The young man told us to grab a table anywhere and after ringing up a pickup order, he came over to wait on us. The shirt he was wearing had been witness to many a pizza, but I didn't hold that against him at all. He's a hard worker, that told me. We discussed a few options, then ordered a small meatball sub with chips and a Diet Coke (of course).

While we waited for our food, I walked next door in the small strip mall to pick up some decongestant, in the teeniest little CVS I have ever seen. I commented to the cashier about its size and she assured me that there was a smaller one than this, in a town nearby. It had been a little family-run pharmacy that CVS had purchased and albeit small, had a very busy pharmacy.

When I returned, our food was already on the table. The meatball sandwich was perfect! Meatballs, plenty of cheese, and a perfectly toasted bun. The young man came over to check on us often, in between the additional folks who came in for pizza. If there was anyone else there with him, I never saw them. He was very adept at handling table service, taking telephone orders, and cashing out the carry outs.

When he brought me the credit card receipt, there was no place to add tips, so I left him a generous one in cash instead. We started a conversation: I handed him the card with "His Road Trip" on it and explained that I had written a book about our travels in these past 15 months, and putting the Gospel in the hands of children. At the rate I was going, our wonderful experience here at Charlestown Famous Pizza would be journaled in Book 3.

I asked him for his name and he explained that he was Steve and his wife's name was Ann. I have a good idea that Steve and Ann own the place, but that's just my assumption. The book is becoming a way to open the door for conversation and to talk openly about Him and what you need to do to accept His free gift of eternal life. Especially about the importance to teach children.

Sharing the gospel can be hard to get started. We have used *His Road Trip* as a tool to open a conversation. You just never know who will be open to the Gospel; where or when your seeds will grow.

---

1 Corinthians 3:6-8
I planted the seed, Apollos watered it,
but God has been making it grow.
[7] So neither the one who plants nor the one who waters is
anything, but only God, who makes things grow.
[8] The one who plants and the one who waters have one
purpose, and they will each be rewarded
according to their own labor.

He quickly stated that he and his family are Catholic, and you could tell he was proud to be a child of the King. He went on to say that if we were curious about the religious aspect of an area, this area is rich with it. I should have taken notes, but online research indeed substantiates his claims. Since 1639, this area—and especially

Newport—has been a hotbed of controversy involving slavery, English and French occupations, export trade, ethnicities, and the greatly conflicting rights and beliefs of Baptists, Quakers, Jews, and Catholics. They were all new to this free world, ever since the Pilgrims arrived at Plymouth Rock. Hence, "New" England. To read the entire article, see the footnote below.[34]

God continues to amaze me with where He leads us.

> Romans 8:14
> For those who are led by the Spirit of God
> are the children of God.

I wasn't even finished writing about Steve's statement of faith, when I heard, "Hello!" through the screen door. There was a couple standing there said they wanted to donate to our Ministry, as the woman had 2 packets in their hand. I opened the door and emphasized it was a free ministry, and sat down on the steps to visit.

They explained that they had taken their 2 granddaughters to Sunday School just that morning and they felt the girls would enjoy the packets. They asked where we were from and I explained our travels. They were so easy to talk to. They knew about Good News Club and Awana. They had seen the banner and said it was so good, in this day and age, to see someone else doing what they can to spread the Gospel.

I told them about His Road Trip and gave them a card. He began reading it while she and I were talking, and then he asked, "May I asked how your son died?" This gave me the opportunity to share how God had spoken to me, assured me that He had my son, that this was no accident, and that He had great plans for all of this. I explained

---

[34] newporthistory.org/about/brief-history-of-newport/

how many have been saved as a snowball effect from Bobby's death, and continue to be saved.

He asked if they could pray for us. Absolutely! We all held hands and bowed our heads. His was a simple prayer that God would continue blessing our efforts for Him, and that He would continue to keep us safe as we serve. They introduced themselves as Jim and Marilee. If you ever get to read this, please know once again, what a blessing you were to me today.

I was sorry that Larry wasn't feeling well and missed all of this. We don't do this for recognition, but it sure is nice when somebody notices that you're working for the Lord. It's great to receive encouragement like that, too. It's an affirmation that God sent those folks special today, to reassure us in our goals. Thank you, Lord.

Larry had complained earlier today that his stomach was queasy, long before we drove to Taylor Swift's house. He ate only a tiny bit of the meatball sub, and continued to get sicker as the evening progressed. He rarely naps during the day, and if he does, it's sitting up on the couch. He had headed to bed as soon as we returned.

I will omit all the torrid details, but I don't think I've ever, in our nearly 45 years together, seen him that sick. He must have caught a bug from NYC being so close to all those people, especially in the subways. Hand sanitizer just hadn't cut it.

Things didn't quiet down until well after 2am. I knew that God was with us, and it was so reassuring to feel his presence here in this remote place. God is good.

Exodus 23:25
Worship the LORD your God,
and his blessing will be on your food and water.
I will take away sickness from among you,

MAY 22

Larry must have had a fever most of the night, because any time I woke up, he was on top of the covers, not cocooned beneath them as he always is. I'm feeling a bit queasy myself, but it's probably a big dose of empathy. Only time will tell.

Yesterday, I sat here and wrote all day with a completely unobstructed view of the Breachway. It was partly sunny, and the water glistened—it was lovely. To that end, let me explain. Picture in your mind 20 large boulders in a long, straight row, numbered with sites 1 thru 20. As instructed, we are pulled up to number 20, at the end of the row. Number 21 is painted on the other side of our rock, and the numbers continue up the row until you're at the back of the first rock, number 40.

We have, for 3 days now been the only RV on row 1-20. I could see a red truck camper up on number 40, way up at the other end. On the other probably 35 sites beyond this row, there are only maybe 6 RV's camping here. I'm sitting here writing and a new camper comes in. Where did they tell him to park? Number 21, of course. His bedroom window is backed up to about 4 feet from my windshield! And because of his nearness, it obstructs nearly all our views of the waterway.

Why, oh why? It's not like there's nowhere else to park him, try numbers 1-15, or 22 or 23? Or even over in 41-50? 68? Oh, well. It is what it is. Lord, thank you for yesterday's view.

Today was a pitiful day. Larry felt terrible and spent the day in bed. Remember that we have no hookups here, so any time I turned on the computer or TV, it sucked juice from the batteries. I could do that, but when they wear down, I would have to run the generator to recharge them. And with our neighbors just an arm's reach away from the generator, I was mindful of just when and for how long I'd run it.

It poured down rain most of the day and the weather reported that it would continue.

You know, a nice long nap sure did sound good. Did I need it? Nope. But I enjoyed it, just because I could.

Larry was still pretty shaky. We were still without utilities, so I had to keep running the generator, because my computer was using up the batteries. As sunset came, I decided to quit writing and just sit in the candle light. The day was done.

Earlier that afternoon, I had noticed both the man and the woman camping in front of us, at separate times, reading books outside. I went over and knocked on their door, wanting to give them a book, but they must have been napping. I left it on one of their chairs.

MAY 23

The worst of Larry's bug has passed, thank you, Jesus. He tried to eat a little for breakfast, but it didn't sit well. He went back to bed for another hour. In the afternoon, he stayed up long enough to get some future reservations done. The sun is shining again, and the temperature is a scooch warmer. Today is our last day here.

MAY 24

As we were hitching up the tow dolly and the car, the lady neighbor came rushing over. She apologized for her looks (she had been in her pajamas and had dressed quickly), but wanted to be sure to thank me for the book I had left on their chair a few days earlier.

She introduced herself as Susan. She had set aside the book I'd seen her reading to open mine—then explained she couldn't put it down! She also offered her condolences for losing Bobby. It seemed to have upset her greatly, but I cheerfully explained how God had used that event—and continues to use it—to lead people to him. I told her how it's all explained in the book. It was my opportunity to witness God's mercy to her.

Despite the fact that Larry's still not well, we set out for our next destination. We spent the first hour on small roads, miles and miles of maple trees, loaded with spinners, the seeds that fall from female trees. I've also seen what must have been hundreds of Crimson King Maples; they are such a magnificent color. There were dogwoods in bloom, lilac bushes galore, and every color of azalea you could imagine. With these past 2 days of rain, spring is bursting forth. Yellow pine pollen dust covers every imaginable surface.

While trying to get the volume to work on the iPad, I missed an instruction from Frankie. I missed her redirect, too. Larry's getting upset and, at that exact moment, a bird poops smack in his line of sight. Not a little poop but a really huge splat! Oh, boy. If he hadn't been so mad, I would have laughed out loud. He pulled the rig over at a gas station to wash the windshield. What a mess! I would describe it in colorful detail, but I think you get the idea.

We followed I-95 then I-195 thru Providence. Then took MA25 to US6 north on Cape Cod. The coolest thing we drove past today was a mailbox made with the cover of an old Evinrude cover.

We had to get some propane before we arrived on Cape Cod, so we stopped at an RV dealer called Majors RV. As I went inside, Larry met with the guy filling up the tank. He didn't get his name, but he was about Larry's age with a long beard. He was their mechanic. He had seen the ministry decals on the rig and asked about our ministry. Larry explained what we did on the road for Him and we discussed Christians in America and how the kids aren't being taught the fundamentals of the Bible. Which in turn, is causing the breakdown of society. This was definitely a gospel stop, on the pretense of getting propane

Back on the road, Frankie told him many times today, "Over speed limit. Larry, slow down." She got one big belly laugh out of me today. Larry had reprogrammed one of the alerts, unbeknownst to me. At one point, we approached a railroad crossing, and she loudly announced, "Railroad crossing ahead. Choo-choo!" I asked Larry, "What did she say?"

We finally arrived at our destination and settled into the Adventure Bound Camping Resort, which Good Sam had rated a 6.5 / 8.5 /8, but Larry rated an overall 2. His biggest complaint, considering all the electrical problems we've had, was that the electric pole didn't even have a breaker. Plugging in, he held his breath, praying that it didn't have wild and crazy voltage that would blow the entire rig. Everything ran smoothly. Thank you, Lord for your every-present hedge of protection.

We drove around Truro, MA then to Providencetown late in the afternoon, and met a couple who told us that half of the huge dune was gone. They had been in exactly this spot one year ago and they mourned aloud what a shame that so much of the dune had been washed away in such a short time. As we continued to talk, we asked them where we should eat. Moby Dick's, they said without hesitation.

We set the GPS for Moby Dick's and arrived there quickly. We've been waiting for North Atlantic lobster, so we ordered 1 ½ pounder with slaw. We also ordered lobster bisque and the lobster arrived with a fresh ear of corn.

We must have looked like we had no clue what we were doing. A kind woman walking through the restaurant asked if we needed anything? Yes, ma'am. We need a lobster lesson. She didn't laugh or anything, she was great and explained it all very well. I suppose we weren't the first lobster newbies she'd met. She explained in detail how to crack it and where the good meat was. We asked her if we were supposed to eat any of the insides?

She cracked it fully open for us to see the liver, and determined it was a female, and pointed out her eggs. She said that the body parts are eaten by some but not by most. It sure didn't look appealing to either one of us, so we agreed to stick with the blissful white meat. We cut the tail meat into pieces and enjoyed every bite, each dipped in warm drawn butter. We worked much harder to get what little meat we could out of its legs and craws. We agreed on one things for sure: this sure is hard work!

The couple at the next table had overheard us discussing traveling, so we had the chance to share Motorhome Ministry as well as His Road Trip to them. More doors were opened, more seeds sown.

On the way out, a man who look looked to be the manager, wished us a great evening, moved closer to Larry and whispered, "I really like your hat." Larry had on his very red ball cap "Make America Great Again" hat. Larry responded loudly, "What?! You need to say that loudly." I heard the manager quietly reply, "I'm a local business owner and I have to be very careful. I'm in the minority here." We quietly sympathized with him and confirmed.

MAY 25

We drove to the Cape Cod National Seashore, so rainy and cold and foggy that we couldn't even see the historic lighthouse. In the visitor center, we watched their park movie and I got my stamps for my passport. There was a walk-up ramp that I suppose offers a spectacular view of the ocean, but it was like looking into a pot of soup. You couldn't see much of anything.

We decided to drive up the end of the cape to visit the quaint little town of Provincetown. When we arrived, the tide was way out. All the "cape cod" style houses reminded me of my childhood because I was raised in one. The town has plenty of shops and restaurants with most having views of the bay or ocean. Again, if it just hadn't been so darn foggy.

We enjoyed The Province Lands visitor center, at the top hook of the cape, as well as the Salt Pond visitor center on the way back. I think it's ironic that many of the photos they posted on the nps.gov site has the same thick fog as the day we were there. It must be a pretty constant state of affairs.

We drove back in the never-ending soup and had a small supper back at the campground. Thanks to the wonderful visitor centers, it was still a precious day of discovery.

MAY 26

Leaving the upper cape, we drove 2 hours to get to Cape Cod Camp Resort & Cabins, East Falmouth, MA. Good Sam rated 10/10/10, Larry would rate a 7 for us, but if you had kids, families would love it here. We had full hook ups and two cold pools one for adults and then one for both kids and their parents. Oh, and a hot tub.

After getting set up we went to the hot tub. We were there with a family of three; a little girl about 6 and her parents. When it was time for them to leave, the parents dried off while the little girl yanked off that bathing suit for the whole world to see. The parents were mortified, but Larry and I just chuckled. The little one went on to explain that she was cold and wanted to get back in her dry clothes.

Kids. You just never know what they're going to do.

Recently, we've been watching *Colony* on Netflix. It's a story about a mysterious alien invasion starring Josh Holloway, who you may remember from the long-running series *Lost*. Segments in that episode had been obviously taken from up at the observatory above Los Angeles. Larry got tired in the middle and went to bed.

Just then, I spotted a street scene that reminded me of Griffith Park. Yes! They didn't name it, but a rendezvous was taking place at the Greek Theater in Griffith Park. The next scene had them meeting inside the theater where Larry and I had personally enjoyed the Norah Jones concert. I've been right there!

MAY 27

Larry was hard at work on his computer this morning and I don't even remember what I did, but I blew the 30amp. He lost everything he'd been working on. He was so mad! It's obvious to us both that our Uninterruptable Power Source (aka UPS) backup batteries had bit the dust. We would have to check the prices on buying 2 new ones.

Larry was understandably grumpy, so I decided to escape for a while. I set the GPS to a Dollar General nearby just for something to do, but when I arrived at my destination, it wasn't a Dollar General Store at all—it was a Staples. Well, perhaps that was a God-thing. I walked right in to check on any UPS they had in stock and was pleasantly surprised that prices were now so low. I think we originally paid over $400 for each of ours years ago, but today I found some APC units for only $65 each. I called up Larry and he agreed it was a good deal. Once they're fully charged, we will no longer have to worry about losing valuable work when we blow a breaker.

I challenged myself to see if I could find my way back to the campground without the assistance of Alice—and I did! That may not seem like much for most of you, but that was a big deal for this directionally-challenged gal! And the drive was beautiful.

MAY 28

Today, the sun finally shined! We got up and put on our Sunday-go-to-meeting clothes and drove the short distance to Cape Cod Church. I'm so glad that we did. The praise band did a terrific job, even though

I didn't know even one of the modern songs. Then Pastor Ben began his sermon regarding "stuff."

This was right up Larry's alley, because he's always had a problem with stuff. He even says the word with obvious disdain. He has no purpose for stuff (unless it's something to eat or an electronic gadget with useful significance to him). He was always annoyed by our house full of stuff. But they were precious memories to me, many of them representing sweet moments that could never come again. I did keep just a couple of small storage bins filled with the most special of things, but all that other stuff went—it was either sold or given to charity—when we decided to live in a motorhome. No room for knickknacks in this little place.

The pastor's message drove home the theory that stuff is not the key to living fully, despite many people who fill their lives with stuff, in the hopes of finding happiness. He spoke with great feeling, listing many easily-understood examples of how stuff fails us in today's life of materialism. When we ground ourselves in God, that next new outfit or new car just doesn't stay special for long.

As for me, I find such satisfaction in the service of others. Offering a kind word to a cashier who seems to be having a bad day blesses me as much as I hope it blesses them. Give a struggling older person a passing smile or a kind word, especially if they're alone. Compliment someone's hair or dress. It doesn't cost you a thing and it may turn out to be the only kind thing they hear today.

Larry and I decided to present Pastor Ben with one of my books. I wrote a note in the front, praying that the book will bless him as much as his message this morning blessed me. He accepted it with gratitude; I hope he enjoys it.

After church, Larry set the GPS for Woods Hole. He wanted to see where the ferries departed and where the parking lots were. Woods Hole turned out to be an old, historic town with really tight roads. By the time cars packed both sides of the road, there really wasn't room for two-way traffic. After turning around a couple of times, we got lucky and found someone pulling out of a metered parking space. We were doubly lucky in the fact that they left 1 hour and 40 minutes on their meter. Thank you!

We walked the streets, looking for someplace to eat, but the restaurants were packed and appeared pricey. The sun is shining and today warmer, but here, close to the water, the breeze was still chilly. Larry spotted a restaurant down a side street called Landfall, and they had plenty of room for us. We ordered a mug of delicious hot and creamy clam chowder and a broiled seafood dinner. It came bubbling fresh from the broiler with whitefish, scallops, and shrimp. There was a huge heap of coleslaw and we'd ordered macaroni salad as our side (I'm sick of French fries).

The food was delicious, and we polished off every bite. It was curious, though that their garnish amounted to 3 different kinds of flowers. No simple parsley for this meal, but a small purple orchid-type flower, two other small flowers, and some bean sprouts on the side. Wonderful presentation, but we didn't know if we should eat them. Larry told me that he would have rather had another piece of shrimp in lieu of the pretty flowers.

We drove back to the motorhome, and I opted for a short nap. When I got back up, I went straight to the computer and began writing on the book.

After today's large lunch, we had chicken salad and fresh fruit for supper. We recently found the most current season of *Bloodline* on Netflix and ran through 3 episodes this evening. Once again, we watched a scene unfold and Larry said aloud, "What city is that?" considering this series is based in the Keys of Florida. One of the characters had moved far away, and it took us both only a few seconds to home in on the Griffith Park Observatory at on the left side of the screen. We knew then the city in the distance was Los Angeles. We've been there!

MAY 29

It was pouring down rain when the alarm went off. Larry was still in bed beside me, so I stayed tucked in. Today is Memorial Day. Most certainly a day to give due respect and thanks to all the thousands of soldiers who have bravely and unselfishly given all they had to give…for me. For my freedom. And yours. I will clearly say that people who disrespect our soldiers, our law enforcement, our flag—they all disgust me. The rights they have to do those despicable acts were paid for long ago, by people they never met. Have some respect, people. What has happened to America?

> Romans 13:7
> Give to everyone what you owe them:
> If you owe taxes, pay taxes; if revenue, then revenue;
> if respect, then respect; if honor, then honor.

> 2 Corinthians 3:17
> Now the Lord is the Spirit,
> and where the Spirit of the Lord is, there is freedom.

I did get up shortly and enjoyed a hot cup of French Toast coffee. It really hit the spot on this rainy morning. I had found it at Marshalls. I worked part-time at the one in North Myrtle Beach for a couple of years. We used to get the neatest stuff in there, especially in the foodie section. And their prices are always great.

The campground had been packed with kids, parents, and grandparents, and filled with bicycles, dogs, and loud laughter. We had given out a dozen or more kids' packets. Everyone was leaving early today, in the pouring rain. With the whole day open to stay in,

I quickly began working on the book. With a headache, I took some Tylenol and covered my head for a half-hour, then got right back to work. I finally called it quits about 5:30 and fixed us some supper.

It's a lot of work to write a book. I was exhausted! Established authors say, "It's easier when you write about what you know." Well, I'm writing about what I know, but it's still not a simple task.

A couple of years ago, we had watched a Netflix series called *Bloodline*, starring Kyle Chandler and Sissy Spacek. It's not been one of our best choices, because it's dark and some episodes get some bad language in them. But the end of Season 2 had been full of cliffhangers and we really wanted to know what happened. We began watching Season 3 a few nights ago and made it to the final episode tonight. To our surprise, it managed to get even darker. Not much was left hanging, so I think they've called it quits.

I made an off-handed remark to Larry afterwards that if I was Kyle Chandler and had to get psychologically deep within his character daily, I may have jumped off of a bridge by now. He laughed. I would never, ever do that—but the remark illustrated just how bad it really was. He's so handsome, a terrific actor, and seems to be a good man. I sure hope his next role is happier than this one.

Anyway, it tried to rain again some more by bedtime. I want to see more sun! We will wait to see what tomorrow brings.

| Isaiah 29:18 |
| In that day the deaf will hear the words of the scroll, and out of gloom and darkness the eyes of the blind will see. |

MAY 30

Another day of no sun, just pouring down rain. After working at our computers for a while, we decided to brave the weather and get out for a while. We drove to the Cape Code Potato Chip factory for their self-guided tour. It was amazing to see the process, from shipments of raw potatoes, through the cleaning and frying processes, right through to packaging. I enjoy Cape Cod chips, because they're thicker and crunchier. The tour ended in the store, where we stocked up on delicious chips.

The tour certainly cheered up an otherwise ugly day.

Supper was another Marie Callender's frozen meal, this time an oriental dish.

We discovered that *House of Cards* had a new season on Netflix, so we dove into it. But, as I now write this part of the book, Kevin Spacey is at the top of the entertainment news headlines. Such a sad legacy of abuse of power.

I had always liked Kevin Spacey. He has such a wide range, from *Pay It Forward*, *American Beauty*, to the time when he ate a banana whole—skin and all—in *K-PAX*. He's so intense in the characters he plays. He makes such amazing villains. In *House of Cards*, the politics and undermining get so complex—well beyond my simple mind—but I would eventually pick up the storyline again. The complicated story sure helped this evening move along. I also learned that the series has been dropped.

Is sun really forecast for tomorrow? I hope it's true, because we just have a few more days here.

MAY 31

It's still raining, wet and gloomy and depressing   When we awoke, we were upset to discover that our Sleep Number mattress wasn't working. Larry's controller displayed ERR, and mine wouldn't work at all. Not good. We had to fix it right away, because sleeping on an uninflated mattress is not an option.

When we initially purchased it, we put the inflator/control unit under the bed, out of the way. Well, to get under an RV bed, you have to lift up the hydraulic base. The inflator is way up under the head of the bed, and the hinges at the top. Larry got out his tools and began.

Hanging over the frame of the bed, with his head stuck into the narrow space at the top, he removed a few screws to look inside of the inflator. It's a lot of electronics, and I ask why he would bother to look inside? He can't fix those little boards. While holding the flashlight for him, I pointed out a burnt spot on the lid he had set aside. Wait a minute. What had caused that?

He followed the wire to my controller, and we discover that the cord has been pinched over time by the bedframe and most probably frayed the wire inside. I rolled the cord between my fingers, and it worked for a moment. Yep! It's the cord. Now that we know the inflator itself isn't damaged—we can fix this. Larry cut the wire, stripped the ends, and re-spliced the wire. A little black electrical tape and then test the inflator. Yay it works!

God was looking down on us considering that right under our heads an electrical component had burned and shorted out as we slept. What a catastrophe that could have been! I would have hated to spend the cash for a new mattress. We had purchased this one used for a fraction of the cost. And there's no Sleep Number store anywhere around here, that's for sure.

In the afternoon, we took the short drive to Hyannis Port, Massachusetts, where President John F. Kennedy was born and raised at the Kennedy Compound, with his brothers, Joe, Robert, and Ted as well as his sisters, Rosemary, Kathleen, Eunice, Patricia, and Jean.

The town is a harbor town full of boats of all sizes and colors, docked near the small beach. We parked and strolled the beach looking for shells and sea glass. The water is so cold, it's like nature's own air conditioner as the wind comes off the ocean. A typical hot day inland is not as hot along the shore this time of year. The town is full of everything "Kennedy," including a museum. The souvenir shops were full of branded t-shirts and trinkets. I always admired the young President and his family, but they did have a colorful past.

I was only in the fourth grade when he was assassinated, but I clearly remember one of his most infamous quotes, "Ask not what your country can do for you, but what you can do for your country." That should be our country's motto. Maybe a lot of folks would quit asking when their country owes them, and approach life with a servant's heart.

What a country we could be!

Galatians 6:9 Let us not become weary in doing good, for at the proper time we will reap a harvest if we do not give up.

JUNE 1

Today, we headed back to Woods Hole, Massachusetts to catch the ferry over to Martha's Vineyard, an island off the coast often visited by the rich and famous. We could have gone to Nantucket as well, but the price of both tickets was just too much.

After our short ride, we strolled through the harbor town of Vineyard Haven. We stopped at Bob's Pizza and Subs for a delicious slice of fresh pizza. It was next to Bernie's Home-Made Ice Cream, so we had to have one big scoop of COOKIE MONSTER--blue vanilla with Oreo pieces and chocolate—for dessert. After lunch, we purchased some bus tickets and caught the next bus around the island.

Ken the bus driver pointed out all kinds of things along the way, like Mr. Norton's house on the hill. You know the guy that started the company for protection from computer viruses called Norton. Who knew there really was a guy named Norton? Across a bridge and to the left he pointed out the beach where the movie "Jaws" was filmed. It looks just like the movie, well, minus the shark.

Then he pointed out a remote place on the island called "Chappaquiddick." Yes, it found its fame when Edward Kennedy crashed his car off a bridge in July of 1969, where he was injured but the woman who was with him in the car was killed. He was a married Senator of the Kennedy Family, so this was hot news and a high-profile scandal at the time. The island is also where Jackie Kennedy owned her last house. Jim Belushi is buried here on the island.

Most of us remember that John F. Kennedy, Jr. was attempting to land his small plane at Martha's Vineyard when he crashed into the waters offshore; he perished along with his beautiful wife, Carolyn Bessette and her sister, Lauren.

Side story here: while I was researching the plane crash, I discovered all sorts of theories that Hillary Clinton was linked to the plane crash. Polls had shown that JFK, Jr. had been in the frontrunning to win the Senate seat ahead of Hillary Clinton; and after his death, she won. There are lots of conspiracy theorists out there.

It's an area with quite a colorful history. Ken was quite a tour guide as we rode his bus.

We got off his bus in Edgartown and walked the town, looking in the windows of quaint shops and reading menus posted outside the restaurants. The town was full of trees and flowers, tediously manicured lawns with views of the ocean. It looked just like a Norman Rockwell Painting.

We boarded another bus to continue our ride around the island. A complete opposite of Ken, this was the driver from Hell. The roads were narrow and winding, and he would accelerate as fast as he could, just to slam on the brakes at the next turn. Every time he braked, we were thrown forward in our seats. I'm grateful no one on board was prone to motion sickness, because if someone else had hurled, I would have hurling right along with them. I think he did it on purpose, getting some delight out of our reactions.

For obvious reasons, there are lighthouses all over the island. One of them is a National Historic Monument called Gayhead Lighthouse. The driver from Hell stopped the bus at the end of the island, allowing passengers to get off. We were so queasy from the ride, we declined and stayed in our seats. He seemed miffed that we were the only ones left on the bus. We came to the assumption that if we stayed on the bus, he had to stay, too. Maybe he desperately needed a smoke break, but I really didn't care. It was all his fault!

Matthew 5:16

In the same way, let your light shine before others,

that they may see your good deeds and

glorify your Father in heaven.

We remained on Hell's bus until we got back to the harbor. Along the route, we passed the golf courses that Presidents Clinton and Obama played golf (at different times) and places the Obamas rented out for their vacations. Some of the homes here would be fit for royalty. The roads were lined with white and purple wildflowers and there were trees everywhere. It was not at all like I had imagined.

Finally, off the bus and back on the ferry, we started to feel human again. We drove to Seafood Sam's on the way back to the motorhome. We enjoyed a delicious shrimp dinner with slaw, baked beans, and clam chowder, at a very affordable price. Cheap and tasty—my kinda meal.

We took the ferry back to Martha's Vineyard We had made a complete circle of the island.

JUNE 2

We were up early to drive to our next destination. We drove to Wompatuck State Park, Hingham, MA which Larry rated a 2. It's just south of Boston.

Today was our 44th wedding anniversary. To celebrate, we went to dinner at Jake's Seafood and the lovely Miss Mari Anna was our delightful waitress. I guess you figured by now, we love seafood.

We enjoyed their delicious Baked Seafood Casserole with scallops, shrimp, and fish, baked in a light sauce with cheese and breadcrumbs. Scrumptious. And the view of the water and nearby docks was beautiful.

We drove to the end of a hook of land called Nantasket to Hull, Massachusetts, which is directly across the bay from Boston. We could view the Boston skyline and the Boston harbor where the famous Boston Tea party took place. We could even see the steeple of The Old North Church, where Paul Revere put up the lanterns. Go back and check your history books for that one.

Silversmith Paul Revere took part in the Boston Tea Party and famously alerted the Lexington Minutemen about the approach of the British in 1775. The phrase, "One, if by land and two, if by sea" was penned by Henry W. Longfellow in his poem, *Paul Revere's Ride.* It was a reference to the secret signal orchestrated by Revere during his historic ride from Boston to Concord on the verge of the American Revolutionary War.

Then it was time to go back to the campground. We passed a graduation ceremony taking place in the football stadium of the local high school. All throughout the town we saw yard signs in front of houses proclaiming this house had a 2017 graduate that resides here. A very neat idea to honor this year's graduates.

Just the thought of Boston brings to mind crafty Boston Rob and Amber from *Survivor*, and especially the frightening bombing of the Boston Marathon in 2013. If you haven't seen the Mark Wahlberg movie, *Patriots Day*, about the bombing be sure to watch it.

JUNE 3

Today was a Saturday, and we had no specific plans. Diana wanted us to go back to the bar that *Cheers* is based on. I had seen it the last time we were in Boston, but we were on the Spyder and there was absolutely no place to park. Larry had dropped me off outside, while he drove around the block.

The outside sign and steps down into the bar are spot-on. But that's where the resemblance ends—abruptly. I stepped inside, expecting the big, open room and the large, four-sided bar you see on TV. But, the real Cheers has only a short bar and a short but wide front room. Then, behind the front room, there's another, larger dining room.

I was confused, because reality did not fulfill expectation. I asked someone at the bar if they sold T-shirts, and they thumbed me toward the opening into the larger dining room. I paid for the shirt and left, sorry that Larry didn't get to see all that. I offered to drive around the block while he went in, but he turned me down. His loss.

So instead—on the way to downtown Boston—we went out of our way to see the first Dunkin Donuts shop located in Quincy, Massachusetts. We went inside to get a couple of donuts. Larry washed his down with chocolate milk. I love their coffee, and I ordered a big one to accompany my sweet stuff. It was just a little place, but now we can say we've been to the place where it all began.

After breakfast, we headed to the Presidential Library of John F. Kennedy, our nation's 35th President, located at the University of

Massachusetts. It was designed by Jackie Kennedy and sits on the bay, out over Boston's skyline. We had to go through a lot of University construction to get there. They were in the process of building expansions, parking lots, and upgrading the roadways. UMass must be doing well.

The Library was well worth the struggle to get there. We have visited as many of these libraries as we could along our route. It has been so interesting to learn about the actual man and his family; his effects on the world as President. It's like finally witnessing what went on behind the news on TV.

We learned of the young Kennedy and his struggles with his health, and his overbearing and demanding father. Also, who knew he was an acclaimed author and that's what brought Jackie and him together. He loved to write and was good at it. He wrote most of his own speeches. He had a way with words.

Outside the Library was his beloved sailboat named RESTOFUS. Kennedy was often photographed enjoying time with his family on that boat; photographs that often landed on TV and national magazines like *Life*.

His chronic back problems were well-known, and his favorite chair in the oval office was a straight-backed rocking chair. It is here on display for all to see. The top hat and suit he wore during his inauguration were on display, and I amazed to learn that he was 6' 1". I always pictured him shorter than that.

There was a grand selection of dresses that Jackie wore at specific events as well as her sketches for the redecorating of the Red, Green, and Blue rooms at the White House. I have stood in those rooms and they are amazing works of art that no other First Lady has deemed to change.

Robert Kennedy's office was on display, too. His brother and Attorney General, can you begin to imagine their discussions during the Cuban Missile Crisis?

He was certainly a man of great dreams. His vision to put a man on the moon before the end of the decade was fulfilled long after his death, when Neil Armstrong walked there on July 20, 1969. What an amazing legacy.

But those dreams ended in Dallas on November 22, 1963 when he was assassinated during a procession on the streets of Dallas. I was 9 years old when they interrupted our quiet elementary school to announce that the President had been shot. As my parents watched the 6pm news, it was a tearful Walter Cronkite who broke the news that the President had later died at Parkland Memorial Hospital.

The news footage was playing on a vintage TV; one of my oldest memories. We have been to the book depository and stood on the grassy knoll, when we were in Dallas last January.

The feelings we experienced here are as real as they were back in Dallas, Texas—as real as they had been back in 1963. Our classes had the TV on all day long during the funeral proceedings. We visited his grave site in Arlington years ago, and I still remember that eternal flame on his marker. You think about Jackie, Caroline and John, Jr.; what they lost as a family and what America lost in a President.

As Americans, what future did we lose that day? Maybe the racial divide of the country would not have happened as it did. Or the Vietnam war would have never been fought, or communism would have ended or…who knows. But God promises…

Jeremiah 29:11
For I know the plans I have for you," declares the LORD,
"plans to prosper you and not to harm you,
plans to give you hope and a future."

We drove on to downtown Boston, perhaps to see Cheers, perhaps not. Big, huge, ginormous mistake. With no specific destination in mind, we tried to get around, and when that proved impossible, we just tried to get out. But with every direction we turned, there was a one-way street that was going the wrong way. The traffic was bumper to bumper, all in gridlocked. We'd go another block, but then that road was shut down for activities. I finally opened Google and discovered there were at least 15 special events in downtown Boston that very day. Oh, my word, get us outta here!

In time, after driving through the maze of street closings and traffic, we found ourselves on the campus of the Massachusetts Institute of Technology, better known at MIT. There were longboat teams practicing on the waterway that follows the main road in downtown Boston. We recognized the waterway from countless movies we've seen. This whole city was hopping!

We were so relieved to finally escape from the city. As we headed back toward the campground, I selected a place called the Red Parrot for supper. The restaurant was up on the second floor of a building on Nantasket Beach, and it offered an unobstructed view of the ocean. We ordered a fried shrimp platter with slaw and the best darned French Fries that we've had in a while.

JUNE 4

The devil wasted no time today. Frankie told us to take a right turn out of the park, and we hesitated. That's not the way we'd come in, and each time we'd gone out, it was always to the left. But Larry went ahead and turned right, trusting the software. We couldn't have been a mile out—in only a matter of minutes—when disaster struck.

You remember I've explained that one of Larry's biggest fears is to wind up in a dead-end, with nowhere to turn around? Well, that's exactly what happened, right in the park! Directly in front of us, on this nicely paved residential road, was a strong, padlocked, steel gate labeled Fire Road, with further instructions not to block the gate. There were cars and pickups parked all around the cul-de-sac, folks who had parked here to walk the trails or ride their bikes. There would be no easy way out of this!

There was a large building just on the other side of the gate, and a lot of heavy equipment parked in the lot. I jumped out of the rig and sprinted to the lot to find someone. I hollered several times, "Is anyone here?" "I need some help!" Then Larry called out my name from the turnaround, now with several men standing by him.

God had sent his angels quickly. The men had seen Larry drive the rig down the road, and knew he would be in trouble. They were headed to help us even before I had a chance to yell. And one of the men—wait for it—had a key to the gate! God is so good.

I asked him to check Frankie's future directions and he carefully reviewed them while one of the young men unlocked the gate. He assured us that we wouldn't have any more problems from here on, to the Interstate, I-95 north. God bless you, all of you! Thank you! They held open the gate and wished us a wonderful day, after telling us that the gate had been right there—and kept locked—for the past 40 years. Thank you, Lord, for sending those angels promptly!

We didn't make it totally unscathed, though. When Larry checked later, low-hanging limbs had cracked both of the plastic AC covers. Duct tape to the rescue, for now. Considering new ones will cost about $150 each to replace, the duct tape will just have to do.

> Romans 5:1-5
> Therefore, since we have been justified through faith,
> we have peace with God through our Lord Jesus Christ,
> [2]Through whom we have gained access by faith into this
> grace in which we now stand.
> [3]Not only so, but we also rejoice in our sufferings, because
> we know that suffering produces perseverance,
> [4]perseverance, character, and character, hope.
> [5]And hope does not disappoint us, because God has poured
> out his love into our hearts by the Holy Spirit,
> whom he has given us.

After getting just a glimpse of the weekend traffic, Larry said earlier there was no way he would risk driving in downtown Boston. He had tweaked the program so that it would take us far west and north of the city, by keeping us on I-93 and I-95 nearly the whole way

We were finally on our way to Salisbury, Massachusetts. We took I-95 north, then off on US1 and US1A to Beach Road and then to State Beach Road. We arrived at the Salisbury Beach State Park, which Larry rated an 8. We would finally be back on 50amp electric, so we can run the heat pumps again! We've already gone through half of the tank of propane we bought recently, because we haven't had the electric to power the heat pumps.

I personally prefer the propane furnaces. They're totally quiet, the ducts are low on the walls instead of up in the ceiling, and the heat is nice and warm. But when you've already paid a fee to use all the electric that you want, why incur the cost of propane? Well, unless it's 30 degrees outside, and then the propane is a must.

JUNE 5

We both stayed in all day today. They had predicted rain for the entire day, so we were planning around it, but they had it all wrong. It was an ugly day, and there's a fog over the nearby Merrimack River, which flows into the Atlantic Ocean at the campground. The tide comes and goes, so the river moves, day and night. The ocean crashes on rocks on the jetties, the opening at the mouth of the river.

It looked like it would pour down rain at any minute, but I sure didn't see or hear any. Since our stay was so short, Larry said I could wash one load of clothes, just to keep things current. I put some thin pork chops in my itty-bitty Crock Pot this morning, then spent the afternoon writing and making phone calls.

June has arrived, but I don't know if we're ever going to see summer on this route. The temperature took a drop again, and it's only made it to 53 degrees today, 52 degrees forecast for tonight. They've been changing the forecast all day—pushing back the rain until later. Now it's coming in at 8:15pm, and 100% chance all day tomorrow. Goodie, at least our move tomorrow is a short one, so I'll just drive the car behind the rig in the morning. We haven't seen any storms for a while, just unrelenting, concurring days of cold, wet, and dreary.

I need some sunshine, Lord. I need a big dose of Vitamin D!

We really enjoyed those pork chops, doused in Sweet Baby Ray's BBQ sauce. I nuked an ear of corn and some French fries.

Isaiah 45:8
You heavens above, rain down my righteousness;
let the clouds shower it down.
Let the earth open wide, let salvation spring up,
let righteousness flourish with it; I, the LORD, have created it.

My co-pilot seat was starting to hurt my hips and butt; and it was making a funky noise when I adjusted the footrest. So, while he had the time this evening, Larry climbed down into the stairwell to check out why. He quickly discovered that the spring had broken under me and the foot rest frame was rubbing up under the seat when I sat down.

Unfortunately, there's not too much he can do to fix it. He did mount a piece of spare plastic up under the seat to add a degree of support to it, then refastened what was left of the spring with electrical ties. It seems to be a little better. He also saw that the electric wires were stripped of their coverings and ready to start shorting out, so it was a good thing that he'd checked it when he did.

When in doubt: black electrical tape and duct tape sure do come in handy.

JUNE 6

It was another dreary day. The sky is the same grey color as yesterday, and it's still spitting, or misting, or whatever you call this not quite raining. We took our time packing up, because our trip today will be short. It's 48 degrees this morning, even colder than predicted. How cold was it? It was so cold, we had to drag out of storage the brown hoodies we bought last year for Alaska. Where in the world is summer?

It was a short trip to get back to I-95. With a low pressure spinning above us, the wind gusted terribly. We headed north, on I-95 and were quickly in New Hampshire. Now in our 41st state, we saw a unique highway sign for the first time: STATE LIQUOR STORE NEXT EXIT. And there it was: The exit was built specifically for that one building. We have state-run liquor stores in Ohio, too but we sure don't have huge signs on the interstate telling you where to exit. We just thought it very peculiar. It was like New

Hampshire wants you to pick up your liquor while traveling on their highways. We saw this not once but twice, and we traveled only about 30 miles before we quickly entered Maine. Weird.

This is the first time either of us has set foot in the state of Maine. Back in 2012, Larry had gotten his Spyder (3-wheel inverted motorcycle). He decided that we were going to take a once-in-a-lifetime trip on the bike, up through what we called New England. That trip was an absolute hoot. There we were, on our white Spyder, towing our little white trailer pod. We'd be zooming up I-95 at 70mph and folks waved at us like we were rock stars. They'd hang out their windows with their cameras, and the drivers would honk their horns.

We got up each morning, without a single plan in place. We would stop only when we needed potty breaks or gas, and when we began to get tired, we'd choose a restaurant where we could take in the iPad and decide in which hotel to spend the night.

That trip was so unlike my husband. As you can tell from my books, he tediously plans everything—hours, weeks, months in advance. This was a real, "by the seat of your pants" trip, and I had a great time. All except for one afternoon…

The plan had led us up the east coast from Myrtle Beach. We planned to get to Maine, then head west, and back south to home. But after we covered Massachusetts, we learned of a big early winter storm heading in our direction. It was only late September, way too early for a winter storm. We agreed to forget Maine and headed west. The front of the storm arrived 6 hours earlier than forecast, and caught us off guard somewhere in Vermont. When the ice-cold freezing rain struck, there wasn't a place for miles to pull over and put on rain gear. No berms, just grass.

By the time we found a place to pull over, we were soaked to the bone. We found a gas station with restrooms where we could change. But weather suits over wet clothes only kept us from getting wetter. We had no choice but to stay soaked and cold. We began to head south, but by that time, we were square in the midst of the storm. Yuck. We nearly froze our toes off. In hindsight, it was laughable. Although at that time, not so much.

Larry had a great time, too. At least up until the time he developed an abscessed tooth and we were grounded in Virginia for several days. I could have driven us home, but he was too sick to even sit up on the bike. Well, that's a story for another day.

Anyway, we never did make it to Maine until today. It's state number 42. I hear the sun will come out tomorrow. I sure hope so.

Right off I-95 north we hit another toll booth. Tolls in New England are adding up. Then up US1 north, we arrived at Moody Beach RV Park in Wells, Maine, which Larry rated a 6. There are a lot of full-time residents here, but that's okay. Maybe it will even get warm enough to hit the hot tub. Today is forecast to be 65 degrees, tomorrow 73. Even Larry should find that comfortable. It was drizzling on and off all day. Larry doesn't like setting up sewer, electric, and water in weather this cold, much less when it's raining. I sure don't envy him that.

JUNE 7

It's a miracle! I woke up to the sun shining this morning! Okay, maybe it's not a miracle. It may just be the passing of a low-pressure system, but it sure does answer MY prayers. Thank you, Lord. It's wonderful to see the sun again.

Psalm 113:3
From the rising of the sun to the place where it sets,
the name of the LORD is to be praised.

I wrote for a couple of hours in the morning, and the words flowed easily. We ate lunch, then drove to Kennebunkport, Maine.

We told Suri (do you think we have too many named electronics in our lives?) to take us to Walker's Point and she complied. It's the summer home of 41st President of the United States George Herbert Walker Bush.

He is #41, the elder Bush, not to be confused with #43, his son President George Walker Bush. This Bush compound has been a summer retreat for Bush's family for over a century. It had been in their family since his Grandfather, George Herbert "Bert" Walker, Sr., on his mother's side, purchased it. Hence it was called "Walkers Point."

Larry told me on the way if there were 3 flags flying, it meant that the Bush Family was at home. Sure enough, when we arrived, the American Flag was flying high, with the state flags of Texas and Maine flying at equal heights below. We were certainly in the right place, as many others were parked along the side of the road, as well. Jeb Bush, his other son, and former Governor of Florida, has built a $1.3 million summer home next door to his father's place, and we could see it, as well.

We stopped at several different places on the road, and took lots of pictures of the compound. We were well above the ocean water crashing below, and the "beach" was comprised of humungous chunks of rocks, pointed in all directions. When the waves crashed into the rocks, white spray flew upwards. There were ducks and seagulls enjoying the day. In the bright sunshine, it was a beautiful sight.

Suddenly, we heard a high-pitched buzz, and a drone appeared in the sky above our heads. It hovered in place for a bit, then sped away. In a few minutes, it reappeared. Whoever was at the controls must have seen Larry's red ball cap stating, "Make America Great Again". Just kidding! We speculated that the secret service was keeping tabs on everybody by watching with a drone.

The main house is fully exposed and not all that far from the road. It would sure be easier and cooler for their security to drone the perimeter rather than walking it. Who knows…perhaps #41 has a new hobby, eavesdropping on those who come to visit.

---

1 Timothy 2:1-3
I urge, then, first of all, that petitions, prayers, intercession and thanksgiving be made for all people—
²for kings and all those in authority, that we may live peaceful and quiet lives in all godliness and holiness.
³ This is good, and pleases God our Savior.

We finally drove on, past the entrance and could see the guard shack about 50 feet up the drive. Just then, Larry abruptly braked the car to a stop in the middle of the road and announced, "You have to give Mrs. Bush a book!" I told him to drive on down the road, as I was not about to park within sight of the guards to root through the back of my car for a book—not unless I wanted to be thrown to the ground and handcuffed. Detain now—ask questions later.

I had picked up Mrs. Bush's (Barbara) book when I visited #41's Presidential Library in College Station, Texas back in January. Ironically, we were there at the same time the President was in the hospital in Houston. The library had a sign in to give best wishes to him to get better.

Larry drove up the road a bit, to another pull off. I wrote a short note to Mrs. Bush in the book, made a U-turn, and we returned to the drive. Larry kept the car by the road, as I apprehensively walked toward the 2 guards. Plain clothes Secret Service for sure, and heavily armed. There were black SUV's parked throughout the compound.

I held the book out in front of me, flipping the pages repeatedly. I called out that I had a book I would like to leave as a gift for Mrs. Bush. Flip, flip, flip.

They were polite, but explained that they don't accept gifts, that I would have to mail it to her. I asked to where, and they told me to Google the address. I whined a bit that it was only a book, but they politely explained that, if they accepted one gift, they would have to accept them all, and they wouldn't be able to do their jobs. All right. Thank you. Have a blessed day.

The secret service was all business, with their sunglasses and black SUV's. I'm sure someone had me in their weapon sight, ready to drop me at the first sign of trouble. I sure wasn't about to hang around to find out.

They stood their positions in the middle of the drive even after we were driving down the road. Well, that was fun! I wondered what they thought of two sixty-year-old farts stopping and coming up the drive. Senior Terrorists! Oh My! A white-haired old woman with book in hand, watch out for her!

It's a testimony of the sad world that we live in today. Later that evening I wrote a letter Mrs. Bush, and put the book into an envelope to mail. I thought she would enjoy reading it since we both have something in common about losing a child—mother to mother.

Larry pointed the car back into Kennebunkport. He said he wanted to go back to a place that sold live lobster, a place on Ocean Avenue he'd seen earlier. He pulled up in front of Port Lobster. It was a little place, with a small counter and price boards posted inside. Larry went up to the counter to ask about purchasing a lobster.

I busied myself at the small glass-doored freezer on the wall. There were small and large containers of all sorts of things, including lobster mac 'n cheese, seafood pie, lobster quiche, crab cakes, lobster pizza, and more. I overheard the lady tell Larry that a 1 ½ pound lobster would be about $15, did he want one? He asked if they would cook it for us? Yes, come back in about 25 minutes.

And that we did. It was steaming hot and double-bagged. I also purchased 4 cheddar biscuits, some of the frozen mac 'n cheese, a small jar of local cocktail sauce, and a mini loaf of chocolate chip banana bread. All of that added together was cheaper than a single lobster meal in a restaurant would have cost. Supper tonight will be fantastic. As we left, Larry peeked into a No Admittance area to see there were dozens of water-filled tanks with what seemed like thousands of live lobsters.

I have explained often that Larry does not like to shop. But, as we were turning off the highway to return to the campground, I mentioned that we should stop at the Farmer's Market we'd noticed earlier along our route. He actually agreed. And he walked with me. I took no cash, but boy did Larry pay for all sorts of goodies to eat!

The first 2 booths offered all sorts of small plants—herbs, vegetables, and flowers. With our rolling home, we had no reason to purchase anything there. The next tent had small baked goods, and Larry commented that a brownie sounded good, so he bought one.

On and on we went, continuing to buy something at almost every vendor. I bought a fresh cinnamon pastry from one tent, then some malt bagels from Clover Hill Breads from Alfred, Maine. We met a vendor from Four Star Fresh Foods with artisan pasta. He had all sorts of stuff I'd never heard of and when asked, he politely explained what polenta was. I purchased some Saffron & White Wine Fettuccine from him, which we'll enjoy tomorrow.

We met a grumpy local farmer, and he didn't have any corn on the cob, which is what we wanted. Yes, I know that it is too early for corn. The last vendor had fresh bread, and we purchased a loaf of rye with caraway seeds from The Olde Craft Bakery which is based up the road in New Hampshire. We had finished the loop of tents and returned to the car. We had surprised ourselves by buying so many items, but it all looked so good. Can you tell we were both hungry?

We carried our haul into the rig, and I began to reheat the lobster. I remembered then that we had no seafood "crackers"—those metal tools for cracking open seafood—so Larry cleaned up a set of channel lock pliers to crack our lobster. We made quite the mess, but supper was lots of fun. It was our first Maine Lobster in Maine!

Genesis 9:3
Everything that lives and moves about will be food for you.
Just as I gave you the green plants,
I now give you everything.

After cleanup was finished, I asked Larry to go up to the hot tub. There was another couple there when we arrived, and they were friendly and quite chatty. They were on a one-year road trip, and we chatted about things we'd seen, factory tours, Presidential libraries, and they greatly appreciated the tip we offered about avoiding the $84 toll for the George Washington Bridge. Then Larry told them about my book.

I told them how the book explains how God has developed our faiths over the years, and how I broke my neck. They listened intently as I told them how God provided for us every step of the way.

As we all decided it was time to get out of the too-hot hot tub, Larry offered to give them a book. They graciously accepted it, and I learned what their names were, Scott and Judy from Seattle, Washington. It was my pleasure, Scott and Judy.

They said they'd be out looking for that lobster place tomorrow, and we would probably see them back in the hot tub.

Psalm 96:3
Declare his glory among the nations,
his marvelous deeds among all peoples.

As I sat and wrote these words for today, even with the windows closed to the cold, I can hear a delightful symphony of birds calling out in the night. There are so many different types of calls that, if I were home in South Carolina, I would swear there were mockingbirds surrounding the rig. I have no clue who these night birds could be, but their songs were beautiful. I will enjoy being lulled to sleep with their sweet, sweet songs.

> Psalm 104:12
> The birds of the sky nest by the waters;
> they sing among the branches.

JUNE 8

Larry had read a review that said if you're in this area, you just have to drive down scenic Shore Road, south to Portsmouth, New Hampshire. And that is exactly what we did.

From the campground, we set out south on US1. We didn't get too far until Larry spotted Banditos Mexican Grill in Ogunquit, so we stopped for lunch. It was a quaint little place, full of bright colors and creaky wooden floors. We were seated right inside the restaurant, screens wide open with a lovely view of the ocean. We soaked in the warm weather today, for tomorrow it will drop back down again. We quickly ate up the fried shrimp in our delicious soft-shelled tacos and were soon ready to get back on the road.

We picked up Shore Road. A few miles into the drive, what impressed me about the lush countryside is that you couldn't see the shore at all. What we did see were many magnificent homes, beautifully landscaped, at the ends of long drives. The rhododendron grows taller and wider than my motorhome, and they sported amazing colors—pinks, purples, and reds throughout the countryside.

We passed the signs to the Cape Neddick Country Club. Driving past Phillips Cove and Phillips Pond, we finally began following the beautiful shore. The waves were crashing into the beach and the rocky shoreline. We drove through all sorts of tiny communities and enjoyed the scenic ride. This is indeed breathtakingly beautiful country.

JUNE 9

We each got into our separate vehicles this morning for a short trip up I-95 north, as it was only a 30-minute drive to our next destination. We exited onto I-195 east to ME5 north to Old Orchard Beach, Maine.

We arrived at Pinehirst RV Resort, which Larry rated a 3. Larry miscalculated his turn from the registration area into the campground and knocked over a small brick wall with the tow dolly. I'm sure this has happened many times before. The entry was narrow, and the bricks weren't even mortared together—they were just stacked. They had them stacked back up in no time.

It was an old campground, and not very tidy. Lots of the sites had seasonal folks there, just arriving to their "summer homes." They only offered 30amp electric, which was very insufficient to battle the heat wave they were having. I really don't think it was full 30amps, either! We kept breaking circuit breakers all day long. The water hookup was rusty and leaking, and the place just smelled bad. When Larry hooked up the sewer, he found the drain open and uncovered. That accounted for some of the smell, but what about snakes and rats in the sewer lines? Ick!

And this is considered a resort by RPI reservation system! I don't think we'll be renewing our membership with them. Their saving grace? The pool area looked like new.

JUNE 10

I started out with a couple hours of book-writing. It was much warmer today, so we cranked up the air conditioning, as much as we could without blowing the less than 30amp.

With the sun directly overhead, we walked up to the pool, well pools. They have a total of 3 sizeable pools, plus the hot tub. One is fenced in a grassy area, a large one is fenced in a concrete area, and another pool is marked adults only. Each area is fenced in, but the adult area has an 8-foot wall to block the screams of joy coming from the kiddie areas.

The hot tub was a scooch too hot, and the pool was like ice. Nonetheless, it felt sooooo good to soak up some sun, after so many days of cloudiness. We were up there less than 30 minutes—even in the hot tub—and I did get a noticeable tan line. The sun sure wasn't like this when we were kids.

After writing a bit more in the air-conditioned motorhome, we went for a drive in the car.

John 8:12
Jesus spoke to all the people, saying,
"I am the Light of the world.
Anyone who follows Me will not walk in darkness.
He will have the Light of Life."

We eventually took back roads all the way to Portland, then enjoyed driving through the historic part of this port town.

We took the quickie way back toward Old Orchard Beach, meaning we paid another $1 toll on I-95, but detoured to Saco to eat supper at the Lobster Claw Pound & Restaurant.

It was a casual place, and we placed our order at the kitchen window before sitting down in one of the dining rooms. They have an indoor room with air-conditioning, an indoor room with huge screened windows all around, and another deck space for outdoor seating. We chose the indoor with screens area, where there was a concrete-paved walking path, then gravel under the table legs. It was quite interesting, I must say. No vacuuming in here, just hose the whole place down with soap and water. It did take a while for our food to arrive, but I think it was because the large party ahead of us had ordered so much.

Larry could see their food arrive, but my back was to them. His eyes turned as big as saucers, looking at the sheer mass of food our waitress delivered to their table. He said they each had a plate with a whole lobster, then another platter heaped with fried "something or another," coleslaw, and mounds of waffle fries. I turned around to look. Oh, my goodness!

Larry said, "How do they eat that much?" He forgets, before his gastric surgery, he ate that much and more. He says that food just doesn't appeal to him anymore. He just never feels hungry, because the part of the stomach that sends those "hungry" signals was surgically removed. I wish I could inactivate that signal section without going through the whole surgery.

That surgery made a huge difference in his quality of life. He went from 2 dozen daily medications to 4, plus vitamins. His weight dropped from 306 to about 180. His 52-inch waist now fits into 38-inch jeans. What a difference indeed. But, the surgery certainly isn't for everyone.

I'd ordered us a Lobster Roll Platter to share. We've seen them advertised everywhere, but tonight was our first experience eating one. I anticipated lobster meat in some sort of hoagie bun, like we have Po' Boys in South Carolina. I was kinda close.

The bun was sorta like a hot dog bun, and about the same size. But this bun had been sliced from a larger slab, so the sides were soft, like a slice of bread. The cook had buttered and grilled both sides of the bun, laid a leaf of lettuce in the top of it, then filled it with a lobster-salad mixture.

It was smaller than I'd hoped, but it did come with coleslaw and waffle fries. I even treated myself to an additional side, cold beet slices. Yum. Larry judged it as, "It was okay," but I would order another one someplace else, just to see the next person's presentation of the same idea. We'll see.

We returned to the motorhome, and I wrote a bit before wanting to go back to the hot tub. Good thing I went when I did, because I only had 20 minutes before the area would be closed for the evening. I went back to write some more. At least with cable TV in this campground, Larry can play the TV in the bedroom without distracting me. We can both do what we want.

It's forecast to be 90+ degrees tomorrow and sunny. We wait and see.

JUNE 11

Well, the forecasters were right, for a change. It crested out at toasty 92 degrees today! And here we are, in a 30amp campground site. We quickly discovered that we couldn't even run the hot water tank with one of the air conditioners, much less both of the air units. And it reached a whopping 89 degrees inside the motorhome.

It was not even 30 amps ... more like 15 or 20 ... we couldn't run hardly anything with the amount of power we were receiving. Yes, we are spoiled rotten campers. We asked our neighbors, who lived there, if they had the same problem with the electric. Yep, the whole park was under-amped where air conditioning was concerned. I had to bite my tongue to keep from asking, "Then why in the world would you want to spend the entire summer here?"

We did head up to the pool area around 3pm. The hot tub was 104, which is pretty spot-on for a hot tub, but I'd come here to cool off. So, I dipped my toes in the grownup pool. Oh, my glory, it's cold! I first took it a step at a time, then just hopped in, up to my neck. Brrrrr! I stayed under, but I was shivering. I just couldn't stay in long.

I laid out in the sun to warm up and finally felt good, while Larry stayed in the shade. But the sun was too strong to stay out there long, so we had to leave within 30 minutes. But it did cool me down.

I took a shower and reminded Larry that it's 89 degrees in here, and we can't even run the microwave without turning off the air conditioning. I googled "restaurants nearby" and quickly found Sea Salt Lobster, only a few miles away. I called ahead to be sure they had an air-conditioned dining room. The girl laughed before confirming that they did.

We arrived. and it was air conditioned, but the restaurant was still pretty warm. We enjoyed 3 grilled lobster tails with rice and coleslaw. It was delicious, but not quite enough to fill us both. Craving carbs, I ordered some hot pretzels to go. They were great.

The sun gave up the day and it finally began to cool. It's only going down to 66 during the night, so the unit will have to continue its quest to cool all night long. We leave in the morning.

Thank you, Lord for this day, in all its glory.

JUNE 12

Today we drove the motorhome to Camden, Maine. We headed up I-95 north to US1 north. The weather is a scorcher, nearly 90 degrees again today. It took a couple of hours, but the drive was nice all the way, mostly on secondary roads. I spotted a small deer by the roadway, standing as frozen as could be—it was so tiny and precious.

We drove through lots of little towns, reading the pretty signs of the butchers and bakers. I was typing notes into my iPhone and was going to write, "but I haven't seen any candlemakers." At that exact moment, what should appear to my left but a store claiming to be candlemakers. Ha!

I had pointed out some beautiful purple flowers, growing wild along the road. I had no idea what they were. They resembled lavender, but I knew it wasn't that. By paying attention to the landscaping places we passed, I learned that it was Lupine. (I later learned it's pronounced "loo pen." Beautiful flowers.

We arrived at Camden Hills State Park, in Camden, Maine, which Larry rated a 4.

After we set up, Larry wanted to drive the car into town, just to get his bearings. It was too bloody hot to stay in the motorhome anyway, and we could enjoy the car's air conditioning while we gave the rig a chance to cool down. We parked by the docks and walked a while.

These folks up here love sailboats. Little ones, big ones, gigantic ones. Single mast, double mast, triple mast, called Tall Ships. "A tall ship is a large, traditionally-rigged sailing vessel. Popular modern tall ship rigs include topsail schooners, brigantines, brigs, and barques."[35]. They were selling tickets for sailings out of the bay, but

---

[35] https://en.wikipedia.org/wiki/Tall_ship

we weren't interested. We owned a 23-foot Hunter sailboat a few years ago, and taught ourselves how to sail it (certainly not without some wild experiences, though). We sailed the low country bays and waterways and even out into the Atlantic along the South Carolina coast. The ships sure were beautiful, though.

James 3:4
Sailing ships are driven by strong winds.
But a small rudder turns a large ship whatever way
the man at the wheel wants the ship to go.

We left the docks to take the scenic drive to Mt. Battie. Although adventure climbers can take the 1.5 round trip hike to the summit, we chose to take the car road as far as we could. The view of the harbor and bay were beautiful, although hazy. We spotted a cruise ship named the American Constitution anchored in Camden Bay. We researched it online when we returned to the rig to discover that it cruises the New England coast and harbors. Rates start at $4,415 PER person. I think we'll pass.

We returned to the motorhome, but it was still brutally hot in there. We could only run 30amp, so we could run only one air conditioner. Here in the thick trees, we hoped that it would cool off as the afternoon progressed. It didn't.

I didn't want to turn off the air conditioning to nuke supper, so Larry and I agreed to just eat some cold sandwiches to hold us over. That poor air conditioner barely shut off the entire day. It did its best, but one unit just isn't enough when it's that hot outside. Perhaps when it "cools down" to a whole 66 degrees tonight, it will catch up. I certainly hope so.

Thank you, Lord for the one air conditioner that we do have. Thank you for making it work at all. Thank you that it's not 90 degrees inside this big rig. Thank you for this beautiful place; thank you for all my blessings.

> Genesis 31:40
> This was my situation: The heat consumed me in the daytime
> and the cold at night, and sleep fled from my eyes.

JUNE 13

Today was forecast to be another hot one. Desperate for entertainment, Larry had discovered how to watch YouTube stuff on the TV through the online feed. He was watching some documentary about how a prince decided to build his own islands in Dubai. The sound was blaring, and it didn't interest me all that much. I know the bedroom's only another 5 feet away from the TV, but the doors in-between do offer a buffer for the sound. I busied myself in there for a while.

When he watched one about the development of the Boeing 747, I sat and watched along with him. We've toured the Boeing plant in Washington, and the information offered in this documentary was in addition to all we had learned there.

He quickly found another documentary, so when he finally finished it, I jumped in. Honey, I can't work on the book with the TV so loud. Could you turn it off for a while? At first, he was upset, so I offered to *not* work on the book at all today. Well, he wanted me to write, so he finally turned off the TV. I had seen earlier on the iPad that he'd been searching how to watch Apple TV on your iPad, and he did just that—with his earphones.

I spent the next 5 hours giving myself a headache, but getting lots of editing done for Book Two.

The air conditioning had been running nearly non-stop all afternoon. I was getting hungry, and I had thawed out the lobster macaroni and cheese we'd purchased last week. We agreed that we didn't want to turn off the air conditioning to run the convection oven for 30 minutes, so we made the decision to eat out, but where?

I searched on my desktop. There are lots of amazing restaurants here in Camden, and I quickly noticed a pattern: a LOT of them are closed on Tuesdays. Well, I guess that will narrow things down a bit. I didn't want a big, fancy meal anyway, I think we've been having way too many of those lately. Our waistlines and our checkbook are all groaning.

After some online research, I decided upon the Camden House of Pizza. When we walked up to the door, I wondered if I'd made a mistake. It was in a very small storefront. We stepped up into the place and discovered how tiny it was inside, too. I think I counted a grand total of maybe 6 tables, and most of them were only 2-tops. I checked the small paper menus and quickly decided on a toasted meatball sub and a slice of pepperoni from the counter. A nice young man with terrific manners took my order and, after I paid, returned to the table with our slice. It was delicious, and it disappeared quickly. Just a bit later, our sub arrived, and it was perfect. We ate every bite. It was a bit warm in there for me, but I'm sure their wall air-conditioner wasn't used to cranking out on days like today, either

It was barely spitting rain as we walked back to the car and returned to the campground. Some folks already had fires burning in their pits and I love the smell of fires. Larry had gathered firewood earlier this afternoon, but I suggested we wait until tomorrow night, when it's supposed to be in the low 60's. It doesn't make much sense to me, to make a fire when it's 85 degrees outside.

We spent the rest of the evening trying to watch stuff on Netflix, but finally gave up on trying to stream data. Larry went off to bed and I wrote some more. By the time I went to bed, I had to remember to switch over the air conditioning to the heat pump. It's supposed to be 53 degrees by morning.

JUNE 14

Today was a lazy day. It was much cooler today, and the windows were wide open. I wrote most of the afternoon, while Larry watched stuff on the iPad. It was so nice and quiet, here in the campground. The tree canopy is so dense, that I kept my desk lamp on for most of the day. I could occasionally hear a truck out on the highway, but the birds were the only constant sounds I heard.

Oh, these days with no scheduled obligations or plans are wonderful. Once again, a day perfect for writing. I broke the news to Larry that we would have to find a laundromat soon, since I couldn't do laundry here. We had sufficient electric and water, but the grey storage tank is slowly filling up. He then decided he'd much rather drive the rig to the dump station here in the park than to have to spend a couple hours at a laundromat.

Okay, then. Laundry it is. I tried to save as much tank space as I could, so I hand-washed the light items in the sink, wrung them out by hand, then put them in the machine to spin. The first load went up on the handy-dandy portable wash line I have inside the motorhome. Load number 2 went through the whole gambit. The national park we're heading to next has no utilities at all, but at least now we're set for the next week.

To get out for a while, we drove up to revisit the view from the mountaintop. The cold front that had blown through had really cleared out the haze. We could see so much more than just a couple of days ago. There was a dozen or more small islands in the distance. We could even see Rockport from up here.

We made a short trip to Mt. Battie Takeout to get some dessert. They didn't have pie, so I made an executive decision to get 2 scoops of ice cream by the name of Confusion. Oh, my goodness, it was unbelievable! It was based with vanilla ice cream, they told me, but you couldn't even taste that. It had peanut butter, cookie dough, chocolate chip cookies, M & M's, and probably a few other things thrown in there. It was amazing. We cheated and tried some before supper, but then stuck it in the freezer until it was time for dessert. My diabetes doesn't make allowances for stuff like this, but I just have to indulge once in a while.

Even though we spend every day in one campground or another, we just don't have the opportunity to enjoy many campfires. A lot of the fancier campgrounds don't allow them, and most of the state and national parks have signs everywhere, telling you not to pick up wood. Others forbid you to enter or exit with firewood, because of the real possibility of the spread of tree disease, so you can't just pick up some cheap stuff by the side of the road.

But this state park had no such signs, so Larry had gone wood hunting yesterday. He got it to burning and, although it was a smoky fire, we enjoyed its warmth and smell. Most of the wood was hardwood, and it was a little harder to get burning. But once he got it going, the fire was very nice.

> Proverbs 26:20
> Without wood a fire goes out;
> without a gossip a quarrel dies down.

Supper was a treat in and of itself. Since we weren't busy running electric to the air conditioners today, the lobster mac & cheese we bought frozen at Port Lobster went into the convection oven and came out perfect. We laughed when we realized that the picnic table we sat down on to eat was right in the path of the smoke! We moved everything over to the folding chairs and enjoyed every delicious bite.

We went in when the fire died down, but Larry doused it with water, just to be sure. We tried to stream TV again, but for every 2 minutes we got to watch, it took another 2 minutes to spool.

It had been a wonderfully peaceful day. It was chilly, but I'd take chilly over hot and sweaty any day. Despite no one camping nearby, kid's packets have disappeared from their hanger.

Thank you, Jesus.

JUNE 15

This everyday lazy stuff is suiting me just fine. It was another great day for writing. At nearly 5pm, Larry suggested we go into town to eat, as it's our last night here. We parked the car in a city lot off Elm, and walked a bit.

Before we made it to the first restaurant, I noticed that the high, long hedge framing the left side of the street was entirely lilac. They bore flowers lighter than the ones I remember as a child, as they were nearly white. But they were most definitely lilacs! The hedge came from around the corner and extended about 50 feet aside the road. And the smell was heavenly. What a sweet flowering fragrance. I stopped every few feet and stuck my face into the hedge, just for another wonderful smell.

The first place we checked was all wood-fired pizza and salads, but we'd had pizza just the night before last. The next place we walked was a bit pricey and too fancy for our moods tonight. We turned the corner and walked up to the main street. A little place called Cuzzy's was on the far side of the street, and we walked right in. There was a great variety of items on the menu, so we had lots to choose from.

I told Larry that since we'd been gorging on seafood these past few weeks, what I really wanted was a great cheeseburger. We ordered it medium-well with lettuce, tomato, and fresh onion. We chose their special Cuzzy fries for our side, which were potato slices deep-fried. They brought it out on 2 plates, each with coleslaw and dill pickle slices. Each had half of the burger, but I think they erred and brought each of us 2 full helpings of everything else. Some of that meal went home in a bag.

We walked back down to the docks, and I made lots of stops to smell those lilac bushes again. I admit that I wanted to steal one to take back to the rig, but I knew that Larry would just say that they stink. It must be a guy thing. We spent more time admiring some of the large sailboats in port.

There were quite a few wooden ships, in various sizes, and having once owned a sailboat, we were awed by the workmanship involved. The polished wood rails and planks, teak decking and trim, and the carved figureheads. Even the poop deck was grand. They were breathtakingly beautiful.

James 3:4
Or take ships as an example.
Although they are so large and are driven by strong winds,
they are steered by a very small rudder
wherever the pilot wants to go.

We put the car on the dolly when we returned, so that's done for departure. We tried some more TV, hoping for a better result, but quickly abandoned that idea. I wrote some more, knowing that the next few days will be on generator and inverter only.

I did notice something noteworthy while Larry was putting on the car. You know, dandelions have 2 faces: the pretty yellow one and the stalk with a head of those little fuzzy flying seeds on them. Our site had lots of both on them, but what caught my attention was the size of the fuzzy ones—I stood next to one that stood halfway up to my hip! I've never seen dandelions that tall. I get to see something new every day.

I spent some time on the phone today with a CVS in Bangor, Maine. Very soon, we will cross the border into Canada, and I wanted to be sure I had the prescription meds I needed to get me through until the end of July. We'll have to go a bit out of our way, but that's okay; I'm sure we'll enjoy the view.

This has been a marvelous 4-day stop, once the temperature cooled down. Parked here among these tall trees, listening to their leaves rustle, watching folks walk their dogs, and enjoying the smell of wood smoke: perfect.

JUNE 16

This morning we left on our next adventure. We had Frankie set for Bangor, Maine first, because I had to go to CVS—the very last CVS to be had in this entire part of Maine.

We changed routes often today. US1 north to ME141, US95 north to Bangor. It was raining just enough to mess up the windshield, but the route to Bangor was pretty. A lot of the trip was spent on US1. Most of it was 2-lane highway, and we passed through dozens of small towns. I saw lots of lupine along the road, many of the purple flowers mixed with pink and crème lupine, as well.

Each town had its own small-town personality. I saw lots of antique shops, and most had at least one pizza place. A man's gotta eat, you know. After passing a few of these little towns, I'd see a large little town, this one with a dentist and a doctor's office. When we were almost to the CVS, I joked that the Bangor McDonald's was the first one I'd seen all day, despite the distance we'd driven.

The CVS was located inside a Target store, so there was plenty of room to park. I'd called ahead yesterday, and they had just about completed my refills. I shopped a bit and purchased a few DVD's knowing we'd have no services for the next few days, but we can watch the TV with power from the inverter.

That done, we headed for Sam's Club. We hadn't been to Sam's in weeks, and probably won't see another for a long while. We probably went a bit overboard, but at least we're all stocked up.

The super Walmart was close by, so we went there to get all the little things you just can't buy at Sam's Club. When we went in, we asked the ladies in the beauty salon if they had 2 openings for haircuts? Sure, come back in a half-hour. That gave us just enough time to shop and check out. I instructed my girl that I didn't just want my hair to look good today, I wanted it to look good in about 2 weeks. She understood completely. It's so much easier to go without electric and limited water when my hair is short.

Back on the road, we traveled a couple more hours through more rural towns. We covered I-95 to I-395 to US1A to ME3. We began seeing signs for blueberry farms, although it's nowhere near the season. In the dismal, cloudy and rainy afternoon, the fields just looked sad this time of year. A lot of the roads need repaving, with lots of stretches with ridges and holes, but the section of I-95 we drove was pretty nice.

We were finally headed to our destination of Blackwoods Campground at Acadia National Park, which Larry rated a 4. That's typical of National Parks, because they have no utilities. But they're safe, well-policed, and full of nature. It was heavily wooded, and all the sites are pull-through. There's enough vegetation that helps absorb the noise of the generator, so we don't feel as bad when we run it. We do have to run it more when there's no sunshine to recharge via the solar panel, and it's supposed to be cloudy the next few days.

Considering there are no utilities to connect, setting up is just a matter of putting out the room extensions. We had purchased some ready-to-eat BBQ ribs at Sam's Club, so I cranked up the generator and put them in the convection oven. The ribs with a single ear of microwaved corn filled us both.

The inverter was fully charged, so we watched the first few episodes of *Friday Night Lights*, which I had purchased at Target. We had never watched the show, but I like Kyle Chandler. We were pleasantly surprised that there's a lot of prayer and faith comments in the show. We will definitely continue to watch this.

We were certainly beat from running all day, and Larry had put in about 4 hours on the road. We went to bed early, listening to the rain on the roof and those furnaces keeping us toasty warm.

Good night, Lord. Thank you for another amazing day.

JUNE 17

It had rained throughout the night and this morning was completely socked in with fog. This must be what Great Britain looks like because we're close to the same Latitude. London Fog is legendary. Larry really wanted to see all of Acadia, so we drove the car out of the campground in hopes of better views.

We drove the entire Park Loop Road, but the socked-in views remained the same. It looked like the homemade potato soup I have a recipe for in the back of the book. The drive was still pretty, though.

We stopped in the Visitors Center to view their park movie and get another stamp. If nothing else, we could see Acadia in the sunlight from the movie. The lady who rang up my souvenir postcard saw my Passport and asked if I wanted a sticker for it. A sticker?

She went on to explain that she could see that my Passport was a Centennial edition, for their 100 years of National Parks in 2016. She handed me a Centennial celebration sticker. I told her, "I've been in dozens of National Parks since I bought this book and you're the very first person who's offered me a sticker. Thank you." She gave me a cocky smile and replied, "I guess that makes me pretty special, doesn't it?" Yes, ma'am, it certainly does.

As we continued to drive the loop, we were delighted at all the variations of ground cover. Sprigs of tiny daisies had popped up everywhere, along with other small yellow flowers. The hearty dandelion was also here—aren't they like everywhere? There were mosses of every color and many varieties of ferns. We also saw a great number of white-barked trees—I think they're birch, which I've never seen as a forest tree.

Along the way, we stopped in the town of Bar Harbor, Maine. Sitting right on the water, there are restaurants and shops in all directions. It was lunch time, so Larry decided we would eat at a place named Stewman's Downtown. There were indoor and outdoor seating areas, and yet another area with outdoor furniture on a deck, but garage doors to convert it from indoor to outdoor. Today was only in the 50's, so the doors were closed against the chilly weather. We were seated well inside.

The scenic views from the restaurant and of the ocean were not to be seen today. Fog was everywhere.

Acts 13:11
"Now the hand of the Lord is against you.
You are going to be blind for a time,
not even able to see the light of the sun."
Immediately mist and darkness came over him, and he
groped about, seeking someone to lead him by the hand."

Rob was our smiling and attentive waiter, who did everything he could to make our lunch enjoyable. He kept my coffee cup full. The chowder was great, as was the shrimp basket we ordered. They offered sweet potato fries, and I shared that I loved them, but Larry does not. Rob offered to split the side, bringing a half-order of the crispiest sweet potato fries I've ever enjoyed, with a half-order of Cape Cod chips for Larry. We ate all we could, but had plenty left to eat tomorrow.

At the very end, I asked Rob if he had a minute for a quick story. Being the terrific water that he was, well, of course he did. I told him that we had already traveled 42 states in the past 15 months and will be heading into Canada in a few days. I explained that we were leaving a brochure and a card for him. The brochure explains our Motorhome Ministry. The card is for the book I'd written about the first part of our trip. I explained that we're about to release *His Road Trip 2*, and that our delightful lunch today with fantastic server Rob would be in *His Road Trip 3*, expected to be released in the fall.

He was touched, I could tell, that we had taken the time to introduce ourselves and that his wonderful service today would be written down and recorded somewhere. He made a point to take the papers and put them safely in his apron. I hope he went to sleep that night, smiling at the memory of the nice folks he'd met today. God bless him in his service to others.

Outside of the restaurant on the dock there was a shop selling and steaming Lobsters. The clerk picked up a large 5 pounder which had a tint of blue. He informed us this old boy would be $125 due to its size. They had some 1 ¼ pounders for $25 and had three big pots steaming and boiling away to cook them for you.

We drove on to Thunder Hole on Park Loop Road. This 21-mile road is a one-way scenic route on Desert Island, the main island for the park. It goes through hills and low areas and around Cadillac Mountain, as well as along the scenic coast. Thunder Hole is aptly named for the noise the crashing water makes in this particular spot.

It's not a simple hole in the rocky shore, but a long, dead-end channel that fills with water as the waves come in. All is dependent upon the timing of the tides and the waves, but it cycles so that eventually, the wave fills the channel so that the water sprays way up and the thunder rolls. There's a fenced observation area you can walk out on, and there were lots of folks here.

We stayed back behind the channel. When the water blows, the empty channel exposes a coating of green moss on the underlaying rocks. Then as the waves swell, they fill it up abruptly, and the sea explodes in a violent crash. The dummies, well the more adventurous people that went down close to the entrance, inevitably walked away soaked to the gills. I hope the pictures they took were worth getting drenched.

> Job 38:8
> Who shut up the sea with doors,
> when it rushed out from its secret place?

We drove back to the campground with the hope that tomorrow afternoon will allow us better views than today. We ate chicken breast from our Sam's hoard, with mashed potatoes and green beans. Filled, we enjoyed several more episodes of *Friday Night Lights*, which seems to be adding innuendo and has a bit too much partying and alcohol for my taste, but the storylines are good.

Is this show an accurate example of what's happening in high schools today? My high school days were nothing like this show! It made us both reconsider what teens are being faced with today, and the urgent need to reach them with the Gospel at a young age, long before they get there. The majority of parents just aren't doing that. It was another peaceful day, thank you, Lord.

> Ephesians 6:4
> Fathers, do not exasperate your children;
> instead, bring them up in the training and instruction
> of the Lord.

JUNE 18

Today is Sunday, Father's Day. Today is another fog-socked-in-at the-campground day. We both lost our dads years ago, but there is still that feeling of missing them. It's a strange feeling when both sets of our fathers and mothers have passed and we are now the oldest of our family. It seems just yesterday we would have looked to our parents and grandparents for advice and approvals. Now, we are the elders. Life is indeed short and in a blink of an eye it's over.

> Psalm 103:13
> The Lord has loving-pity on those who fear Him,
> as a father has loving-pity on his children.

At first, my husband was confused when I told him the air temperature was 66 and the dew point 47, yet we had fog. During his pilot training many years ago, he learned that fog happens when the temperature and the dew point are near the same temperature. This weather-freak girl was the one who figured it out: it's not the *air* temperature causing this fog, it's the surrounding *water* temperature! Yep, we knew the water was cold, so it must be 47 degrees to do this.

I did write a bit while we ran the generator this afternoon. Our close neighbors had left early this morning, and I felt sorry for them. Tent campers, in the cold and rain, their fires dampened by the misty rain. I don't know if they left because their visit time was over or if they left out of utter frustration, due to the weather.

It was past time to defrost the freezer, so I managed to get that done, too. Even though it was full of stuff from our recent stocking rampage, it was completed in a record time of 20 minutes. Wow, I guess practice does make perfect.

We headed out in the car, hoping that it wasn't as bad everywhere else, but it was. We drove to the Bass Harbor Head Lighthouse, the only point of interest we hadn't yet seen. The view reminded me of a beautiful Thomas Kincaid painting I'd once seen, of a lighthouse on a rocky shore. The drive was foggy, as was our entire visit there. We walked down the paved trail, then descended 3 flights of wooden steps. After that, the walk got real interesting.

This area of Maine has a lot of natural granite. There were large, irregular steps constructed of granite, which led out onto the rocky shore. Not rocky as in pebbles or rocks the size of bricks, but large rocks, some the size of Smart Cars, thrown haphazardly by nature itself. People were everywhere, out on the rocks. There were parents who'd taken their toddlers out there, which I personally thought was nuts. One slip and they'd both be hurt.

Larry decided he was going to climb out on the far rocks, to get a good shot of the lighthouse perched on the ledge above. I opted to sit securely at the top, being the woman of age that I am. Larry confessed to me later that he shouldn't have gone way out there. His mind still thinks it's 20, but the body is definitely not. If he had slipped while jumping from one rock to another, he would have wound up with a broken bone for sure, or even a broken head. But God had sent angels to keep that hedge of protection around him, so he would not be hurt. And he sure hated to admit just how sore that jumping adventure left him later. Getting old is not for sissies.

I noticed a woman about my age descending cautiously down the granite stairway. Her husband was standing near my perch, and he showed surprise that she had walked down. She replied, "Probably not one of my wiser moves." When her husband caught my smile, he told me she'd had hip surgery. Oh.

Larry finally found his way back to where I was sitting, and the 4 of us headed up the trail at the same time. I rooted her on, "C'mon. If I can do it, you can, too." She smiled at my encouragement. When she reached the stair platform I was resting on, I asked when her surgery was. Even though it was 2 years ago, she's recently had a fall and badly damaged some nerves. I commiserated, and explained my broken neck. The husband called me lucky. I call myself blessed.

Back up in the parking lot, I gave them a His Road Trip card. I hope they check it out. Perhaps it will give her encouragement in recovering from her injury.

Psalm 119:105
Your Word is a lamp to my feet and a light to my path.

We continued our journey through this foggy but pretty area. We've been in lots of national parks, and seen lots of ways the NPS protects you from running off the road. Considering the granite in this area, the folks of Arcadia have used thousands of large chunks of it to make an impenetrable guardrail that ran alongside the road, everywhere in the park. We're talking chunks half the size of hay rolls. Pretty effective, I'd say.

I continue to see spring everywhere. I know I've been saying that for a few months now, but it's still true. Lilac is in bloom, as is huge rhododendron of all colors, various blooming trees, and beautiful iris in purple and yellow. And these folks have used these various colors to decorate their yards in amazing ways. Occasionally, I've seen brilliant red poppies and there's another flowering bush with bright orange flowers that I've had yet to figure out. Just awesome. We are following spring as we travel north…or spring is following us.

Late in the afternoon, Larry was grumping something like, "What a Father's Day this is." Feeling sorry for himself, I reminded him that Diana had explained in a text on Saturday that she had a 7am-3pm shift at Paula Dean's gift shop today. I'll bet she calls right after she gets off work.

She texted to say hi about 4:30pm, probably to see if we were able to receive and respond. Larry was driving the car, so I responded on his cell. Another 10 minutes later, she called to wish him a Happy Father's Day. Larry tries to shake off all kinds of mushy stuff, but I knew his heart swelled to know that his grown daughter would make sure to call to wish him a happy day. They talked a pretty good while,

Larry driving all the way. I warned them we were almost back to the campground, so we said goodbyes before we were dropped off with no service. God is good.

We heated up another Marie Colander's, turkey and the works this time, and watched another few *Friday Night Lights.*

And went to sleep in the fog. God is good.

JUNE 19

We awoke to another day of fog. Does the sun ever shine up here? Larry recalled the mini-cruise ship down in the bay at Camden. Those poor folks had paid $4,400 each to see the coast socked in.

We left Acadia early, to get a head start on the day. The rain had weighed down lower branches on trees, and we hit a lot of them on the way out of the park. We drove first up Route 3 west, then Route 179 north. We picked up 9 north to US 1 south. US1 takes you right over the border into Canada, where they just call it Route 1. Here, it's part of the Trans-Canada Highway.

Trip Advisor claims that "The Trans-Canada Highway is the world's longest national highway. Stretching 7,821 km (4,860 miles), across Canada, it connects all ten provinces, from the Pacific…to the Atlantic."[36]

Not long after we passed through Canadian Customs, we followed a sign for a Visitor Center. At the exit, we ate at the Burger King and walked to the information center. The lady who offered to help was very nice. After telling her our route and how long we'd already been on the road, she recommended parking overnight at the Rockwood Park Campground in downtown Saint John, New

---

[36] tripadvisor.com

Brunswick, Canada. She assured us that there would be available sites this time of year and they offered full hookups.

We drove in the fog, another 80 miles or so. And I must say that Canada Route 1 is sure is a lot better shape than US1. The road looked nearly brand new, there is absolutely no trash, and the wildflowers were beautiful. They're doing something right up here!

On the way, I thought it was due time to download a Unit Converter App, so I could convert these km to miles and know that the $40 I paid with my US debit card will eventually clear for around $30 USD.

We quickly checked in and the info lady had been quite right—there was plenty of room. The "campground" is actually a large level parking lot, covered in gravel. The sites were defined by yellow lines that had been spray-painted on the gravel. It was neat and tidy, just not much on aesthetics. The utilities were easy to access, although we're back to 30amp again. Water heater? Propane. Heat? Propane. Just so that I could use the electric to get the laundry all caught up. Larry rated Rockwood Park Campground a 4.

After vacuuming all the junk Larry had tracked into the rig from Acadia, I had lots of laundry to wash, while I snuck in some writing. I have one clothesline in the rig, and filled it up with the first load. I hung the wet second load on hangers, in the hopes they will dry by morning. Load 3 was jeans, so it'll take a few hours to get them good and dry in my little unit.

With the help of Stouffers, we enjoyed delicious stuffed peppers and a fresh ear of corn.

Let me stop now and tell you a funny story about stuffed peppers. The year was 1975, and we had recently moved to Winston-Salem, North Carolina. Larry had moved us there to take a job with Lowe's Foods, and I was hired at Integon, a large insurance company downtown, to work in their investment department. Larry came home from work one day and said a coworker had invited both of us to dinner. How exciting! We would make some new friends.

Well, the time came, and I met John and his wife, Diane at their home. Diane had gone to great lengths to prepare a homemade meal for our first night together. Their place was small (as was ours) and we sat at the table, as she served from the stove. She handed Larry a plate with a single stuffed pepper on it. In all honesty, neither one of us had ever seen such a thing as a stuffed pepper.

Larry was, at that time, a very basic meat-and-potato eater. He took one look at that "thing" and his eyes met mine in sheer panic. I gave him one of those, "Now what are you gonna do?" looks, because he would never try anything new for me, he would just turn it away. After John said a blessing for our meal, Larry braved a pithy little bite. Hmm. Then another. Along with mounds of homemade mashed potatoes, he finished off the whole thing and asked if he could have another. I remember that night so well. That look was priceless!

We enjoyed another couple *Friday Night Lights* episodes. No cable, no satellite here. I'm so glad I picked up those DVD's at Target.

Larry drove a lot of hours today, and we lost an hour of time. He went to bed early, while I enjoyed being able to write with electric on demand. It's been a good day. Please continue to keep that hedge of protection on duty, Lord. We are here, we are safe, we are sound. We're still in Fog, but we're in Canada.

Thank you, Lord that our adventure safely continues.

JUNE 20

We took our time getting ready this morning, knowing full well that there was nobody waiting in a foggy line to get our campsite. This place is socked in worse than ever. I took down all my now-dry laundry and put it away, while Larry spent his time reviewing (and adding to) my book entries for the past few days. Hot cream of wheat and a fresh cup of coffee really hit the spot on such a gloomy morning.

Larry quietly told me about an "episode" that he had experienced earlier that morning. He said he was just sitting in front of the computer reading, when he found it difficult to focus on the letters of the words. Blinking, he began seeing little prisms of color floating around. Nothing seemed to help, as he opened and closed his eyes, or pushed on them with his fingers. In time, they passed as suddenly as they'd appeared.

Curious, he Googled "seeing prisms in eyes" and there it was. It said they were associated with migraines, or what they call "visual migraines" but sometimes not. He's never had a migraine and rarely has headaches. What really concerned us was the prisms could indicate a stroke. His blood pressure is getting high again. Later in the morning, I requested that if he ever begins to see prisms while driving, please make every attempt to bring the rig to a stop and park it before he has a stroke. Please. Not funny at all.

We finally pulled the motorhome out of the campground and, with all credit due to Frankie, I instructed Larry to take a wrong turn. It wasn't fatal, of course, and we were quickly back on the route. As we approached a traffic light, both lights were flashing green. A green flashing light? We weren't exactly sure what that meant, but the coast was clear, and we sailed on through.

We would spend the entire day on the Trans-Canada Highway. The road was good, but the fog was horrible—it was indeed like driving through potato soup. I don't know how long Larry will want to drive today.

We learned that the TCH is one Highway, but it's comprised of different route numbers. We started out on Route 1, which ended and became Route 2. Eventually it became Route 104, but still the Trans-Canada Highway. The exits are well-marked and few and far between. The traffic was very light, and in many places, we had the road all to ourselves. Much of the scenery was covered in evergreen forests with stretches of farms or homes near to the exits. Past one exit, we spotted a covered bridge, but was going too fast to get a pic.

Around the Norton exit, a break in the fog revealed a large valley to my left. There were lots of farms, with barns and silos; large fields tilled for planting. There were homes scattered about. It was lush and beautiful.

I will say again that this is the cleanest stretch of highway I've ever been on, in all our travels. There is virtually no trash, no blown out tires or retreads on the roadsides here, as it should be everywhere. What a shame that Americans take so little pride and choose to litter. We also noticed not many billboards along the highway. Each Province has large, uniform attraction signs. These signs have up-to-date graphics and blend in well with the surroundings. We did hit one long stretch of highway that had its share of potholes and erosion, but then the route turned pristine again.

One thing is for sure, Canadians seem more respectful to their country than we Americans do as a people. Sure, there are some on both sides of the spectrum. But, you can see their character in the way they treat you as a person and the way the roads, farms, houses, and cities look. Canadians should be proud.

Something else to note. Construction crews on the highway actually work in the rain! In America, if rain is predicted—even if it doesn't show up—it seems that all work gets called off. Not so in Canada. They were all busy working with rain suits on in the pouring rain. Whether building bridges, laying asphalt, or grading roads—whatever they were doing, they were doing it in the rain. Also, in America it seems to take 4 guys to watch one guy dig a hole. We never saw that once in Canada. Everyone was working doing their own particular job.

> 2 Thessalonians 3:10-12
>
> For even when we were with you, we gave you this rule: "The one who is unwilling to work shall not eat."
> [11] We hear that some among you are idle and disruptive. They are not busy; they are busybodies.
> [12] Such people we command and urge in the Lord Jesus Christ to settle down and earn the food they eat.

The fog finally dissipated when we traveled far enough away from the coast. It's overcast, but at least we can see the road ahead.

We stopped to fill up with diesel and we nuked a small lunch in the rig. At the truck stop was a mobile chapel in a semi-trailer called Transport for Christ. They counsel, give out Bibles, and offer church services for truckers on the road.

Jesus and His apostles never stayed inside a church to preach the word. He met the people outside of the church walls, where the people were along the roads and in the cities. Church is fine for believers to gather and be with each other.

Larry says, "You have to step away from the church to see the real world and the real work that needs to be done. Because our main goal for life is to reach the lost, anyway we can." The lost aren't in church. You have to go meet them where they are.

As the afternoon progressed, it began to rain intermittently. It was annoying. It would rain, then stop. Turn the wipers on, then off. Then someone would pass us and spray the windshield.

It was still raining once we stopped for the day around 4pm. I just didn't want Larry to drive much more today. We tried to find a Walmart on the way, but here in this part of Canada, they aren't every couple of miles, like they are back home in the USA. I opened my trusty Allstays app and found Elm River Park in Debert, Nova Scotia, which Larry rated a 4. It's well-maintained, but the sites are on one large, grassy field. The folks at check-in were real nice. I'm sure the pouring rain had something to do with the rating, too.

I decided to do a load of towels while we had 50amp, and while it was pouring down rain. We enjoyed P.F. Chang's for supper and watched some more *Friday Night Lights*.

Thank you, Lord for bringing us safely to this place.

JUNE 21

The sun tried hard to burn off the foggy skies. We got an early start with the motorhome, because today would be a long day of travel. And we had errands to do on the way.

We went through a period of months that it seemed like something constantly was in desperate need of repair. I don't want to tempt the devil, but things had been quiet for a while. Please keep those "bloopers" away, but bring on the "blessings." But, after all the bouncing and bumping on the roads these past few days, the support that holds up the rod in our closet pulled itself right out of the ceiling. Larry's fixed it a couple of times before, and I remember the last time he claimed, "This will never come down again." Yeah, well, it did.

We headed out for a short time back on the TCH. We had Frankie set for the campground at the end of the day, and Frack was set to get us to the Home Depot in Halifax. Along the way, we spotted a young doe not 25 feet from the highway. I sure hope she stayed on that side of the forest!

Proverbs 5:19
Let her be like a loving, female deer.
Let her breasts please you at all times.
Be filled with great joy always because of her love.

We passed a sign for Stewiacke, which declared that the town was noted for being the halfway point between the equator and the north pole. Now, you know.

Larry continues to be amazed by the cleanliness of the highways. There's no trash, no blown-out retreads, and a real scarcity of billboards. But, there are plenty of wildflowers—daisies, yellow flowers, and even cattails in wet areas. All beautiful. This Canadian landscape is good for the soul.

My Ford Escape has both miles per hour (mph) and kilometers per hour (kph) on the speedometer, but the motorhome does not. Well, actually it does, but the numbers are so tiny that you can't read them. We quickly learned that 110 kph is equivalent to 68 mph and that's common for the highway. Seeing a sign for 80 on a ramp (50mph) seems so odd.

For a while, the road was following a small river. Going through a rural area, my highlight was seeing 2 folks in a canoe, paddling. Between them was a large hand-written sign that clearly stated, "We got this." I'm not sure exactly what they had, but...

We stopped to get our stuff at the Home Depot.

The campground tomorrow had warned us that they accept only Canadian cash as payment, so I walked to a nearby bank to get some. We would watch the rest of the first season of *Friday Night Lights* tonight, so I ran into Walmart to search for the second season. No luck. The cashier suggested we go to Best Buy, just down the street. No luck there, either; they didn't even have it in their computer to order! I'll find it online later.

We took Route 333 toward the campground. It was a winding road, but the view of the water was great. We arrived at King Neptune Campground, which Larry rated a 4. The little, very old lady who took my Canadian cash was so funny. I told her that I was grateful they'd told me in advance that they took Canadian cash only. She deadpanned, "Well, when we opened this place 55 years ago, there was no such thing as a credit card." Yeah, I thought to myself, but uh, times do change. Her son-in-law came in and told me to choose any site I wanted. While I walked to the lower end, down by the water, I saw him talking to Larry, who had already chosen an upper level site. We parked on the grass, and set up.

We had a wonderful view of the North Atlantic Ocean at Margaret's Bay. The blue water was breaking along the nearby rocky shore, making a pleasant sound. There was a red and white wooden fishing boat docked in the small bay next to the campground.

| Psalm 139:9 |
| If I take the wings of the morning or |
| live in the farthest part of the sea |

It was only in the mid 60's when we left Halifax, but here—only 20 feet from the water—it was probably 50 degrees outside. Water is certainly nature's air conditioner.

I've mentioned that our air conditioner covers have been in bad shape. Larry had them held together with duct tape, but the sun and weather has caused it to quickly peel and dry out. While at Walmart, he purchased some black (matches the AC covers) Gorilla duct tape and some of that stuff you see on TV, black Flex Seal. He took the ladder up to the top of the rig and got to work. He plastered the covers with Gorilla duct tape, then sealed them with Flex Seal. There, that ought to hold them for a while. From down below, they looked brand new.

While he was up there, he decided to give the roof a good scrub. He said it was a total mess, covered in tree sap. I handed him up the brush and hoses. When he finally came in, he said all he needed now was a good rain to rinse off the rest of the degreaser. I reported there was no chance of rain this evening. Sorry.

However, within a couple of hours, it not only rained hard, it even thundered. God provided what we needed.

Philippians 4:19
And my God will give you everything you need because of
His great riches in Christ Jesus.

I fixed a pork chop and an ear of corn for supper. It was very good, if I do say so myself. We watched the last 2 episodes of *Friday Night Lights*, which made me sad. Even if I order them right away, we won't get to watch them until Diana brings them to us. In the meantime, I sure will miss it.

JUNE 22

Today was a wonderful day of adventure! It's finally in the high 70's with a beautiful blue sky and intermittent puffy white clouds. We took a right out of the campground on Route 333 to follow the Lighthouse Route. Larry had been doing some reading right before we left to learn that back in 1998, a Swissair flight crashed in the bay just a couple of miles from our campground; there were no survivors. That was our first stop, to see the memorial.

From the parking lot, we followed a winding path to the memorial. "On September 2, 1998, Swissair Flight 111 crashed into St. Margaret's Bay with the loss of all aboard. One of two memorials to the victims of the disaster is located at The Whalesback, a promontory approximately one km northwest of Peggy's Cove. The other is located at Bayswater, Nova Scotia, on the Aspotogan Peninsula on the western shore of the bay. The 2 monuments and the actual crash site are at the vertices on a roughly equilateral triangle across the bay. In layman's terms 5 miles out into the bay, in a straight line.

"The monument at Whalesback reads in English and French: 'In memory of the 229 men, women, and children aboard Swissair Flight 111 who perished off these shores September 2, 1998. They have been joined to the sea, and the sky. May they rest in peace.'"[37] I read that the monument at Bayswater contains each of the victims' names.

En mémoire des 229 hommes, femmes et enfants à bord de Swissair Flight 111 qui ont péri sur ces rives le 2 septembre 1998. Ils ont été joints à la mer et au ciel. Qu'ils reposent en paix. "J'ai lu que le monument à Bayswater contient chacun des noms des victimes.

---

[37] en.wikipedia.org/wiki/Peggy's Cove, Nova Scotia

As you stare 5 miles out to sea where it happened you begin to wonder what these people were thinking as their time on earth was coming to an end. Did they know Christ? As the plane fell from the sky, did they know their eternal destination? Heaven or Hell?

They had to be frightened in those last moments. There was fire and smoke throughout the aircraft. The pilots lost control as the fire spread throughout the cabin. Whether you have decades or seconds to live, it is never too late to accept, believe, confess, and invite Christ into your heart to have everlasting life. We hope and pray those souls are with Him.

Everyone was quiet and respectful of the memorial, and spent their quiet time listening to the sound of the surf crashing against the rocky coast. It was somber indeed. We could see the popular Peggy's Cove Lighthouse in the distance up the rocky coast. The sky was blue and the sun was high in the sky.

It was a short drive on to Peggy's Cove, a small rural community, but quite the tourist attraction. They restrict property development to keep it rustic. There were lots of small, quaint shops lining the twisting road out to the Lighthouse. We parked the car and walked up the paved path to the no-frills structure. The large granite boulders at the shoreline around the lighthouse were worn smooth, and folks were walking in every direction. One family of a dozen folks had carried 2 large coolers up to the top of the giant granite boulders, and were sitting down to eat lunch there. What a great idea.

Since Larry's not a shopper, we got back in the car and passed a little food booth with lobster rolls and cooked fish. He was doing quite the business with the crowd, but Larry had other plans.

We headed back the way we'd come, then back to the campground. He had seen a small lobster shack nearly next door to the campground. We parked at Ryer Lobsters and entered the small building. It was a simple setup inside, with 2 gas boilers and a long L-shaped service/prep counter. All the lobsters were in a large steel tank behind the counter, with circulating water.

Apparently, it was a husband and wife team, and the wife took our order, and the husband cooked and cracked the lobster. We asked for a 1 ¼ pounder and was charged $16 Canadian. That is $12.81 US for a lobster. Wow, what a deal! We've been using our credit card when we can, so the bank can handle the exchange. I bought a Diet Coke and we shared it outside in the sun, waiting for lobster to cook.

One highlight of our visit there was when the owner, Dave, introduced us to Harry Potter. He put a gargantuan lobster up on the counter, and it dwarfed the lobster next to him. Harry was not the least impressed with us, despite us being very impressed with him. Dave explained that he weighed 12 pounds and was probably about 10 years old. He said they'd had him for about a week. They keep him fed with pieces of fish, as Harry particularly likes Halibut. Dave showed him while sharing his plans to put him back in the sea next week. Harry, I hope the next guy who catches you will be as kind.

Just in case you ever want to know, it takes lobster 7 long years to weigh in at one pound. After that seventh birthday, he gains about a half-pound a year. Lobster 101…so, now you know.

Genesis 9:3
Everything that lives and moves about
will be food for you. Just as I gave you the green plants,
I now give you everything.

We drove to the campground and put dinner in the fridge for supper tonight, then headed out again, because Larry had read about the Lighthouse Trail drive, and wanted to drive it.

We drove through town after town: Hackett's Cove, Glen Margaret, Seabright, French Village, Upper Tantallon. The winding road never wandered far from the water, which was peppered with anchored boats in all colors—sail boats, fishing boats, dinghies, and skiffs. I guess when summer arrives for good, they'll all be busy playing in the open water. We did notice a school sign posted June 30 as the last day of school. No wonder we haven't seen many kids around here. Perhaps they had enjoyed a bunch of snow days.

We drove on through Boutiliers Point, Queensland, Hubbard's Beach, and East Chester. In Chester Basin, we spotted the Seaside Shanty, and we decided we would have lunch here. We walked into a patio deck with wide-opened screens on 2 sides. It was a small place, and our waitress seated us at a table for 2, just feet from the waterfront. The tables and chairs are all wood and painted in different bright colors. A small breeze was unencumbered by the screens and the day was perfect.

I decided we would get the Shanty Combo, "The ultimate seafood combo…a cup of Seafood Chowder paired with a Lobster Roll." We were delighted when the food arrived. Their creamy chowder was so thick with scallops, shrimp, mussels, clams, and haddock, we could have easily eaten it with a fork. The lobster roll was the largest I'd seen yet, and it was delicious. This one had twice as much lobster in it than the one we had back in Maine a few weeks ago, and a lot cheaper.

When we had devoured it all, I asked our waitress Jill about the "Blueberry Grunt" we saw written on the dessert chalkboard. She explained that her mother didn't cook her blueberries on the stove, but baked them in the oven. She always grunted when she pulled out the large, full pans. Hence, Blueberry Grunt. The baked blueberries were served hot in their own syrup, with a type of dumpling and vanilla ice cream. Larry's not a blueberry lover, but he sure ate more than his share of this! Delicious!

We continued the Lighthouse Route, passing through Oakland Lake, the beautiful town of Mahone Bay, Martin's Brook, and Lunenburg. We even crossed the Mushamush River.

The one storefront that really caught my eye was appropriately named "Loonies and Toonies." You have to think Canadian to find the humor in it. They don't have one-dollar bills in Canada, their bills begin with Fives. Their one-dollar coin is referred to as a Loonie, nicknamed because of the Loon on the back of the coin. And then there's the Toonie, a two-toned $2 coin. Loosely translated, the "Loonies and Toonies" was simply a dollar store. Cute.

Taking Route 103 for an hour's trip back to the campground, I admit to taking a short nap. When we got back to the rig, I took an icepack to my neck, quite sore from rubber-necking all afternoon.

Then it was time to fix the lobster. I put water on to boil.

I could hear Larry talking to a woman outside, explaining our Motorhome Ministry. I heard him give her a book to read, and when she asked how to return it, he requested only that she pass it on to someone else. I picked up a pen and walked to the door. Would you like for me to sign it for you? Oh, yes please.

I asked her name, and I signed it for Verity. She was probably about my age, and excitedly gave me details of many ways that God has accompanied her on her adventure, and even gone before her to make perfect arrangements. Yes, I agreed wholeheartedly. God travels before us, too. We enjoyed a short chat and she went on her way. She was from the West side of Canada, in Victoria, British Columbia. She had indeed traveled a very long way.

When we were in Washington state last year, we stayed at Fort Worden State Park. It was located in Port Townsend, along Admiralty Inlet. As we sat in our motorhome, she was probably enjoying a spot of tea in her home across the inlet, in Canada. It is such a small world.

I finished preparing our lobster and nuked 2 fresh ears of corn. We made a terrible mess at the table, but it was probably the cheapest meal we'd had all week. Thank you, Jesus for such tasty creatures.

> 1 Chronicles 16:34
> Give thanks to the LORD, for he is good;
> His love endures forever.

I was cleaning up when I heard a knock at the door. When I answered, there was Verity standing there. After exchanging hellos, she handed me a check. Assuming it was to pay for the book, I told her that she didn't have to do that. She laughed and said, "Yes, I do." And pointing skyward, she said, "He told me to." She extended blessings for our continued ministry, and the hopes her contribution would cover costs for additional materials for the kids. She had told me earlier about how God had impressed upon her heart to leave tracts wherever she goes. I voiced my blessings on her continued "ministry", as well.

Go in peace. Serve the Lord.

> 1 Samuel 1:17
> Eli answered, "Go in peace,
> and may the God of Israel grant you
> what you have asked of him."

After I wrote for a while, we walked down to the rocky shore in the campground to takes some pictures of the magnificent sky. The sun was still up, but the clouds and the sky and the sun were just breathtaking. There was even a rainbow in the clouds. God's promise. Even after we returned to the rig, the sky stayed brilliant throughout the sunset and an hour beyond.

Thank you, Lord, for all your promises.

Genesis 9:16
Whenever the rainbow appears in the clouds,
I will see it and remember the everlasting covenant
between God
and all living creatures of every kind on the earth."

JUNE 23

We were just about ready to leave the campground to hit the road. Larry was outside shutting down the utilities when a man hurried up to him. He said that he thought we'd be staying longer, and his wife wanted to get a kid's packet. We had no idea where he got that idea, but Larry was happy to get him a packet from the basement of the rig.

We spent quite a few hours on the TCH today, heading northeast. The terrain was a little hillier (more hilly?) today, once again filled with forests. I busied my hands crocheting little yarn bracelets to contribute to Operation Christmas Child. I haven't done it in a while, and I certainly enjoyed it today.

We decided to stop at a Taco Bell for lunch. I know in the US, PepsiCo owns both Kentucky Fried Chicken and Taco Bell. This restaurant had both, behind the same counter. I could have ordered Taco Bell for Larry and KFC for me, at one register. They offered a Create Your Own Box for $5.99. Choice of 2 tacos, chips with cheese, your choice of dessert and a drink. What a bargain! That figured out to be about $4.50 in US money for all that food.

Later in the afternoon, we came upon a wreck that had just happened—car versus motorcycle. I looked for the motorcyclist and was grateful to see a group of bikers standing, one of them sitting on the guard rail, apparently unharmed. What a relief. Another couple of miles down the road, we saw 3 different police cruisers were responding to the accident. The motorcycle was indeed a mess of scrap metal; there were pieces scattered everywhere.

Here's a tidbit to remember, should you ride a motorcycle: Don't dress for the ride, dress for the slide. Truer words could not be spoken. I see folks on those zippy crotch-rockets, wearing tiny little shorts and tank tops. What if they were thrown from the bike? It would take them months to heal from skidding across the pavement, body parts exposed. The guy we saw had been dressed for the slide.

Following Frankie and the road signs, we arrived without unnecessary drama at the Hyclass Ocean Campground in Navre Boucher, Nova Scotia, which Larry rated a 5. We didn't have reservations and Larry's instructions were specific: he wanted a pull-through with utilities and a view of the water. God went before us, and there were 3 unreserved such sites awaiting our choosing.

I put ice on my neck for a short rest, while Larry was washing the bugs off the dirty windshield. I set out a ground patty for supper, and began writing. The sun sparkling off the rippling water was inspiring.

Larry grilled the meat and I served it with tator tots and baked beans. We watched the DVD, *Captain Phillips*, starring Tom Hanks. What a nail-biting movie. Just as the movie was coming to an end, it began sprinkling rain, although the 6 kids playing baseball in the sites across from us didn't give a whit. Those happy voices are great to hear. As you get older and don't have kids around anymore, you sure do miss being around them.

Matthew 19:14
Jesus said, "Let the little children come to me,
and do not hinder them, for the kingdom of heaven
belongs to such as these."

There's no beautiful sunset, like we enjoyed last night, just an overcast sky. Tonight will be early to bed, because it was a long day of driving. Tomorrow is a short trip. The slight breeze coming in the window was nice, as I wrote about the day. Thank you, Lord for another blessed day.

JUNE 24

It did my heart good to see a dad and his son pitching ball right in front of our rig this morning. The young man was probably 10, and he was really throwing them hard. While I was packing up, a cute bespectacled girl dressed in one-piece pink jammies and pink rain boots showed some interest in the packets. She seemed too shy to take one, so I quietly opened the door and offered her one myself. I asked if there were other kids with her who'd want one, and she innocently shrugged her shoulders. I knew there were over half-dozen kids of all ages nearby, so I put 3 more in her hands. She smiled and ran away.

It was a short drive to get back on the TCH, in this area also known as the Fleur de Lis Trail. Today's scheduled drive in the motorhome was short, less than 2 hours. The hills are getting a bit higher and the when the views from the winding road don't reveal small towns, we continue to be surrounded by forest and views of the bays and inlets of the North Atlantic. There were quite a few miles of highway in terrible disrepair, then quite a few that were being prepped to be repaved. Today was a bumpy ride for sure. But the scenery was just beautiful.

About noon, Larry spotted a good price for diesel and decided to fill up again. Since our plan was to leave the car on the dolly for the next 2 days, I asked him to take me to lunch at Tim Horton's, right next to the gas station. We'd been seeing them everywhere, but never tried them.

Larry scoffed as we entered, saying it was just like a Dunkin Donuts. Perhaps because of their donuts and coffee, but they sure had a lot more to offer in the lunch department.

I ordered chicken salad on a croissant for us and it was delicious. Along with chicken soup, we were filled. Almost. They had lots of unique flavors of fresh bagels, so I ordered a couple to fix for breakfast tomorrow. But I wanted something sweet now. I went back to order a 20-count box of Timbits, donuts holes in 5 flavors.

While we were eating, a man came into the restaurant and immediately asked if that was our rig parked out there. He was amazed at all the state stickers. Then we told him that we had done all that in just the past 16 months. He asked where the Canada map was, and we both quickly replied, "It's on order." I gave him a card and explained our motorhome ministry. We talked a little longer and he wished us well. Then he told us, "My job is on the road but, but my wife doesn't like to leave home." I thought that perhaps my book will convince her to see what she is missing, and I told him about www.HisRoadTrip.com.

While we were still eating, the wind picked up outside. I saw something flapping underneath the motorhome. I pointed it out to Larry. His remark was, "Whatever that is, it's not good." He would make a point to check it when we set up.

It had been overcast and spitting rain the entire route today. What I haven't seen so far on our travels here in Canada is farmland. Occasionally, I will see a barn, but I can't figure out what its purpose is or was, because I've yet to see herds of cattle or horses, either. It's the end of June, and I don't even see little vegetable gardens. I guess their season is just too short to grow much of anything.

We finally arrive at Adventures East Campground, Baddeck, Nova Scotia. Several men were busy putting up flags in the hammock of trees coming into the campground. Canada Day is just a week away! The lady in the small office was very cordial. I explained that we had placed our reservations through Coast to Coast. She quickly found the reservation. While deciding what site to put us on, she kept repeating that we were here for "only 2 days." That seemed to matter greatly to her. She finally pointed up the hill behind me. She explained that they'd had lots of rain recently, and our motorhome would be too heavy for the sites on the right side, which was lower. The left side should be okay, just don't pull back too far, because where there's no grass, they had just put in fresh dirt.

I ask about the pool. They had just had a new liner installed in the pool yesterday, and the chemicals weren't perfected yet. No one was allowed in the pool. Oh, well.

We were to pull into site 46, which was the skinniest site I have ever seen, and by this time, I've seen a LOT of sites! It was one of 25 in a row—only a few of them occupied—each had a picnic table, a fire rim, and utilities. We couldn't back all the way in because of the wet, fresh dirt in the back. When we backed in on the left side of the narrow site, there was no room for the car. We moved the rig out, then backed it into the right side, but then our generator was hanging right over the potential neighbor's fire ring. For us to back in 3 times and still not fit right, Larry was ready to explode. Everything was muddy, and the site was just too small.

When we had pulled off the highway, there was a sign for a Good Sam Park directly across the road. Larry looked them up on Allstays, and I called them. I explained our current situation at Adventures East. I asked if they had a pull-thru available. Yes. "And it's got gravel or pavement on it, so I won't sink?" I asked. The lady kindly chuckled and replied, "No, you won't sink." I assured her that we would be right there.

I went back and explained to the nice lady in the office that the site just doesn't suit our needs. We drove across the street.

When I walked in the front door of the Baddeck Cabot Trail Campground, that Larry rated a 6, the young lady at the counter smiled at me. I knew right away she was the one I had whined to, and I quickly introduced myself as such: "Hi, I'm Mrs. Hammond and I just called and whined to someone about sinking in the mud." According to the map she marked the site on, there are many generous sites throughout the campground, but the site she chose for us seems to be one of less than a dozen ginormous sites in the park. Yes, we paid a premium for it, but I have everything I could have asked for: water, sewer, 50amp, and a fantastic, unobstructed view from this long and generous site on the perimeter of the campground. And they have a heated pool. Wow.

For the sake of rating, Larry would rate Adventures East a very low 1. BUT, a gentleman at Baddeck Cabot spoke very kindly of them to me. The owners had just recently purchased the park from someone who had really run it into the ground. I could see that they were making improvements, but it just wasn't in time for us. I bear them no ill will and wish them the best of luck with their new endeavor. Perhaps by the time you read this, they'll have created a beautiful campground.

I put some chicken tenderloins on the stove to cook while Larry completed the repairs outside. The flapping I had seen from Tim Horton's was under skirting in one place that had worked itself loose. He took some small screws and reattached the under skirting. Then he took the Flex Seal and sprayed it and him with it.

Larry has never understood the concept of "work clothes." He just jumps into whatever job comes to mind with whatever he has on. He was wearing a T-shirt I'd recently bought him that he's gotten compliments on several times. It reads, "I have OCD. Obsessive Camping Disorder." It was particularly suiting because he does have OCD. He was an absolute mess with all this black gooey stuff all over his arms, in his hair, and on his cute shirt. His excuse was, "the wind was blowing as I sprayed".

When he came in, he said he was planning to take me out to dinner tonight. I finished cooking the chicken breasts, then packed them in the fridge, and we drove the car into town. As Larry drove past a sign I thought said Baddeck Lobster Suppers, I mentioned it. He turned the car around and when he went to turn in, I apologized, "Oh, I'm sorry. That sign actually says Baddeck Lobster Supplies." What? He laughed out loud. It must have been the red font with the blue shadow behind it that made it so hard to read. Suppers, it said. The trials of getting old.

> Isaiah 46:4
> Even when you are old I will be the same.
> And even when your hair turns white, I will help you.
> I will take care of what I have made.
> I will carry you, and will save you.

Their menu was short and sweet of 4 main dishes: locally fished lobster, fire-planked Atlantic salmon, Cape Breton snow crab, or grilled strip loin steak. You could order all you can eat for one price, served with chowder and dessert. Or, you could pick one of the 4 different items served with tomato and cucumber salad, coleslaw, and potato salad. I chose the snow crab dinner plus a bowl of seafood chowder with potatoes, haddock, pollock, scallops, and shrimp.

They brought us a basket of nibbles while we waited that included oat biscuits, a dinner roll, and a flour biscuit. We polished off every crumb. Jill was a delightful server who kept my coffee cup full. To lots of other patrons, they were serving large bowls of mussels; the menu said you could order a "big ole bucket full."

Stuffed, we came back and watched some Netflix until the campground wifi started slowing down. The sky remained overcast all evening, but no rain so far. I hoped for rain—the car is absolutely filthy. It's cool enough to have the windows open tonight. Thank you, Lord, for your hedge of protection today.

> Psalm 5:11
> But let all who take refuge in you be glad;
> let them ever sing for joy.
> Spread your protection over them,
> that those who love your name may rejoice in you.

JUNE 25

Today was another stay inside, get some work done day. I stripped the bed linens and got them all washed. I love the smell of clean sheets and pillowcases, don't you? I wrote most of the day, while Larry labored outside. I'm trying so hard to get to the end of Book 2. It's another great read with lots of great places to visit.

Larry had a long list of periodic maintenance he had to do, while the weather was nice. He greased the levellers as well as the rig bearings. He checked the fluid levels in the batteries, engine, and generator and topped off them all. He greased the bearings in the tow dolly, then topped off the brake fluid. I made him go take a shower when he came in—he had grease all over him.

We grilled chicken for supper and corn on the cob, then watched Netflix until it spent more time spooling than we did viewing. That gets old quick. The sunsets came later this time of year and it was a beautiful, clear, and colourful sky.

I wrote some more after Larry went to bed. It's nice and quiet then. A day of earthly accomplishments, thank you, Lord.

JUNE 26

I had just a couple of things I wanted to pick up, so we stopped at the local CoOp, the only supermarket I could find in Baddeck, Nova Scotia. I know I'm in another country, but it seemed like another world! I wanted to purchase just a few ground beef patties, but the fresh meat cooler had none, only frozen. I finally found a package of Johnsonville "Sausage Burgers" in several varieties. What is this? I chose a package of "Original Recipe Bratwurst." We like beef and we like Bratwurst. We should like them.

We headed to Breton National Park today, one of the most popular Canadian National Parks. We will be traveling the world-famous Cabot Trail along the beautiful coast. We did get behind a big vehicle that was repainting the highway stripes, down the middle and the curb at the same time. We could see the faded lines of the previous stripes and were amazed at how precise the operator was painting the new ones on this very curvy road. Larry wondered aloud if perhaps they run automatically by GPS. Hmm. I wonder?

We saw a lot of Canada flags today. This Saturday will be July 1, and everyone was preparing to celebrate their country's Sesquicentennial, or 150th birthday.

The road was getting progressively worse until we hit a blissfully new stretch of the Cabot Trail. It was like floating on air.

Just as we were about to arrive at the campground, Larry pulled into the Sea Gull Restaurant in Ingonish. It was on the Atlantic Ocean waterfront, with indoor and windowed deck seating. You could tell it was a family-run restaurant—all the family members were working, even the kids. We ordered fish and chips, 2 fillets of haddock with coleslaw, and an enormous pile of fries. The haddock and coleslaw were great, but there was no way to eat all those fries, so we carted them back to the motorhome.

We finally arrived at Broad Cove Campground at Breton National Park, which Larry rated a 6. It had been a very long day.

We enjoyed watching *The Blind Side* with Sandra Bullock. What a great, great movie.

I wrote until late. Everything was edited through December 20, the original cutoff date for Book 2, but the book needs to be longer. It was a good time to stop and get some sleep. Tomorrow will be spent adding more dates to the book. I can finally see the end of this project through the tunnel.

JUNE 27

I had left Larry a note, telling him not to change a single thing in Book 2, unless he cleared it with me. He had reread everything up to the middle of October, and hadn't found much of anything that needed to be changed. Thank heaven.

I shooed him away from my computer so that I could write some more. About 1pm, he wanted to go for a drive, to check out a couple places the park ranger had told us not to miss.

We first headed south through Ingonish, down to a turnoff marked for Middle Head. It took us past the Highlands Links and the Keltic Lodge, which I found to be quite impressive. The flowers were beautiful. There were purples, reds, yellow, white, and orange blossoms, all overlooking the cliffs and the blue North Atlantic. The sky was a bright sunlit blue. The view was so impressive. I took some pictures from one of their overlooks, with 4 bright red Adirondack chairs sitting at the edge. It was an award-winning shot for sure.

We finally arrived at the Middle Head Trailhead. I had already told him that the Trail was meant to be a 2 ½-hour hike out and back. Instead of hiking just a short while, he decided he wanted no part of it. He turned around the car to leave.

We stopped at a small snack bar by the beach to get a couple of bottled drinks. A conversation ensued about loonies and toonies with the 3 young men working there. One explained that the government prefers coins, because they last longer than paper money. Point taken. He asked if I'd seen one of their "new twenties?" I pulled one from my wallet. It felt like a thin sheet of plastic. He went on to tell me that if you wash them, they do hold up better than the old paper money. However, if you dry them, you wind up with a little ball of plastic. Wow. That would-be heartbreaking, to lose a twenty in the dryer, and it seems he was speaking from painful personal experience.

They didn't have ice, so Larry didn't want the drink I bought him. I told him again about a couple of waterfalls that were north of the campground. Since we were going right past the camper, could we stop for a potty break and get him a Diet Coke with ice? We wound up staying in the cool for nearly an hour, then I asked to go see the waterfalls. I think he would have preferred not to, but he said he would go. It turned out to be the best part ever.

We followed the signs toward Black Brook Beach, but wound up on Black Brook Cove, and couldn't find a waterfall. We were ready to hike back up to the car, when I spotted it on the far side of the bay. Now we knew where we were going!

We got back in the car, and drove to the Beach parking lot. There was a set of steps to begin down toward the beach, but it dead-ended into a massive hill of granite rocks, worn-smooth by the ocean. You know how driftwood is still wood, but it's light, all its weight gone? That's what these rocks were like: they looked like rocks, but they were light and sounded hollow when you walked on them.

We carefully picked our way down through the dry but slippery rocks to the sandy beach. We walked to the left, in the direction of the waterfalls. But to get close to the falls, there were chunks of granite the size of cows we had to climb over and through.

Larry went charging in again—the boy of 20 trying to get there first. Well, the old fart of 62 lost his balance and nearly went head-first into one of those chunks. He regained his stance, but then lost it again and nearly fell for the second time. His angels were there to hold him up safely. At least we had driven past the medical center yesterday, so I knew where it was.

I stayed way back and took my photos from there. The cove, the beach, the waterfall, the Northern Atlantic...everything was incredibly beautiful. They call this the Highlands of Canada.

Psalm 42:7
Deep calls to deep in the roar of your waterfalls;
all your waves and breakers have swept over me.

And everywhere we looked at the blue Atlantic, we saw hundreds, collectively thousands of buoys, each marking a lobster trap. Neon yellow, green, and pink, with white and blue and red on others. If each one of those traps catches just one lobster—no wonder they're sold everywhere you look. They looked like little dots of color throughout the bay waters.

We negotiated our way back down the granite and stood on the beach. We watched as 2 preteen boys charged into the ice-cold water. Brothers, they appeared to be. The older just had to prove himself by heading out neck-deep before coming back into shore. There were also a pair of girls, probably around 8 years old. They went screaming into the water, then ran right back out, screaming their little-girl screams. As they ran past us, I heard one of them say, "I'm not going in there, it's too cold!"

Smart girls. Silly boys. The water was like 40 degrees! As I tried to maneuver my way back up through those smooth rocks, I slid, my right foot losing its footing. I lost a layer of skin off my right knee, but it didn't even bleed. My right ring finger also suffered a bit, too. But hey, if nothing broke, that's great!

We headed then for the other waterfall, named Mary Ann Falls. The map showed a dotted line for the road, which the ranger had told me was a dusty dirt road. It was the bumpiest, tooth-jangling ride ever! It was basically a one-laner, but there were 3 different cars coming out while we were still heading up, and we managed without incident. A pull-off at the top had a magnificent view overlooking the blue Atlantic and bay.

When we arrived at the trailhead, there were nearly a dozen cars already there. There was a closed auto gate and a mileage sign. I left Larry behind in the car to read how far it was to the falls: 0.2 m. I kept him in suspense while I entered the number into my metric converter. "It's 656 feet to the falls," I explained. "Okay, we can do that." Off we went.

It was a pleasant walk, with a gradual decline. Then we came to a set of nicely-maintained steps—probably 100 of them—leading down to the stream and falls, all in a forest setting. About halfway down, I said to Larry, "It's going to be a lot harder getting back up than it was getting down here." The steps were very steep. He agreed. His Myositis will be screaming on the return trip.

When we arrived at the bottom platform, we had a full view of the magnificent falls and the gathering pool at the bottom. There were more than a dozen folks either swimming in the water or sitting on the rocks with their feet submerged.

On a relative note, the City of Myrtle Beach has Can-Am days every March. We have always laughed at the "Crazy Canadians" who love to swim in our ocean in March. Now I know why. Our Atlantic in March is already warmer than their Atlantic ever gets! Now it all makes perfect sense.

As we took our pictures of the falls, a group of young men (really boys) began jumping off the cliffs into the water. It had to be sixty feet up those cliffs. Watching those healthy but slightly chunky young men jump into those unknown depths made me a nervous wreck. I guess the risk of a broken neck affects me more than any of them. I think they were trying to impress the two teenaged girls in bikinis that were swimming in the tidepool below them. They were giggling with each other. Probably making fun of the "Macho" boys jumping off the cliffs.

Ezekiel 38:20

The fish in the sea, the birds in the sky,

the beasts of the field, every creature that

moves along the ground, and

all the people on the face of the earth

will tremble at my presence.

The mountains will be overturned, the cliffs

will crumble and every wall will fall to the ground.

We made it back up the steps without incident and only stopped once to catch our breath. We were nearly back to the car when I asked Larry what made this hike so special today? And, he actually knew. I had done all the steps, the walking, the granite-climbing, all of it—without the back brace. Plus, His legs seem to make it back without too much pain. Praise the Lord!

Remember the Johnsonville "Sausage Burgers" we bought yesterday? We grilled one for supper tonight. It was everything it claimed to be and had the most delicious taste of Bratwurst. I would buy these again. Served with reheated French Fries from the Sea Gull Restaurant, we were filled.

Larry spent most of his evening kibitzing about how slow the internet is out here. I hear that most days, so I tend to ignore it. The only DVD in a wrapper I had left was *Remember the Titans*, but Larry complained that he'd already seen it a couple of times, so he went to bed to stare at his iPhone as well as give his legs a rest from today's activities. I enjoyed the movie again, then succumbed to the sunshine and fresh air of the day.

What a wonderful day it was. Thank you, Lord for yet another remarkable day. I know I say this at the end of every day, but who else can you thank but Him. I am alive, I'm well, and living the dream.

Psalm 128:2

You will eat the fruit of your labor;

blessings and prosperity will be yours.

JUNE 28

This day was not an easy day. We packed everything up as usual, to hit the road. We started out heading north on Cabot Trail. Today we would transverse Nova Scotia from Broad Cove, halfway up the eastern coast, to Cheticamp on the lower western coast. Little did we know what adventures awaited us.

The roads are in really poor shape up here. At times, we felt like a yo-yo. We couldn't even see where they've been patched over the years, they're simply old and full of pot holes. When we checked into Broad Cove, the Park ranger had told me that there are a lot of repaving projects going on this summer. They even printed an entire brochure about the projects—what the project is, where it is, and what type of delay or closure you should expect. The first detour was only a few miles into the day.

I think we passed through every single work project today.

There were bridge projects being built right next to old bridges, so there were no delays. There were several places where the road was closed to one lane with a temporary traffic light, because the workers were busy building up a wider lane. There was a section more than a mile long where the old road had either been torn up or buried.

They were laying a high bed of large crushed rock, then covering it with packed dirt. That was down to one lane for a while, then they allowed us to drive on the new rock/dirt base. No asphalt, no lines, just a wide bed of dirt. And you know what? I commented to Larry that it was the smoothest section of road we'd been on all day. He laughingly agreed.

We stopped at a couple scenic overlooks, just to give Larry a break. At one stop, we cranked up the generator and nuked White Castles to eat for lunch. The section of the Cabot Trail we traveled today went from sea level to 1,400 feet and back down again. None of it was in a straight line. It was curvy and winding and up and down and horribly bumpy and under construction. It was a very difficult drive in trying to keep the rig and tow vehicle on such a road. He was completely tuckered out when we finally arrived.

Luke 3:5
Every valley shall be filled in,
every mountain and hill made low.
The crooked roads shall become straight,
the rough ways smooth.

As we entered the Cheticamp campground, which Larry rated a 6, the small registration booth had a sign on it that it was closed. Please register at the Visitors Center. Okay. I'd be happy to do just that, if I knew where the Visitors Center was! But God was with us as a young woman employee parked her car and walked over to us, seeing our obvious confusion. She was heading to the Visitors Center anyway, and she led me there.

The ranger who checked me in was very nice. In general, everyone I've met here in Canada has been happy and polite. She noted our reservations for Site 98 and voiced some concern. She showed me on a detailed map of the campground just how we would normally drive, then back right into the site. Not today. They had a sewer line break yesterday, and had that lane blocked off (more construction), so we'd have to come in from the other direction. Our success will depend on how angled the campsite is.

Larry had taken the car off the dolly while I was gone, so I got in the car and led him to the site. It didn't look too bad, because the site was perfectly perpendicular to the road. What we failed to take into consideration were the fire ring, the trees and stump opposite the site, or the trees on the left side of the site. At one point, he was perfectly tucked in cater-cornered between the stump and the fire ring. Uh oh. He is not in the mood for this.

At that point, a nicely-dressed man in a neon vest walking toward the sewer repairs took pity on us and jumped right in. I would have never directed Larry to drive into the mowed grassy field right next to our site, but the man suggested it, so we did. I don't think we could have wiggled our way into our site without the guy in the orange vest. As always, God knew our needs and sent an angel in a vest and a cool head to help us. Thank you, Lord.

Luke 4:9-11
He will command his angels concerning you
to guard you carefully;
[11]they will lift you up in their hands,
so that you will not strike your foot against a stone.

We took a car ride into nearby Cheticamp. It's a tidy small town, spread all along the coast. Little businesses with cute names are tucked between tidy houses. Larry jerked the car to the right when he spotted a car wash. Our poor silver Escape needed a bath so badly. I went inside the convenience store beside the wash and asked the man what coins I needed for the wash. I pulled out a $5 Canadian bill. "It only takes toonies," he said. "It needs 2 or sometimes 3 to wash my car." He gave me back 2 toonies and a loonie for my bill. I thanked him and left.

I inserted the 2 toonies into the box and Larry went to work. I truly believe he did his best to spray me as much as he possibly could, although he wouldn't admit it. After he brushed soap all over the car, it was my turn to take over. I was halfway through the wax cycle when the machine abruptly stopped. I went back to buy another toonie, and we quickly finished the job. Since I already had a couple of loonies, we inserted them into the vacuum. At least for a moment, we have a nice, clean car.

We hunted for a place to eat supper. We reached the end of town, having seen everything, we turned around. Larry pulled into a place named Harbour Restaurant & Bar. It was waterfront, and we were seated right by the window. The view was lovely, once again.

We ordered a sampler with a pan-fried haddock fillet, broiled scallops, and shrimp. It was delicious. In fact, I told Lisette our waitress, that it was about the sweetest and flakiest piece of fish I'd ever enjoyed. The coleslaw and huge baked gold potato were great, too. The sampler price included a small dessert and my iced tea. The dessert was a type of warm apple cake with nuts, served in a delectable sauce and whipped cream. Roll me outta here!

We drove straight back to the campground with full tummies and a clean car. It was indeed another memory for the record books.

I had one DVD that I'd bought for $2 that we'd never watched. It starred Kevin Spacey, so we thought we'd enjoy it. But, most of the scenes were spoken in Chinese and had thousands of closed captions. Kevin was great, as usual, but the movie was bad. We didn't watch that for very long!

There are tent campers across from us. They've been sitting in front of their campfire most of the evening, and appear as though they're staring right over here, into the motorhome. Their fire is nice, but it's weird with them looking in this direction. It's just me, I know.

It's been another wonderful day, sunny and not too hot, not too cold. Tomorrow is another day of travel. Please let us sleep well.

Psalm 62:5

Yes, my soul, find rest in God; my hope comes from him.

JUNE 29

We had quite a storm come through last night—lots of thunder, lightning, and rain. We were up early for a travel day. It was still cloudy, but it is trying to clear up. It was 59 degrees this morning; will we ever see summer this year?

We headed out on Cabot Trail again, then drove a long way on Route 219 south, then Canada 19 and then north and west on Canada 104 and 106. This late morning must be the time of day that the lobster fishermen check their traps. As we had seen thousands of buoys out on the water, now we were watching as lobster boats crisscrossed the area. One bonus sighting we enjoyed was a large deer, standing aside the road. He decided to run across the road far enough ahead that we didn't even have to brake for him. He was beautiful. My hope is still that we see a moose in the wild before we leave this area.

Road conditions changed by the mile. Some were nice and wide with breakdown lanes, while others are barely big enough to fit 2 Mini Coopers across, much less a motorhome. Some are in great shape while others haven't seen a patch crew—much less pavers—for a long, long while.

But the scenery is amazing. What would otherwise be a majestic glide through scenic waterways, pastures, forest, and farmlands was quite literally a comedy of bumps and grunts from the motorhome. What's that, did you say?

We stopped to fill up the diesel tank. Whenever we stop, Larry checks the straps on the tow dolly. He returned to where I was pumping diesel to say the news was bad. One of the straps had loosened from the ratchet clamp and as it waved madly in the wind, finally wrapped itself completely around the axle of the dolly, right behind the braking mechanism. It was wrapped so tight, he had to ruin the strap by cutting it out. If it had locked up the mechanism, the result could have been disastrous. Good thing he checked! And, it's a good thing we carry an extra set of straps.

After a little luck at the store, we headed to a nearby Walmart. It was a small one and still didn't have most of what we needed. The pattern I see is that no one in Canada carries grab-and-go breakfasts. There are only frozen waffles, frozen pancakes, and Toaster Strudel. They don't carry much in family meals to heat and serve, either. They're not big on snacks, where Walmart at home carries an entire aisle-full as well as impulse displays down the main aisles. Yogurt selections are small; laundry items are limited, too. Everything is so different here.

Now in Western Nova Scotia, I'm seeing some cattle, a few horses, and even one vegetable garden! By afternoon, the brilliant blue sky had filled with big white and puffy clouds. A few of them just might make some rain later in the day.

Then it was time to board the ferry! The PEI (Prince Edward Island) ferry was huge. I couldn't count the cars that drove on, but there were 5 RV's and 2 semi-tractor trailers. Up on the passenger deck, it was the nicest ferry I've ever traveled on. We walked out on the deck a couple of times, and the day was beautiful. Inside, they had comfortable chairs, a small snack bar in one section and another full-service cafeteria line in the other section. The food must have been good, because there were lots of folks gobbling it down. The ride took one hour and fifteen minutes and it was certainly fair sailing. We crossed over the Northumberland Straight from Caribou, Nova Scotia to Wood Island, Prince Edward Isle.

We still had an hour and a half to go before arriving at Red Point Provincial Park on PEI, which Larry rated a 6. We traveled along PEI 315, routes 4 and 2 north, through the small harbor town of Souris. The campsites were spread far and wide on several grassy levels above the water of the North Atlantic. We looked forward to the view we would have over the next few days.

We were beat from the long day. I nuked something that wasn't worthy to write down and it was too late to start a movie. I took a shower and went to bed. Thank you, Lord for the hedge of protection that surrounded us to bring us safely here.

JUNE 30

Happy birthday to me, happy birthday to me…I turned off the alarm when it went off, happy to stay warm and cozy in my bed. It was a cloudy day, a 90% chance of rain, and the wind was buffeting against the motorhome. I was in no hurry to go anywhere. I was grateful that my iPhone was working again, having gone through yet another crazy spell last night. I thought it was a goner, for sure.

Larry scoffed when I asked him where we were going today, because it was ugly and raining outside. I told him that I didn't care, we could still ride in the car, and see the area. He said he would take me wherever I wanted to go. I didn't know if he was being sarcastic or not, but I took him up on his offer.

During our ferry ride yesterday, we had spoken to a lady with the tourist information booth. She took a PEI map and made all sorts of notes on it for us. With the map, I asked Larry to drive us northward to the East Point Lighthouse. There is a small lighthouse there, but to walk up inside, you had to pay admission. I didn't need to go up that badly. They did have a delightful gift shop that offered lots of area crafts for sale. There was also a café, but we didn't go in there.

Standing outside on the point, the wind was gusting, and I couldn't tell whether it was spitting rain, or blowing mist from the sea. We didn't stay there long, but we witnessed a fascinating thing: the point where the tide hitting the eastern side of the island and the tide hitting the western side of the island meet. The tide on the eastern side was full of white caps from the winds; the tide coming in on the western side was flat and unruffled. The phenomena of the 2 oceans meeting was very interesting.

> Genesis 1:6
> And God said, "Let there be a vault between the waters
> to separate water from water."

We left the lighthouse and I directed him down the eastern side of the island on route 16 through North Lake, the tuna capital of PEI, then on through Fairfield and Campbells Cove. At Priest Pond, we took route 302 southeastward to finish the circle back to Red Point, where we started.

Then we headed to Souris, which the locals pronounced Soo-ree. I had gotten directions to the Artisans on Main, who was said to have sea glass jewelry for sale.

Larry filled up on gas first, then we stopped at the Evergreen Café for lunch, just because of its location, which was directly across the street from the Artisans.

The Café was a tiny little place, mostly selling herbal teas and wraps. We sat down at a table with our menus, and Larry went straight to his iPhone. After much consideration, I decided that I had a hankering for some eggs. I ordered a Breakfast Wrap, which included 3 scrambled eggs, bacon, cheese, and any veges I wanted. Our waiter was new at this order-taking stuff, I could tell. I decided to add bean sprouts and green peppers. I ordered Larry a cup of corn chowder.

The wrap was large and cut in half when it arrived. He took one bite and decided he didn't like it at all. He must not have been in the mood for eggs, because I thought it was delicious, and I ate every single bite. The chowder wasn't as creamy as I'm used to seeing, but it was very good. We ordered a choco-peanut-butter cookie for dessert. I just love to taste and discover new foods of the areas we visit. The culture of the locals comes out in the foods they enjoy.

> Genesis 1:29
> Then God said, "I give you every seed-bearing plant
> on the face of the whole earth and every tree that has fruit
> with seed in it. They will be yours for food.

When I had asked the info woman at the lighthouse about sea glass jewelry, she proudly showed me her earrings, then told me they were designed by an artist by the name of Teri Hall.

We walked across the street to the artisans. When I asked the greeter where I might find sea glass jewelry, she pointed to the glass case. Much to my delight, she also pointed out the woman aside the counter, Lisa Freeman, who was also a sea glass jewelry designer. She was a pleasant woman, and never for a moment did she try to encourage me to purchase her work instead of Teri Hall's.

But because of her presence, I DID want to purchase a piece of hers. Each set of drop earrings she had on display was unique and beautiful—it was so hard to choose! I finally decided on buying a pair that contained some rare cobalt blue sea glass. They will probably become a gift to my lovely daughter.

Then, just for fun, I asked Larry to take me to the dollar store, at the opposite end of the block. Nothing of huge interest there, but it was fun to see the different things they offer for sale up here.

Back at the motorhome, it continued to lightly spit rain. I wrote a bit, but then told Larry I was going to snuggle up in a warm cover my friend Sue had given me and rest, just because I could. Right as I covered up, my iPhone rang. It was my best buddy Deb, who always, without fail, calls me on my special day to sing Happy Birthday to me. This year, she encouraged her small grandson, Hank to sing along. It was precious. She passed him the phone when they were finished singing, so I could talk to him, but oh no, not me, too shy to talk. That's okay. I sure loved him singing along. Friends from far and away bring me so much joy.

I did have a nice rest and eventually went back to writing. Larry grilled a large burger for us to share and I fixed a fresh cucumber-tomato salad with Paula Dean's Vidalia Onion Poppyseed Dressing. My daughter works in the gift shop of the new Paula Dean's restaurant in Myrtle Beach, SC. This stuff is yummy!

We had picked up some more DVD's at Walmart, so tonight we watched *Wyatt Earp*, starring Kevin Costner. There were at least a dozen actors who weren't too famous then, but sure are famous now. It was a long movie and well worth the $5 we paid for it.

My sister-in-law Sherri called late, and everyone there at her house sang to me. Back in the days when all 5 of her kids were small, it was quite a production and hilarious to hear them trying to out-scream each other. Now everyone's an adult. It's still a lot of fun. We talked for a while and I hadn't realized until then that we'd be meeting up with them in only 5 weeks, in early August.

Back in March, when we were together when Mom was sick, they mentioned that they were planning a family trip to Mackinac, on the Upper Peninsula of Michigan. We said we were scheduled to come down through that area in August. She gave us the exact dates of their reservations and we will meet up with them then. Some of our nieces and nephews will be there, too. I can't wait to see them all.

Friends sent me over 100 birthday wishes through Facebook today. Sitting there, in the dark quiet, I praised God for all the places we've lived, all the jobs I've worked, all the church to which I've belonged, and all the friends I've made.

God is always good.

> 1 Samuel 20:42
> Jonathan said to David, "Go in peace,
> for we have sworn friendship with each other
> in the name of the LORD, saying,
> 'The LORD is witness between you and me,
> and between your descendants and my descendants forever.'"

JULY 1

Happy Canada Day! During our journey through Canada, we have seen thousands of bright white and red maple leaf Canada Flags. I remember well the crowded streets of Vancouver when we happened upon their 149th birthday last year.

I'm grateful that we're way out in the country, away from any large metropolis in mainland Canada. It was overcast all day, despite the sun's attempts to shine through the clouds.

It was a hard-work day here at the Hammond home. I know it's small, but it really needed a good twice-over. Every time we've opened the windows somewhere (which has been often), dust comes in to settle on everything. You can't dust everything every day, so it does accumulate. Larry was never taught to wipe his feet when coming in from outside. Considering all the days lately that it's rained, it was easy to track in every little thing. Larry scoffs off my scolding and says, "It's a guy thing."

The tedious nook-and-cranny cleaning was long overdue.

I didn't get to sit down to write until nearly supper time, and it sure felt good to sit. But it's done; until we open the windows again.

I grilled a ribeye steak for supper tonight and nuked some mashed potatoes. Meat and potatoes—simple and delicious.

I had been hoping to get some photographs today, but it was just too dismal. I have described constantly the masses of purple flowers along the highways—the Lupines. The entrance to this campground is loaded with them. She went on to say that last summer there weren't many at all, but this year—wow! There were so many here, and I wouldn't have to wander off the main road to get some great close-up pics. There are purples, in several different shades, a couple of shades of pinks, and cream-colored ones. Perhaps the sun will shine in the morning, before we must leave.

Isaiah 40:8

The grass withers and the flowers fall,

but the word of our God endures forever.

We watched another DVD this evening, *Jack Ryan, Shadow Recruit*. Chris Pine, Kevin Costner, and Keira Knightley. Lots of action. Kevin's gotten older (he's 6 months younger than me), but he's still great.

It's staying so light so late, that I wonder what time the Canada Day fireworks down in Souris will be? We're an hour ahead of EDT, and at 9pm, as I wrote this, it's way too light for fireworks. I'll be in bed by the time it gets dark. We probably can't see them anyway.

JULY 2

Well, my hopes of getting pics of the Lupines has drowned. Literally. It was pouring down rain when the alarm went off this morning. When I checked Weather Underground radar, it looked as though someone had painted the screen in green. Rain, rain, and more rain. We both got dressed and was ready to go. It stopped raining just long enough for Larry to disconnect the utilities without getting drenched. Thank you for that kindness, Lord.

> Leviticus 26:4
>
> I will send you rain in its season, and the ground will yield its crops and the trees their fruit

A good part of the trip was spent on Highway 2, the Veterans Highway. Some parts of the road were crummy, and some looked brand new. As we passed through Souris, I couldn't help but notice how many of the businesses were closed on this Sunday morning. Would they be closed all day, or just open late. After being in retail for nearly 2 decades, I think that's great to close down during church hours. Our leases always prohibited that—non-negotiable.

As the rain continued sporadically, I mentioned to Larry that I'd bet the farmers are happy with this rain. I wondered in Nova Scotia where all the farms were? I now know that they're all over Prince Edward Island! Picture rolling hills, fields laid out like a patchwork quilt, with small bands of trees defining their boundaries. The dirt here is redder than that of southern Georgia. Potatoes are their primary crop, although there are others, all planted in perfect rows. Consider this their spring planting, and the plants are young. A day-long gentle rain is just what the farmers ordered.

I did notice in the grain fields that there were signs of recent wind damage, as the stalks were bent over in places. I hope tomorrow's sunshine will perk them right back up again.

We continued on Highway 13, until we got close to the campground. It was rougher and skinnier than any of Route 2 had been. In addition to the crop fields, we saw lots of fields filled with grazing cattle. We passed one pen full of horses and I saw the cutest thing. One horse seemed to be trying to "kiss" another horse, but that horse would not have it. The second horse raised his entire neck and head to push the first horse away. The first horse went back in for another try, to the same response. By then, they were out of sight. I hope (s)he eventually got their kiss.

The Lupines in this area seem to be past their prime. They're faded and I'm so disappointed that I didn't get my pictures back at the campground. Perhaps our travels along the coast tomorrow will present some in their prime.

We finally arrived at Prince Edward Island National Park in Cavendish, PEI, Canada, which Larry rated a 6. The roads and sites are crushed rock, which have been cut into the forest, with as much of the lush trees and undergrowth left in place. As a result, the sites are very private and quiet. But, Oh My Lord, the mosquitos! There were swarms of them outside. I know this is to be expected when you are camping but not this many. We became their meal ticket!

Deuteronomy 14:19

All flying insects are unclean to you; do not eat them.

Once we were set up, we drove to the Cavendish Beach at the campground. I quickly found a beautiful piece of bright green sea glass, as well as some blue mussel shells. I've never seen a shell such bright blue—it was pearlescent and nearly purple. Then Larry drove to the public park, down the road on the same beach. The sand is loose and difficult to walk in, until you get down to the water.

As good as my back has been lately, I was so disappointed when it chose that very moment to scream loudly with pain. I wanted to discover some more sea glass and shells, but these weren't scattered across the sand, they were heaped in piles, along with rocks. I just couldn't do it, and I asked Larry to take me back to the car.

We went for a long car ride that didn't require any walking. We traveled several rural routes and wound up down on Route 2. We followed it back to Hunter Grove, then headed up Route 13 to New Glasgow. It was an afternoon filled with beautiful scenery of beautiful, fertile farmland.

Larry had decided from the information he'd read about PEI said one absolutely MUST go to New Glasgow Lobster Supper, so we did. We arrived at 3:30 to learn that they didn't open until 4pm. By then, there were lots of folks in line. Their menu was short and to the point. You paid for your choice of entrée as you entered. We thought it a bit pricey, so it had better be good. They were kind in hearing about Larry's surgery and allowed him to eat off one plate, with no extra charge. Thank you, Lord for that favor.

Our sweet waitress greeted us with a basket of yeast rolls and a warm slice of wheat bread. I already liked her. Since we had never been there before, she explained how supper works here. It was a 5-course meal, and you can reorder as much of any course you wish, except your main seafood course. All inclusive, with a beverage.

The first course would be mussels. "Do you like mussels?" she asked. Yes. Would you like a plate of them, or—she pointed to a gallon container on the table for discarded shells—a half bucket or full bucket? "You can always order more." Wow.

When the plate of mussels was done, she brought a cup of seafood chowder, along with a plate that contained a tossed salad, potato salad, and coleslaw. Then our lobster arrived, all 2 pounds of him. God bless them, the crustacean was already precut in every important place, so he was so easy to eat. No cracking was required on our part. But those black eyes were staring at us.

Just like with our crayfish dining so long ago, neither one of us was brave enough to eat that nasty-looking green stuff inside the main body and behind the beady eyes. I'll stick to the white meat, thank you very much.

When she returned to clean off the table, she had the audacity to offer us a selection from 6 different types of house-made pie as well as 4 different cakes for dessert. I chose the blueberry pie they'd made today from scratch.

Larry enjoyed Diet Coke and I had sweet tea to wash everything down. We were both stuffed. How could one person have eaten all that? No way.

We stopped at the campground beach to try to look for shells, as it was closer to low tide. I wore my back brace this time, and felt much better. I did find another piece of sea glass; this one was brown and bigger than a silver dollar.

On the ride back to the rig, we kept noticing long pieces of wood in the bodies of inland water. They were perfectly spaced apart—not random at all. We learned later that those were mussel beds, where mussels grow to maturity. We were amazed to learn that PEI raises 90% of all mussels in Canada—over 50 million pounds annually! Check out peimussel.com to learn more about these nutritious little critters.

When we returned to the motorhome, we moved quickly, trying our best to dodge the thousands of little bugs swarming around us. We assumed they were mosquitoes, and we weren't letting them land on us to find out. We got the bug zapper down from a closet for the first time on this trip, just in case any of the little buggers managed to get inside.

We watched *Cloud Atlas* with Tom Hanks and Halle Berry. It is a strange movie indeed, with each star performing as different characters in about 5 different eras. Very confusing, but Tom was great, as always.

JULY 3

We'd driven much of the area yesterday, but there was one particular place we wanted to see today: Green Gables. It seems everyone in my world has read the book, *Anne of Green Gables*, or at least seen the video—except me. Our daughter, Diana insisted we visit this place, because it was on her bucket list. We went as instructed, and we were not disappointed.

We drove to "Green Gables Heritage Place, part of L. M. Montgomery's Cavendish National Historic Site of Canada," which commemorates L. M. Montgomery as a person of national historic significance. Her full name was Lucy Maud Montgomery, who lived from 1874 to 1942. She published her infamous book in 1908, then went on to write many more, both fiction and non-fiction.

Per the park brochure, "In real life, this farm was the home of David, Jr. and his sister Margaret, cousins of Montgomery's grandfather. Although Montgomery never lived at Green Gables, she came to know her cousin's farm through her explorations of the surrounding woodlands. The special places she discovered and named such as the Haunted Wood and Lover's Lane still exist at Green Gables."

The 2-story house is painted white with dark green shutters. The inside has been decorated per descriptions Montgomery gave in her writings. Each wall is papered in bold and colorful prints, each room with a different personality. Even the stairway and the ceiling of the stairway to the upstairs was papered. The rooms were small and cozy, probably easier to heat in the colder months. It was beautifully furnished and would have been a wonderful place to live.

"Anne" was there in her red pig tails as well as her friend for the tourists to take pictures with her. All dressed up in period era clothes, the little girls as well as grownups were busy taking photos with "Anne".

We walked the trail loop down Lover's Lane. It was a worn dirt path through a wooded area of the farm. There was just enough break in the clouds and trees to allow the sun to shine through in places. There was a small brook that snaked through the woods, making cheerful trickling sounds as we passed by. There were wild ferns and wildflowers everywhere. There was an old milk bottle tied to a rope, bobbling in the stream, with a placard which explained that Anne would have kept her lunch milk cold in the same way.

What a wonderful place this must have been for a young woman to get lost in her own thoughts. There was another trail that headed out from the front flower garden, but we didn't go there. The flower beds were expertly planted in rainbows of colors. We walked through the barn, and finally the gift shop.

By the time we left, we were hungry and drove to the Lost Anchor Pub for lunch. It was in a newish strip center with several other businesses, just up the road from Green Gables. We took a table inside and ordered a lobster roll with onion rings. Yes, more lobster! The folks at the next table had ordered lemonades, so we ordered them, too. They were served in Mason jars, refreshingly tart, and were made with some type of lemon-lime soda. It bubbled.

They were packed with diners inside, outside, and up on the deck. The food was taking some time to arrive, and Larry had his face in his iPhone. I took my wallet and went to explore the other stores.

The first one was a T-shirt shop and I skipped that one. The PEI Dirt Shirt Store was interesting, and their work room was a mess, with red dirt everywhere. Check out PEIDirtShirt.org.

Then I followed my nose into the great-smelling Great Canadian Soap Company. Their flier claims they're "Canada's largest handmade goat milk soap producer!" This shop was small and seasonal, and the young lady was pleasant. I gave her a card and told her about our ministry. I was the only person in the shop at that time and she answered all my questions well. I purchased a bar of mango & Papaya Soap, a small travel bar, and an applicator with Healing Butter in it, with Lavender and Tea Tree essential oils.

I returned to Larry already diving into our lunch, but it didn't take long for me to catch up. It was yet the largest lobster roll we'd enjoyed. Our waiter's name was James and whether he was serving us or running upstairs to deliver food to the deck diners, a smile never left his face. Great job, James.

We returned to a cool motorhome and I began to write. Tomorrow is yet another travel day, so I knew I had to get this stuff caught up today. I nuked a Shepherd's Pie for supper. And we love shepherd's pie.

The last time we purchased some DVD's, I showed Larry a copy of *The Outsiders*. I told him that I'd never seen it. Francis Ford Coppola directed the movie that was released in 1983, starring 7 young men who would eventually become some of the biggest names in Hollywood: Patrick Swayze, Tom Cruise, Ralph Macchio, Emelio Estevez, C. Thomas Howell, Matt Dillon, and Rob Lowe, even Leif Garrett and Diane Lane. It was a film about the haves and the have nots, and it was fascinating to watch these guys before their prime.

Rain came late, but we were tucked into bed by then. It had been yet another wonderful day.

JULY 4

As the date above states, today is the Fourth of July. America's Independence Day. Back when we were in business in Myrtle Beach, this would have been our largest sales date all year. You prayed for the cash to come for the bills, but then you prayed harder to have the strength to live through it.

The day did not begin well. Larry spotted something on our online banking that got him really upset, and it gnawed at him while he drove. At every break in driving, he was back emailing a company to find out what was going on.

We headed out on Route 6, then Route 8. We traveled mile after mile of gently rolling hills. There were lots of farmers working in their fields, but the only crop I recognized were potatoes and corn, both in their early stages. There was a lot of work going on in the hay fields, some were cutting while others were baling.

On the road, we approached a monstrosity of a farm machine. As it sped past, Larry asked, "What in the world was that?" I laughed and told him that was my exact response when I saw my first John Deere High Boy. I was riding in a car with Deb and as it came over the crest of a hill, I said it looked like a UFO. She had loudly laughed at me, too.

We drove on Route 109, then a dozen different roads, 3 miles on this one, 2 miles on the next one. We finally funneled onto the TCH right before the bridge.

"The Confederation Bridge joins the eastern Canadian provinces of Prince Edward Island and New Brunswick, making travel throughout the Maritimes easy and convenient. The curved, 12.9 kilometer (8 mile) long bridge is the longest in the world crossing ice-covered water, and continues to endure as one of Canada's top engineering achievements of the 20th century."[38] Larry kept his eyes on the road while I scanned the water for whales among the whitecaps.

I've seen plenty of seagulls. The gulls back home are solid white, with a tinge of grey. Earlier this week, I saw gulls that I would call brown. Now these are different yet, white with black wing tips.

We were back in New Brunswick, far away from the point that we'd crossed into New Brunswick originally. We took Route 955 west. It was a terrible road, but we had no choice but to travel 16 rough and tumble miles on it.

We were finally back to Route 15, and we praised the Lord that it was nicely paved. Mostly. Then we got back on the Trans-Canada Highway, Route 2, heading Northwest.

We stopped at Irving in Frederiction for diesel. What a story! We inserted our credit card, and it grumbled a few things back at us. We lifted the handle and it was authorized to dispense. We filled the tank to the top. We were going to eat at the restaurant inside. I told Larry I'd go order while he parked the rig.

Well, the line to get in to eat was much too long, and the inside much too packed. It was, after all, the noon hour. I met him in the store to suggest we just get a wrapped sandwich and get back on the road, when an employee came up to him and asked, "Is that your motorhome?" Larry replied that it was, and the man said, "Oh, good. You're still here." He turned and walked away.

We went to the register to pay for the sandwiches and they were talking about us—they're the folks with the motorhome—and one said that so-and-so is still outside looking for them. Tell him to come back in. What was this all about?

---

[38] confederationbridge.com/about/confederation-bridge.html

After some more discussion, it became apparent that the card had not been charged for the diesel. We expressed our confusion, explaining that we had inserted the card and the fuel was dispensed. It was at that moment that we learned that Canada is not prepay. The pumps dispense for everyone. Our card had not been charged.

We were so embarrassed. We knew without a doubt that we had paid and would have never given it a second thought. We apologized repeatedly, and they were very nice about it. They had seen the signs for Motorhome Ministry. I told Larry if we hadn't gone in to buy sandwiches, and just driven off, I'll bet they would have called the Canadian Mounties on us, for sure. How embarrassing that would have been. Headlines: "Ministry arrested in Canada!"

Mark 13:11

Whenever you are arrested and brought to trial,

do not worry beforehand about what to say.

Just say whatever is given you at the time,

for it is not you speaking, but the Holy Spirit

It was 4pm by the time we entered Quebec. It had already been a very long day. We were grateful to gain back the hour we lost a while ago. All through New Brunswick, Nova Scotia, and Prince Edward Island the signs had been bilingual, French and English. Not here. All in French only. Well, Lord be with us.

It wasn't long before we saw a sign that designated an exit for "Saint-Louis-du-Ha! Ha!" I quickly Googled that one, to find out that it's the only town in the world with 2 exclamation points in its name. Go figure. You know this is true; I just can't make this stuff up.

The sky stayed blue, with big white, puffy clouds forming as the afternoon progressed. We rolled into a Walmart in Riviere-du-Loup, Quebec. There had been friendly reviews on Allstays and they were spot on. When we arrived, there were already more than a dozen

RV's parked in the outer parts of the lot. We went in with our shopping list. Canada frozen breakfasts are still limited to waffles, pancakes, and Toaster Strudel, but we did pretty well on the rest of the list. We bought lots of meat on sale for Diana's upcoming visit, so we will probably grill out each evening. And, we forgot to bring in the shopping bags again, and they charge you a nickel apiece. No, thanks. We'll just take it loose in the cart.

It was at that store we first discovered "milk bags." If you wanted to purchase a small amount of milk, they had cardboard cartons like we have in the US. But, if you wanted more—4 liters are close to a gallon—you had to buy a milk bag, which contained 2 clear plastic bags of milk, tucked into a larger clear plastic bag. No plastic milk jugs in this place!

I fixed BLT's for supper and they really hit the spot. Then God blessed us with a beautiful sunset. As we settled in to boondoggle for the evening, more and more campers arrived, there were probably close to 50 by the time we went to bed. Some folks were sitting in chairs outside, greeting other campers. It looked like an RV show.

I learned from Facebook that a sweet friend of mine, Jacqueline--wife and mother of 3 precious children—had been bitten by a copperhead and was suffering terribly from its effects. I prayed for quick healing and less pain. Poor thing. I will continue to pray.

Jeremiah 33:6
Nevertheless, I will bring health and healing to it; I will heal my people and will let them enjoy abundant peace and security.

Larry went to bed earlier than normal; all that driving had worn him out. When the Walmart closed at 9pm, it became blissfully quiet. The RV City at Walmart slept well.

UH, JUST A FEW MORE THINGS...

Once again, I hope you've enjoyed reading my book. It has been a most amazing wild ride!

Although I don't include specifics on a daily basis, we have distributed hundreds of ministry packets for kids. We've given hundreds of cards and brochures about Motorhome Ministry to everyone who has served us in public. We've touched hundreds with *His Road Trip* and *His Road Trip 2*. We post our whereabouts on numerous Facebook Feeds and Larry tweets a lot. I don't tweet at all. I do a lot of things, but tweeting isn't one of them.

His Road Trip 4 will be yet another chock-full-of-nuts edition. We continue our adventures in Canada, with another sticky map on the side of the motorhome. The antics of Frick, Frack, Frankie, and Alice are all greatly detailed. And one day, Lois joined us on a day of great navigational need.

Diana spends another week of vacation with us, and we experience lots of interesting things. We have problems with potatoes and the Border Patrol and explore Niagara Falls as a family.

After her departure, we drive on to spend some time with friends in Ontario. We meet up with family in Mackinac and biked around the entire island. Nearly killed me! Did you know it's pronounced Mack-in-aw? For real!

We learn about pasties (they're not what you think), Chicago Pizza, and purchase delicious goods from a bakery of monks.

We visit lots of Provincial and National Parks and witnessed an errant helicopter landing really too close. We did lots more boondoggling and witnessed the eclipse. We were restricted to only a half-gig of internet each day, which nearly killed my poor husband.

Have you ever encountered a "bug storm?" We have, and all the amazing details are in the book. We spent a day at the Mall of American and visited factories and watched as luxurious motorhomes were being built.

We had several bouts of complicated mechanical difficulties and were busted by store management while doing an EasyShift evaluation. That was interesting!

Larry's Trump hat still gets a lot of attention, as he wears it everywhere. We were amazed by the Creation Museum and The Ark, then and traveled to Gatlinburg, Tennessee to see the aftermath of the tragic fire that burned thousands of acres in late 2016.

As I said in every book, my greatest hope is that, despite my humanness, you have been able to see Christ in me, well, Christ in both of us. And, my prayer is that you desire a personal relationship with Him yourself.

Some folks have the misconception that Christians think they're better other people. We are most definitely not. We are sinners, just like you, but stand strong in the security that we have been forgiven by the Grace of God.

We have confessed our sins, asked that God would forgive us, and have become new creatures in Christ. It's really very simple. You can become a new creature, too.

Romans 10:9-10
If you declare with your mouth, "Jesus is Lord,"
and believe in your heart that God
raised him from the dead,
YOU WILL BE SAVED.
[10] For it is with your heart that you believe
and are justified,
and it is with your mouth that you profess
your faith and are saved.

Billy Graham Ministries' website explains that, "Jesus Christ says that we must be born again. How do we become born again? By repenting of sin. That means we are willing to change our way of living. We say to God, "I'm a sinner, and I'm sorry." It's simple and childlike. Then, by faith we receive Jesus Christ as our Lord and Savior. We are willing to follow Him in a new life of obedience, in which the Holy Spirit helps us as we read the Bible and pray and witness."[39]

John 3:5-7
Jesus answered, "Very truly I tell you,
no one can enter the kingdom of God
unless they are born of water and the Spirit.
[6]Flesh gives birth to flesh, but the Spirit gives birth to spirit
[7]You should not be surprised at my saying,
'YOU MUST BE BORN AGAIN.'

---

2 Peter 3:9
The Lord is not slow in keeping his promise,
as some understand slowness.
Instead he is patient with you, not wanting anyone to perish,
but everyone to come to repentance.

I personally believe that, "Those who leave everything in God's hand will eventually see God's hand in everything." I see God's hand in everything, every day. I hope you can understand why, after reading my words of faith.

May God bless you richly.

---

[39] billygraham.org

By the will of God, the adventure will continue.

On to book 4!

MORE OF MY FAVORITE RECIPES

RECIPE FOR CROCK POT HAWAIIAN CHICKEN

SHOPPING LIST:

2-4 boneless chicken breasts

1 large can crushed pineapple

1 cup BBQ sauce

Mix together pineapple and BBQ sauce in a bowl

Lay chicken in bottom of Crock Pot

Cover chicken with pineapple mixture

Cook on low 5-6 hours

Eat as cooked, or throw on the grill for a little crispy!

RECIPE FOR EASY CROCK POT POTATO SOUP

SHOPPING LIST and some prep work:

32 oz bag	Ore Ida Frozen Shredded Hash Browns
32 box	chicken broth
10 oz can	condensed cream of chicken soup
8 oz pkg	Philadelphia Cream Cheese
1 ½ cups	shredded sharp cheddar
¾ cup	bacon, crumbled
½ tsp fresh	rosemary, minced (I left this out)
	salt & pepper to taste

Combine all ingredients except rosemary in a 6-quart Crock Pot.

Cook on HIGH 3 hours.
Garnish with rosemary, if desired.
Soup thickens as it cools; enjoy with your favorite crackers.

I cut this recipe in half and managed to get it in my mini Crock Pot.

I've also just cooked this on the stove—it cooks up quickly.

RECIPE FOR SWEET POTATOES AND APPLES

This is another delicious recipe from my best buddy, Deb. She had some sweet potatoes left in her garden when we went to visit, and she whipped this up for supper one night. Larry liked it, and he doesn't even like sweet tators!

SHOPPING LIST and some prep work:

3-4	medium sweet potatoes, cut into 2" cubes
3-4	apples, cored and cubed—do NOT peel. For best flavor, mix Red Delicious, Braeburn, and Golden Delicious.
12 oz	Orange Juice OR substitute a 12oz can of apricot nectar. It was delish!
2 TBSP	butter
2-3 TBSP	brown sugar
Dash	ground cinnamon

Heat a 12" skillet.

Add butter, sweet potatoes and apples.

Add brown sugar, dash of cinnamon, and juice.

Cover and low simmer until apples and tators can be easily pricked with a fork. BE SURE NOT TO OVERCOOK! The juice should reduce and make a tasty sauce for the fruit and veges. Enjoy!

RECIPE FOR WILD PLUM TEA

I purchased this recipe printed on a nice gift card back in 1994, after enjoying lunch at the Wild Plum Tea Room. We lived in Gatlinburg, Tennessee at the time, and the Great Smoky Arts and Crafts Community has an amazing driving trail full of unique crafters. The Tea Room sits among those crafters and offers unique and delicious eats, far from the city. You're served mini plum muffins with plum jelly on exquisite china. Your meal--remarkable

If you're ever in the area, be sure to go. Check out www.wildplumtearoom.com for pics and all the amazing details.

SHOPPING LIST and some prep work:

4 family-size tea bags

2 quarts water

2 cups sugar

2 cups orange juice

½ cup lemon juice

Cold water

In a one-gallon pitcher, steep tea bags in 1 quart of hot water.

Mix the remaining quart of water and sugar, heat over high heat until sugar is dissolved.

Pour over tea and water in pitcher. Steep 15 minutes.

Strain out tea bags, add orange juice and lemon juice and enough water to make one gallon.

Serve cold and over ice OR if you prefer, serve hot.

RECIPE FOR GOOD OLE' CHICKEN BOG

According to discoversouthcarolina.com, "Chicken bog is a delicious chicken, rice and sausage dish, and it's very much a South Carolina thing…Specifically, chicken bog is most popular in Horry County, the home of Myrtle Beach and Conway, and west to Florence…

"The name 'bog' probably comes from the wetness of the dish, although some speculate that it may come from the bogginess of the area where it is popular.

"While there are recipes around that include green peppers and other vegetables, purists insist that the only ingredients should be chicken, smoked sausage, rice, salt and pepper and perhaps onion."

I love this "purist" handwritten recipe I received from my friend, Bootsie, when we first moved to Myrtle Beach.

SHOPPING LIST and some prep work:

1 fryer cooked and deboned (save broth)**
1-pound package of Hillshire Smoked Pork Sausage (I fix mine with Kielbasa—I am from the North, after all)
1 box Uncle Ben's Original Wild Rice (4 cups in 14oz box needs 8 cups water and/or broth)

**If you need this quickly, substitute canned chicken and boxed broth.

Cut up the chicken and sausage into bite-sized pieces and set aside. In a large pot, bring chicken broth to a boil. Add rice, chicken, and sausage. Cover and cook on low until done. Salt and pepper to taste.

You can really play around with this basic recipe, adding onion or lots of other things. Check online for more ideas. Top with your favorite hot sauce, if you want to spice it up. It saved me from catastrophe one Christmas when family showed up unannounced!

RECIPE FOR PASTA FAGIOLI

JUST AS DELICIOUS AS THE OLIVE GARDEN'S

SHOPPING LIST and some prep work:

2 pounds ground beef

1 onion, chopped

3 carrots, chopped

4 stalks celery, chopped

2 28-oz cans diced tomatoes, do not drain

1 16-oz can white kidney beans, drained

3 10-oz cans beef stock

3 tsp oregano

2 tsp pepper

5 tsp parsley

1 tsp Tabasco sauce (optional)

1 20-oz jar spaghetti sauce

8 ounces dried pasta

Brown beef in a skillet, drain fat off and discard.

In a Crock Pot, combine all ingredients **except pasta**.

Cook on high 4-5 hours, or cook on low for 7-8 hours.

Add pasta 30 minutes before you're ready to serve.

Add a nice crisp salad and some hot cheesy bread for a perfect meal.

A REALLY GREAT SOUP THAT I MADE UP!

Dump all the following in a large kettle. **Each time** you dump in the contents of a can, fill that can with water and put it in the pot, too.

  1 large baker potato, diced into small pieces

  1   2-pound can diced tomatoes

  1-pound can stewed tomatoes

  2 stalks celery, split and sliced

  1/2 large onion, halved and sliced thin

  1 small can of lima beans, drained and rinsed

  1 cup barley

  6 cups of shredded cabbage (I bought a bag of cole slaw

      cabbage at the store

  1 pound can of corn, drained

  1 cup of Minute Rice

  1 pound can French-style green beans SEASONED

      w/peppers & onions

  1   2-pound can of VegAl for Stew

  1 TBSP salt

  1 TBSP Mrs. Dash original blend.)

Cook on medium-high heat until vegetables are tender.

BACK OF THE BOOK STUFF

Republished from the original His Road Trip

and we added a few more ...

Some folks wonder how we can possibly live full-time in about 350 square feet?

We downsized from a 2,300 square-foot home with a huge kitchen, 3 bathrooms and a 2-car garage for storage, so YES, there were some adjustments to be made! We had yard sales for three weekends running, sold all our furniture, and brokered our antiques. I gave dozens of books to a senior living facility and some to our county library. Some precious memories could not be parted with, and could not accompany us, so they did go into storage for a time.

During the yard sales, a woman introduced herself as a worker from a local Habitat for Humanity store. Not only would they pick up furniture, she said the local store would pick up anything and everything we had left over, as long as it was all in boxes, and easy to load. When we had packed, sold, donated, and brokered everything that we could, I gave her a call. It was a tremendous service to me.

Now on the road, there are times, I must admit, that I just have to get out by myself for a while. I usually feign a need for something and take the car and Frack out on a drive to Walmart, Dollar General, or whatever's available in the area. I feel much better when I get back.

And even though Larry nibbles in little bits all day, he has finally come to understand that I like to eat out, especially to sample unique area cuisine. If I've been inside for days—because of writing, weather, or whatever—much he's better now at suggesting that we go out to shop, eat, or go to a movie.

But get used to the idea that there are going to be times that both of you want to be in exactly the same place at the exactly the same time...usually the bathroom! Just be considerate of who's whining the loudest.

Some folks wonder if we could give them some pointers?

Larry would say that planning is of the utmost importance, especially if you travel when school is out of session. At those times, you can't just roll in somewhere and expect there to be vacancy. Plan your route well, because at 8 miles to the gallon, you sure don't want to backtrack!

Larry's really great at drilling in and planning, and had all of our National Park reservations in advance of our departure, most of our State Parks, and a great deal of our private parks, as well. He put in a lot of time, while I was recovering, searching the routes, computing travel times, comparing rates and ratings of campgrounds. He had searched areas to see what attractions were there. The out-of-season weather has been our biggest surprise, but you can't control Mother Nature!

Some folks wonder if there are any apps out there, to help them on the way?

Larry's phone is chuck full of helpful apps!

#1 App! ALLSTAYS is an app that every person with an RV should have. You can search campgrounds and read personal reviews, find Walmarts who allow boondoggling with reviews, truck stops, rest stops, propane, dump stations, height clearances along a route, rig maintenance and repair. Their reviews have helped us avoid poor choices on the road. We use this the most in our travels. Plus, it maps it all out for you.

GOOD SAM has an app that is good for checking campgrounds near you and if they are a member with a discount as well their rating of the campground.

ULTIMATE CG app shows where there is free camping allowed on public lands. This is how we had the opportunity to stay at White Sands.

CHIMANI is an app that gives you great information on all National Parks, national monuments, historic sites, memorials, recreational areas and more.

TRIPOSO is an app that gives you everything you need to know about the places and cities you plan to visit.

GAS BUDDY is an app for finding the cheapest fuel on your route. Members are constantly updating prices, and a recently reported drop of even a few cents on diesel can save you lots of cash on 100 gallons. TIP: if you can, always fill up away from the interstate. We have seen interstate truck plazas charge up to forty cents more than a small-town guy just off the interstate, less than a mile away. Gas Buddy will help you find those deals. But also, Google it, to be sure their lot has room for your big rig.

MY MEDICAL is an app for keeping your medical records with you, wherever you go, whether you're traveling away from home, or not.

WUNDERGROUND is an app from Weather Underground that will show you live weather from every weather station out there. When you open it, it automatically homes in on exactly where you are and what weather forecast, live radar, and any weather alerts that are active at that time. Priceless!

GOOGLE MAPS (aka Frack) is an app that everybody should have for everyday use. Frack is pretty great on the long haul, but sometimes needs some human interpretation. It also has no idea that you're a high-profile vehicle with another vehicle in tow, so it may take you somewhere you really shouldn't be.

SYGIC TRUCKERS GPS (aka Frankie) is what we primarily depend upon. You begin by telling the program how long you are, what height you are, and what load you are, so it keeps you away from places you shouldn't be. One important talent loudly warns you of exceeding speed limits, upcoming rest areas, and railroad crossings.

RVingVIP is a maintenance app, a desktop program to keep track of all the maintenance issues of your RV.

DISHALIGN and **DishForMyRv** are invaluable tools to assist you in manually setting your dish antenna to satellite feeds.

TOLL CALCULATOR GPS helps you determine which route costs less when traveling on toll roads with a large motorhome and a "toad" (tow vehicle). This could save you hundreds of dollars, if you plan to be in areas with multiple toll roads. Personal No-Brainer: Avoid the George Washington Bridge into NY or it will cost you BIG time!

TOLLSMART is another toll calculator app.

Find a good **LEVELING TOOL**. Every single time we pull into a new campground, we need to level. There are lots of apps out there that can assist you with this. I recently discovered that my Compass app on my iPhone has a second screen, a level. It is, by far, the easiest to use to date, and now my favorite.

BANK AND INVESTMENT apps are very important. One thing we learned years ago, the hard way. When you leave on a trip, your debit card company wants you to call ahead of time. We had lived in South Carolina for so long that, one year when we went home to Cincinnati and used our debit card, the bank declined it. They continued to decline it until I called in and asked what was going on? Their security assumed that my card has been stolen, because it was being used in an area that I never frequented—it went against my spending pattern. They made a note of where I was and for how long, and the problem was solved. Now I'm sure to notify them before I go anywhere out-of-state, to avoid surprises.

Some folks wonder what to do with their mail?

If you're a member of Good Sam, they offer forwarding services. They assign you an address that you give out, they collect your mail until you ask them to forward it to you. We personally, have a PO Box back home. Diana picks up everything, opens anything unusual and screen shots us copies, in case it's something urgent.

Some folks wonder about using their computers on the road?

This has been our biggest challenge and for a while, our largest expense. We initially chose Verizon for our cellular service because they had the best coverage across America. The Verizon Jet Pack is mobile and works wherever our Verizon cell service works. AND, they recently changed to Unlimited Service. This rocked our world completely! Most private and some state campgrounds advertise FREE wifi, but it's usually just a token offering, and rarely works well, except in the middle of the night. So, don't depend on what campgrounds offer. Make solid, dependable plans of your own.

Some folks wonder if there are any National Park programs they should join?

If you are 65 or older, or permanently disabled, you should definitely apply for a lifetime Access Pass and pay the one-time $10 fee. Every National Park has an impact fee they charge for entering the Park. The Access Pass will have your name and photo on it, and it's good for you and anyone in your vehicle.

Larry has one, so I don't need one because I'm always with him. Some federal campgrounds even offer a 50% discount on campground fees. It's saved us hundreds of dollars this past year.

I've heard that the federal government is making changes to the current permanent pass in 2018, so if you qualify, you should scoop one up before it becomes an annual, renewable pass.

Some folks wonder if there are clubs or memberships they should consider joining?

We use several camping clubs. Just for your information, the average we've spent per night on the road is around $40 for full hookups, where high-end resorts could cost you $70-$100 per night. Special events like Mardi Gras, in New Orleans, one campground (we did *not* stay here) was charging nearly $300 per night. National Parks and State parks average around $30. Casinos sometimes offer a cheap night of camping, $20 or less—one even let us stay for free—in the hopes they get you in their casino.

Of course, you can't beat Boondoggling, it's FREE! Here are some of our personal thoughts about each:

GOOD SAM CLUB is a great value for the annual fee. It saves us 10% each time we use it and most private campgrounds do accept it. Their website has the BEST reviews of campgrounds, and Larry based most of our reservations on those reviews. They offer supplemental programs that you can sign up for, as well: Roadside Assistance, Motorhome Insurance, Travel Assist Medical, Extended Warranty, Motorhome Financing, Coast to Coast, Discounts at Camping World, Flying J, Pilot, and others, RV Forum, Mail Forwarding Services, and much, much more.

PASSPORT AMERICA is another good value for some half-priced stays. The drawback is that there are a lot of rules regarding its use and there are many campgrounds that don't accept it. You really can't use this in prime seasons.

COAST TO COAST. We have saved money with this membership, but it's costly to join up front. Usually the campgrounds are older and off the beaten path, but for $10 a night, sometimes it's worth the trip. Before buying, I'd suggest you search the internet for discounters and other agents, and be sure there would be participating campgrounds in the area you'll be visiting. Some of them can be nice and cheap, but we've stayed in others that have been mediocre, at best.

Your nightly fee may be $10, but then it's $5 more for 50-amp electric, $5 more for wifi, $3 more for cable (you cannot opt-out—true story). They $5 you to death, until what you pay is closer to their normal rates.

KOA VALUE KARD. Many KOA campgrounds are aging, but there are still some really nice ones out there, just be sure to check out the reviews. We pay an annual fee and receive 10% at KOA across America. They don't accept any other discounts, not even Good Sam.

RESORT PARKS INTERNATIONAL / RPI. We do have this, but haven't used it at all this past year, because we have the Coast to Coast membership. The 2 programs are similar, and we have it because we have Coast to Coast. We have found that the resorts they offer are not in the best of shape and most are old. We have not renewed our membership.

ENCORE is also benefit of Coast to Coast, and we have used it for a 10% discount.

THOUSAND TRAILS. We don't use this since we have Coast to Coast. Some of the participating parks are old and outdated as well as being out of the way. I think it's their way of attempting to attract folks that would not come otherwise.

ENJOY AMERICA. We have used this to save 50%, but like Passport America, there are some rules you must follow. This came with our RPI membership, as well.

Some folks wonder if we could offer any tips to making reservations?

Accept the fact that reservations are a MUST for popular destinations and/or popular times. Any time kids are out of school—even for a three-day holiday—people are out and about.

Make reservations at least 60-90 days out. If you want to stay in the post popular places like Yellowstone, Yosemite or Cades Cove in the Great Smoky Mountains National Park, you must make them a YEAR in advance of your date. For example, we wanted to enjoy a White House tour in 2017. We learned that, post 9/11, you must request that reservation through your State Congressman or Senator, 3 to 4 months in advance of our desired date. Research your destinations. Avoid surprises.

Print out everything you reserved, your dates, an exact address or for your GPS, and any confirmation numbers. Keep them in date order, organized and ready for your arrival. We keep ours on a clip board on the dash.

We use www.Recreation.gov and www.ReserveAmerica.com, a great deal for park reservations.

We are weather wussies. We have been through multiple hurricanes and 3 blizzards in our lives. We like warm weather, so if you're in search of 70-degree weather in the winter like us, I have news: so is everybody else! Places like Key West, Florida, the Gulf Coast Beaches, South Padre Island, and Galveston, Texas fill up fast for the winter. You should probably make those reservations a YEAR in advance, too.

In Texas, they called us Winter Texans. In Florida, they'll call us Snowbirds. We love being called names.

Some folks wonder if we could help them get organized?

Organization is a must. I have only a tiny fraction of the space I had in my nice home. I brought one piece of Corning Ware and rarely use it. I have two skillets, three saucepans, again, which I rarely use, because I nuke or Crock Pot almost everything. I brought 4 plates, 4 bowls, and 2 large bowls. If we ever have company, we'll eat off paper, no problem.

BUY SMALL. When I went back to work several years ago, and Larry started shopping, he would bring home huge packages of stuff from Sam's Club and Costco. Early on this trip, we had 36 rolls of toilet paper stuck away in every cabinet, nook and cranny, under the dinette, and under the bed. "But it was cheap," he said. He has finally learned that a 9- or 12-pack of Scott is just fine.

My washer/dryer uses one tablespoon of detergent per load. I had purchased Mrs. Meyers in a bottle with 68 loads. He bought a gigantic Tide that will probably last me two years. There's just no need for that, with such precious limited space.

Larry's sense of humor often tells me, "If you can't eat it and poop it, then don't buy it." Not Funny. And then he buys 6 huge tubes of toothpaste, that we will take up precious space until he turns 70.

Buy small. You're on the road—you can always buy more.

Some folks wonder if we have any tips for repairs and maintenance?

I would recommend first getting online to use an RV forum at www.rvforum.net or www.rv.net/forum for information regarding your specific rig and maintenance. There's a strong chance that other folks have experienced the same problem you have, so you should be able to easily find solutions to your problem.

Always carry a good set of basic tools and a drill set because, believe me, you WILL need them. Other basic needs would include backups of: engine oil, coolant, silicone, sealant, distilled water for your batteries, Gorilla Glue, duct tape, and water filters. We have found out recently about a "duct tape" from the Gorilla Glue people, and it's amazing! Larry recently fixed holes in our plastic AC shrouds with this tape and then sprayed them with black Flex Seal. They look good as new! We have Flex Seal in white, black and clear. We use them all.

Basic facts you may know, but you may not:

Always use a water regulator. Many campgrounds will warn you that they have high water pressure, so I always use a regulator, regardless. And always carry a spare—they fail without any warning whatsoever.

You should carry at least 25 feet of water hose, and a spare. Since typical hoses take up room and kink, we bought one that shrinks up when not in use for maintenance, and another rubber blue EZ coil one for our fresh water uses. Also, keep on hand a couple of 3-foot sections of regular water hose. If the campsite spigots are too low to the ground, they really come in handy.

They also make rinsing your holding tank a whole lot easier. We leave one 3-foot section connected to the black tank rinse all the time. This makes it easier to rinse the tank when its time. Don't forget those extra water hose washers! These go missing out of your hoses all the time. They cost like $1 for a package of a dozen or so but if you don't have one you have a leaky faucet.

You will also need 30 feet of <u>electric cable</u> (I've never needed more than that). One for 50-amp and one for 30-amp. You can always use the extra 30-amp one for an extension cord if you ever needed one. A good <u>surge protector</u> is needed as well, for your electrical connection, and <u>adapters</u> to connect to different amps offered.

After a major electric failure with costly repairs and not knowing if it was the campgrounds fault, we invested in a TRC electrical monitor for about $300. Here's what the box said: "Portable whole-RV surge and spike protectors which now offer more than twice the rated protection of earlier models. They have easy-to-see LCD display uses plain, easy to understand language to keep you informed of status at a glance. Built-in intelligence lets these units reset automatically at power restoration. Each now shuts off power in the event of an open ground or thermal line/load overtemperature condition, as well as in the event of an open neutral, low (under 102 volts) and high (over 132 volts) voltage or reverse polarity to protect your RV and its electrical components from damage and fire.

"Continuously monitors for voltage and amp draw (RMS) and reverse polarity (miswired pedestal or elevated ground voltage). Built-in 128-second reset delay protects air conditioner compressors. Two-light LED backup indicators for power and faults. More compact design for easier storage. Easy pull handles on connectors for safety and convenience."

To avoid any problems, you should have FOUR 10-15-foot sections of <u>sewer hoses</u>. Carry extras because you constantly get pin holes in the hoses. We use the more expensive Rhino Extreme brand hoses; they cost more but last a lot longer than the cheaper brands.

To access <u>cable</u> connections, a good quality 25-foot coax should do.

We also carry a small Shopvac for fast clean ups.

We have small flashlights all over the place in handy storage spots for easy excess as well as plenty of AA and AAA batteries.

To help us maneuver the rig in campgrounds and tight places we use walkie talkies to help us communicate with each other. Some campgrounds have huge trees, rocks, fences in really bad places when trying to back the rig. We used to scream and yell—the radios are a so much easier and quieter way to give moment-to-moment directions.

Some folks wonder about Camping World?

We do use this RV supply store. But, they can be expensive! If you can find what you need at Walmart, buy there. But, as a last resort, you can usually find or order what you need. Amazon is also a great site to search and order from if you don't need something fast and can have it delivered to you down the road.

We usually try to get maintenance done at a Freightliner chassis dealer instead of Camping World but shop around. Another thing we have learned, all RV repair places and dealers are not the same, especially mobile operators. Some are just plain and simple rip-offs! Do your research and look at reviews before letting anyone touch your rig. You can usually fix things yourself if you think through the problem and search on line for solutions. Figure out how it works before attempting the repairs yourself and if you are physically capable of doing it.

Some folks wonder how we handle keeping up with our doctors?

We sat down with our doctors before we left our home base. We explained our plans to travel and requested that they write our prescriptions in a way that would enable us to get them filled as needed, for the next 12 months. None of our doctors had any problems in doing just that.

I can personally recommend CVS Pharmacy for this. They seem to be almost everywhere, and your refill information is right there in every computer. Other national chains like Walmart or Walgreens probably do this, too. As long as there were refills left, I never had a problem in getting prescriptions filled. But if you take any controlled prescriptions, the rules are different, so talk to your home pharmacy about these.

When we planned our trip, we planned to return to our home base in the spring, when the weather would be warm. We'll spend 30 days back home to take care of dentist and doctor appointments, and get those refills rewritten for another year.

Some folks wonder about all of those factory tours we took?

Other than the scenery and wildlife at the National Parks, those tours were some of our best times! Each time we arrived in a new area, we Googled it. Most cities and city Chambers of Commerce have official sites to encourage travelers to visit there. All you need is the name, and you go to their official site for possible tours, times, and prices. Most have been absolutely FREE, and those that charged, the fees were minimal.

We have already been to the following points of interest:
- Jelly Belly, Fairfield, CA
- Freightliner, Gaffney, SC
- Harry & David, Medford, OR
- Gibson Guitar, Memphis, TN
- Hallmark, Kansas City, MO
- Tabasco, Avery Island, LA
- Budweiser, St. Louis, MO
- Celestial Teas, Boulder, CO
- Boeing, Everett, WA
- SAS Shoes, San Antonio, TX
- Hammonds Candies, Denver, CO
- Pendleton Blankets, Washougal, WA

- Jim Beam, Clermont, KY
- Landstrom's Black Hills Gold, Rapid City, SD
- Cape Cod Potato Chips, Hyannis, MA
- Ben & Jerry's, Waterbury, VT
- The White House, Washington, DC
- The Smithsonian
- A show on Broadway, New York City
- The 9/11 memorial
- Niagara Falls
- Winnebago, Forest City, IA

I don't know if you'd call these factory tours, but

- The US Mint in Denver, CO was amazing too.
- The Money Museum Federal Res. Bank of St. Louis
- US Bureau of Engraving & Printing, Wash. DC

Don't miss the Presidential Libraries … Buy a membership if you are going to visit more than one in a year. Check it out—it can save you money.

ODYSSEY MAPS

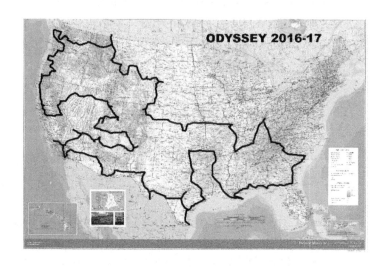

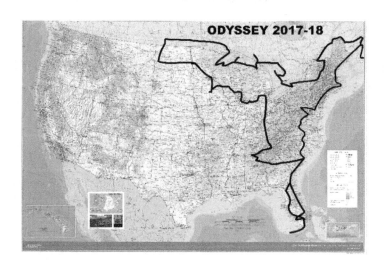

CAMPGROUND LIST 2017

February~ Jude Travel Park. New Orleans, LA, Rating 3

March~ Buccaneer State Park, Waveland, MS, Rating 6

March~ Davis Bayou State Park, Oceanview, FL, Rating 6

March~ Fort Pickens CG, Pensacola, FL, Rating 4

March~ Myrtle Beach Travel Park, Myrtle Beach, SC, Rating 7

March~ Cypress Camping Resort, Myrtle Beach, SC, Rating 7

April~ Myrtle Beach State Park, Myrtle Beach, SC, Rating 6

April~ Briarcliff RV Park, Myrtle Beach, SC, Rating 7

April~ Rollingview, Falls Lake, Wake Forrest, NC, Rating 5

May~ Yogi Bear, Luray, VA, Rating 7

May~ Greenbelt NP, Greenbelt, MD (Washington DC), Rating 4

May~ KOA Harpers Ferry, Harpers Ferry, WV, Rating 6

May~ Gettysburg Battlefield RV Resort, Gettysburg, PA, Rating 6

May~ Spring Gulch RV CG, New Holland, PA, Rating 3

May~ Timberlane KOA, Clarksboro, NJ (Philly), Rating 4

May~ Liberty Harbour RV Park, Jersey City, NJ (NYC), Rating 2

May~ Fisherman's Memorial State Park, Narragansett, RI, Rating 7

May~ Charlestown Breachway, Charlestown, RI, Rating 1

May~ Adventure Bound, North Truro, MA, Rating 2

May~ Cape Cod Camp Resort, East Falmouth, MA, Rating 7

June~ Wompatuck State Park, Hingham, MA, Rating 2

June~ Salisbury Beach State Res., MA, Rating 8

June~ Moody Beach RV CG, Wells, ME, Rating 6

June~ Pinehirst RV Resort, Orchard Beach, ME, Rating 3

June~ Camden Hills Maine State Park, ME, Rating 4

June~ Blackwoods Campground, Acadia NP, ME Rating 4

CAMPGROUND LIST CANADA 2017

June~ Rockwood Park CG, Saint John, New Brunswick, Rating 4

June~ Elm River RV Park Ltd, Glenholm, Nova Scotia, Rating 4

June~ King Neptune CG (Peggy's Cove) Indian Harbour, Nova
Scotia, Rating 4

June~ Hyclass Ocean CG, Havre Boucher, Nova Scotia, Rating 5

June~ Adventures East CG, Baddeck, Nova Scotia, Rating 1

June~ Baddeck Cabot Trail CG, Baddeck, Nova Scotia, Rating 6

June~ Broad Cove, Cape Breton Highlands Park of Canada, Nova
Scotia, Canada Rating 6

June~ Cheticamp, Cape Breton Highlands Park of Canada, Nova
Scotia, Canada Rating 6

July~ Red Point Provincial Park, Red Point, PEI, Rating 5

July~ Cavendish, Prince Edward Island NP, PEI, Rating 6

Proverbs 19:17
Kindness to the poor is a loan to the Lord,
and He will give a reward to the lender.

2 Timothy 4:6-8
For I am already being poured out like a drink offering,
and the time for my departure is near.
I have fought the good fight, I have finished the race,
I have kept the faith.

Now, there is in store for me the Crown of Righteousness,
which the Lord, the Righteous Judge,
will award to me on that day—and not only to me,
but also to all who have longed for His appearing.

2 Timothy 3:14-17
But as for you, continue in what you have learned and
have become convinced of,
because you know those from whom you learned it,
[15]and how from infancy you have known the Holy Scriptures,
which are able to make you wise for salvation
through faith in Christ Jesus.
[16]All Scripture is God-breathed and is useful for
teaching, rebuking, correcting and
training in righteousness,
[17]so that the servant of God may be thoroughly
equipped for every good work.

Made in the USA
Middletown, DE
29 April 2021